Jayne Steel

Demons, Hamlets and Femmes Fatales

Representations of
Irish Republicanism
in Popular Fiction

PETER LANG

Oxford · Bern · Berlin · Bruxelles · Frankfurt am Main · New York · Wien

Bibliographic information published by Die Deutsche Bibliothek
Die Deutsche Bibliothek lists this publication in the Deutsche
Nationalbibliografie; detailed bibliographic data is available on
the Internet at ‹http://dnb.ddb.de›.

British Library and Library of Congress Cataloguing-in-Publication
Data:
A catalogue record for this book is available from The British Library,
Great Britain, and from The Library of Congress, USA

ISBN 978-3-03911-007-0

© Peter Lang AG, International Academic Publishers, Bern 2007
Hochfeldstrasse 32, Postfach 746, CH-3000 Bern 9, Switzerland
info@peterlang.com, www.peterlang.com, www.peterlang.net

Printed in Germany

Demons, Hamlets
and Femmes Fatales

For Ken

Contents

Preface

Demons, Hamlets and Femmes Fatales is a lively, rigorous, and perhaps contentious, interrogation of the ways in which popular fiction appropriates the figure of the Provisional IRA and the political conflict within the north of Ireland; a conflict euphemistically termed the 'Troubles'. Throughout, I look at how British and Irish recreations, or hysterical repetitions, of Irish republicanism reveal, at both a conscious and unconscious level, self-referential images that are, ultimately, a product of human subjectivity, national identity and/or gender politics. These images include a recurrence of 'pleasurable' stereotypes which include comic, demonic and guilt-ridden Hamlet figures. Although I concentrate upon popular fiction, the significance of film and the media to my analyses cannot be ignored. For instance, many of the novels that I discuss have been adapted to film. For this reason I have, where relevant, included discussion about such texts.

An important focus my study resides in the interrogation of the British and male fascination and fixation with the Provisional IRA and its 'trauma'. Importantly, though, I compare and contrast novels written by male and Irish authors that deploy the same generic conventions as male and British authors (frequently through the thriller genre) but, sometimes, for different reasons. These reasons often focus upon gender politics.

By way of a response to these male-authored narratives, I also analyse female-authored texts to establish whether or not women writers might be able to challenge the, previously dominant, male narratives through, for example, the deconstruction of female stereotypes. These stereotypes include the iconic Mother Ireland or the terrorist *femme fatale*, and a politicizing of the private realm of home and family.

Crucially, following a psychoanalytical and cultural materialist methodology, I argue how the texts explored signal a failure to supply 'reality' through the conventions of 'realism'; a failure that triggers desire, trauma and lack.

Acknowledgements

I would like to thank Alexis Kirschbaum at Peter Lang for her enthusiasm and support for this project. Her advice throughout has been invaluable. So too Helena Sedgwick for her assistance with preparing the manuscript.

Introduction

> If God invented whiskey to prevent the Irish from
> ruling the world, then who invented Ireland?[1]

Commencing in 1968, for over thirty years, complex political issues fuelled Irish paramilitary activity within the north of Ireland. While it is impossible to debate and explore all these issues, the following brief overview provides an historical context for the main focus of my study.

This focus concerns British and Irish, male and female, representations of the Provisional IRA (PIRA) and the 'Troubles' within, predominantly, popular fiction but also, where relevant, film and the media.

The north of Ireland and 1968 supplied the political environment for the birth of the PIRA and rebirth of violent political conflict. At a global level, since the 1960s, people had already been protesting over, for example, Vietnam, Chile and Black civil rights.[2] In 1968, 'the civil rights movement [within the north of Ireland] marked the transition from a period of peace to a renewal of [...] an unresolved conflict'.[3] This conflict was euphemistically termed the Troubles.

Tracing the inception of the civil rights movement within the north of Ireland, which included Protestant as well as Catholic student voices, Tim Pat Coogan writes that 'on 24 August 1968 [...] four thousand people took part in a march [...] from Coalisland to Dungannon'.[4] The march was in protest over inequalities suffered by the Catholic majority in terms of the electoral system, housing, employ-

---

1   Declan Kiberd, *Inventing Ireland: The Literature of the Modern Nation* (London: Jonathan Cape, 1995), p.1.
2   Bob Purdie, *Politics in the Streets* (Belfast: Blackstaff, 1990), p.2.
3   Ibid., p.1.
4   Tim Pat Coogan, *The Troubles: Ireland's Ordeal (1966–1995) and the Search for Peace* (London: Hutchinson, 1995), p.60.

ment and education. These initial protests were peaceful demon-strations. However, incidents such as 'the baton charge by the Royal Ulster Constabulary in Derry on 5 October 1968 helped to create a mass movement'.[5] This movement 'became involved in communal tensions [whereby] more and more of its time was spent trying to damp down sectarian out-breaks as the old fracture lines between Catholics and Protestants began to reappear'.[6] Eventually, 'the re-sulting violence led to the intervention of British troops in August 1969'.[7]

Coogan recalls how the then IRA 'posed very little threat to anyone during those days'.[8] In fact, when the IRA failed to mobilize against the Protestants who were burning Catholics from their Belfast homes, the Catholic community dubbed the IRA 'Irish Ran Away'.[9] The ensuing split in IRA ranks created the Official IRA versus the Provisional IRA, the latter favouring more forceful paramilitary action against Protestant bullying and British rule.

From 1968, Britain's and Ireland's self-image and self-con-fidence has been shaped and tested both culturally and politically by the threat posed from the Provisional IRA and the Troubles: a threat which, in spite of the on-going peace process, continues. The Troubles vis-à-vis 'a threat' has galvanized British and Irish fiction, film and the media to produce a remarkably diverse, and highly revealing, body of work that discloses the shifting self-perceptions of Britain and Britishness (or Englishness), Ireland and (Irishness), and gender. In this book I argue that, paradoxically, many recreations, or trans-formations, of Irish republicanism often reveal *self-referential* im-ages that are, ultimately, a product of notions about national identity, self and other, and gender. I examine how, at both a conscious and unconscious level, fictional representations of the PIRA and the Troubles can reveal much about human subjectivity.

5   Purdie, *Politics in the Streets*, p.3.
6   Ibid.
7   Ibid.
8   Coogan, *The Troubles: Ireland's Ordeal*, p.89.
9   Ibid.

While political attitudes towards the Troubles obviously influence their fictionalization, especially within the thriller genre, I am primarily concerned with the way that *repetition of* generic conventions and stereotypes informs specific and varied ideological viewpoints. Although the corpus of works interrogated throughout includes texts from various nations such as Canada and America, the majority are 'British' or 'Irish'. I am particularly interested in how so many British and male-authored texts facilitate the imagining of the PIRA as an intimate enemy. This said, British viewpoints do not always summon negative or stereotypical representations of the Irish, but rather point to self-conscious attempts to acknowledge some kind of responsibility for the *trauma* of the violent conflict within the United Kingdom. When comparing and contrasting Irish and male-authored texts, I show how these texts often deploy the same generic conventions and stereotypes as those from Britain but sometimes for different reasons. These reasons include issues relating to male-dominated national identity and gender politics. Because gender politics are so crucial to this study, I also examine female-authored novels to discover how women rewrite the Troubles.

Thus, in Chapter 1 (*Dempira*), I explore how many of the 'Godfathers' of the PIRA represented in spy, detective and thriller genres are, perhaps surprisingly, represented as being English, homosexual, public school educated, malcontents (recalling Burgess, Blunt, Philby and Maclean), suggesting that at its core the enemy is perceived as a symptom of English decadence, resentment and political failure. This idea recalls Burke's observations about 'English stereotypes of the Irish' in the sense that such stereotypes are 'projections onto a neighbouring people of those elements which the English den[y] or despise in themselves'.[10]

Alternatively, in Chapter 2 (*Hampira*), I discuss why, within both British and Irish fictions, the high frequency of references to Hamlet reproduces the structure of Shakespeare's play in which a young protagonist agonizes over ethics and the tragic implications of violent political action. Here, then, a high cultural, quintessentially English 'subject' (a symbol for liberal humanist values) is located at the heart

10   Kiberd, *Inventing Ireland*, p.20.

of the Irish 'subject' – as both self and other. In various ways, Shakespeare's Gertrude is the mother figure accompanying these quintessentially English Hamlets. Therefore, psychoanalytical questions relating to the desire of the mother are included in my close readings of Campbell Armstrong's 1987 novel *Jig* and Bernard MacLaverty's 1984 novella *Cal*. Here, Jacques Lacan's interpretation of *Hamlet* will be shown to offer a useful framework.

Chapter 3 (*Vampira*) looks at British as well as Irish male-authored representations of women in the PIRA, which range from deadly and seductive *femme fatales* to monstrous Mother Ireland figures, and how such representations 'contain' British women such as Miranda Richardson, Myra Hindley, Ruth Ellis and Margaret Thatcher as well as the archetypal imago of the Mother in terms of the scape-goat or the 'woman to blame'. Connections are drawn between the ways that, historically, writers have exploited the age-old meta-phorical equivalence between death and orgasm yet, at the same time, found it necessary to keep a psychological distance from this equiv-alence. As gender politics looms large here, where relevant I also look at Irish, male-authored representations of *Vampira*.

Lastly, in Chapter 4 (*Fempira*), I concentrate upon female-authored texts to discover whether or not 'women writing the Troubles' do so differently from their male counterparts. Novels from authors such as Mary Costello, Jennifer Johnston and Deidre Madden will be considered to see if female authors can deconstruct what have been traditionally male-dominated texts and stereotypes. The women writers I discuss all forward attempts to challenge the stereotypical ways in which the north of Ireland has been written as a male 'thriller' narrative.

There are numerous examples that disclose the complex and changing ways in which the PIRA have been demonized, glamorized, fetishized and sometimes sentimentalized in representations that locate the traumatic 'Troubles' as the defining point not only of the changing political map of Britain and Ireland, but the 'internal' map of the British and Irish psyche and its sense of identity. I explore many of these examples throughout this book which, in turn, provides both a cultural history of British and Irish self-perceptions since 1968 and plots and co-ordinates the terrain of British and Irish subjectivity in the form of fictional representations that manifest symptoms of deep cultural introspection and political anxiety, symptoms that, as mentioned, also recur in representations of the female paramilitary.

During my research, I long debated the distinction between 'Britishness' and 'Englishness', but, ultimately, I believe that it is impossible to maintain these types of exclusive national boundaries; even, to some extent, in relation to the north of Ireland where many individuals within the Loyalist community consider themselves to be British as opposed to English or Irish. Indeed, I have deliberately limited my discussion to representations of the PIRA and the Troubles, excluding novels that depict representations of Loyalist paramilitaries. This is because issues relating to national identity and Loyalist groups are not the same as those relating to Republican groups. Thus, without rejecting the importance of authors such as Glenn Patterson, Eoin McNamee and Maurice Leitch, I contend that a discussion of their texts belongs to a different project.

It could be further argued that, following the suggestion made by the Runnymeade Trust's report on the Future of Multi-ethnic Britain (*The Parekh Report*, 2000), Britain is a coded term for whiteness, as exemplified by the Loyalists. This whiteness is also coded as Protestant and centred on the Queen of England, English institutions and Literature.[11] Consequently, 'British' is a signifier that binds together the Scottish, the Welsh and the Loyalist Northern Irish in a subordinate relation to the white Protestant Englishness of which they form an inferior copy. Fittingly, then, while referring to Oscar Wilde, Henry Craik asked 'was there ever an Irishman of genius who did not get himself turned into an Englishman as fast as he could'.[12] Wilde's excessive, parodic Englishness further confirmed, rather than subverted, the idea of Irish – Britishness as a derivative copy of an English original. Although I am not suggesting that Irish subjects, especially republican subjects, consciously adopt Britishness, or vice versa, I am suggesting that national identities feed into one another. Jacques Lacan's 'neologism' termed 'extimacy' is a key word here because 'extimacy [...] neatly expresses the way in which psycho-

---

11   Bhikhu Parekh, *The Parekh Report* (London: Profile Books, 2000).
12   Kiberd, *Inventing Ireland*, p.33. Cit. Kiberd.

analysis problematizes the opposition between inside and outside, between container and contained [whereby] the Other is "something strange to me, although it is at the heart of me".[13]

In terms of methodology, this study draws upon Lacanian psychoanalysis and cultural materialism as both of these theoretical perspectives are compatible with my exploration of ideas concerning how the conscious and unconscious psyche mediates aspects of the self in conjunction with, often mirrored, images of the other. This other can, of course, be either British or Irish, male or female. As stated by Jonathan Dollimore and Alan Sinfield, a cultural materialist approach involves:

> A combination of historical context, theoretical method, political commitment and textual analysis. Historical context undermines the transcendent significance traditionally accorded to the literary text and allows us to recover its histories; theoretical method detaches the text from immanent criticism which seeks only to reproduce it in its own terms; socialist and feminist commitment confronts conservative categories in which most criticism has hitherto been conducted; textual analysis locates the critique of traditional approaches where it cannot be ignored. We call this 'cultural materialism'.[14]

Coinciding with this definition offered by Dollimore and Sinfield, I examine representations of the PIRA through historical context (the north of Ireland from 1968 to the present date), theoretical method (psychoanalysis), political commitment (an interrogation of ideology), and textual analysis (close readings of texts vis-à-vis their historical, unconscious, and ideological subtexts).

At a psychoanalytical level, Slavoj Zizek's readings of Lacan, especially those concerning 'desire' and 'lack', are also important to this study. For instance, according to Zizek, 'the object which func-

---

13   Dylan Evans, *An Introductory Dictionary of Lacanian Psychoanalysis* (New York: Routledge, 1996), pp.58, 59. See also Jacques Lacan, *The Seminar. Book VII. The Ethics of Psychoanalysis (1959–1960)*, trans. Dennis Porter, notes Dennis Porter (London: Routledge, 1992), pp.139, 71.

14   *Political Shakespeare: New Essays in Cultural Materialism*, eds. Jonathan Dollimore and Alan Sinfield (Manchester: Manchester University Press, 1985), p.vii. See also Scott Wilson, *Cultural Materialism: Theory and Practice* (Oxford: Blackwell, 1995).

tions as the "cause of desire" must be in itself a metonymy of lack'. Agreeing with this principle, I maintain that the PIRA are an 'object' that triggers 'desire', that *causes* desire, but whose metonymic representations supply only lack and, therefore, continue to stimulate desire and perpetuate more and more failed representations.

In addition to scholarly works focusing upon the north of Ireland and its culture, several texts concerning 'nation' and 'national identity' have offered some interesting and relevant perspectives for the grounding of my work.[15] Edited by David Boswell and Jessica Evans, I found *Representing the Nation: A Reader* a useful eclectic study of 'nation' from various academic points of view.[16] So too Kiberd's *Inventing Ireland* which is an exhaustive literary exploration of how 'the English helped to invent Ireland'.[17]

In *Representing the Nation*, Jessica Evans writes about how 'in recent years "The Nation" has come to be seen not merely as the object of political, geographical or economic analysis, but as one of *cultural* analysis'.[18] Evans's acknowledgement of the importance of culture is of course analogous to my own focus upon fiction and film, whereas David Boswell's comment about the way in which 'nationalism [...] entail[s], fundamentally, the perception of difference from others' is germane to my focus upon the self and the other.[19]

---

15 These texts include: *Representing the Troubles: Texts and Images*, eds. Brian Cliff and Èibhear Walshe (Dublin: Four Courts, 2004); *Contemporary Irish Fiction: Themes, Tropes, Theories*, eds. Liam Harte and Michael Parker (London: Macmillan, 2000); Elmer Kennedy Andrews, *(De)constructing the North: Fiction and the Northern Ireland Troubles* (Dublin: Four Courts, 2003); Richard Kirkland, *Identity Parades: Northern Irish Culture and Dissident Subjects* (Liverpool: Liverpool University Press, 2002); *Irish Women and Nationalism: Soldiers, New Women and Wicked Hags*, eds. Louise Ryan and Margaret Ward (Dublin: Irish Academic Press, 2004); Gerry Smythe, *Decolonization and Criticism: The Construction of Irish Literature* (London: Pluto, 1998); Christine St. Peter, *Changing Ireland: Strategies in Contemporary Women's Fiction* (Basingstoke: Macmillan, 2000).

16 *Representing the Nation: A Reader*, eds. David Boswell and Jessica Evans (London: Routledge, 1999).

17 Kiberd, *Inventing Ireland*, p.xi.

18 *Representing the Nation: A Reader*, eds. Boswell and Evans, p.1.

19 Ibid., p.11.

From an alternative perspective, Anthony Easthope's *English-ness and National Culture* provides incisive psychoanalytical readings of national identity.[20] For Easthope:

> National identity [is] an unconscious structure [...] that [...] works at deeper strata than simply the *content* of the various overtly national practices, narratives, discourses, symbols and tropes through which national identity is conventionally presented (4–5).

Indeed, Easthope offers a compelling argument for 'nation as an identity that can speak us even when we think we are speaking for ourselves' (5). Easthope also accords with a cultural materialist viewpoint when he claims that nation is 'material' as well as 'ideal' (12). 'National cultures', writes Easthope, 'are material in that they are produced through institutions, practices and traditions [...] but national cultures are also reproduced through narratives and discourses' (12). Following Easthope, I will demonstrate how both the material (for instance the law) and the ideal (for instance Hamlet as a universal human subject) are shown to be instrumental in the process whereby the PIRA and the Troubles are 'reproduced through narratives and discourses'.

Easthope's emphasis upon the importance of 'trauma' as well as 'desire and lack' is also worth noting. For instance, Easthope reminds us that 'a traumatic experience is one the subject repeats because he or she cannot work it through' (31). Hence, the traumatic experience of the Troubles in the north of Ireland (the bombs and dead bodies which the individual psyche 'cannot work through') becomes repeated, often through metonymic constructs of the PIRA. As for 'desire' and 'lack', Easthope repeats the Lacanian premise that 'lack in being (*manque-a-etre*) is the cause of desire, which can never be satisfied because it is constituted as desire for what is missing' (37). For Easthope, 'in this definition national desire is desire for a being nation seems to offer but never provide' (37).

---

20   Anthony Easthope, *Englishness and National Culture* (London: Routledge, 1999). Further consecutive references to this edition are given after quotations in the text.

There are, not surprisingly, numerous texts about the Troubles. Social historian Coogan has written from an Irish Republican perspective.[21] So too Patrick Bishop and Eamonn Mallie.[22] Other studies include those from Bill Rolston,[23] Liz Curtis,[24] and David Miller,[25] who have all supplied in-depth analyses concerning how the Troubles are misrepresented within the British media. Moreover, the exhaustive bibliography 'compiled using bibliographies produced by [...] Rolston at the University of Ulster and Robert Bell of the political collection at the Linenhall Library' provided an invaluable resource for my own initial readings of the many novels discussed in the following pages.[26]

Themes concerning misrepresentation of the PIRA in fiction and film occur within articles by, for example, Margaret Scanlan, John Hill, Alan Titley, Joseph McMinn and Stephen Watt; all of which I refer to at relevant points throughout. Indeed, the politics of representation, or misrepresentation, signal one of my key themes. But it is not my task to discredit one set of ostensibly 'false' representations and replace them with another set of ostensibly 'true' representations. On the contrary, it seems to me that *all* representations are to a greater or lesser extent 'fictive'. Representations do not emerge as a unified whole from the individual psyche of a writer but are, instead, selected and constructed from a range of pre-existing *repeated* images. My book explores how these repeated images are used to both consciously and unconsciously express specific cultural fixations that fashion, nourish and articulate shared anxieties. Representations of the PIRA are not, then, created from a psychological

21   See Coogan, *The Troubles: Ireland's Ordeal (1966–1995) and the Search for Peace,* See also Coogan, *The IRA* (London: Harper Collins, 1995).

22   See Patrick Bishop and Eamonn Mallie, *The Provisional IRA* (London: Corgi, 1988).

23   See *War and Words: The Northern Ireland Media Reader*, eds. Bill Rolston and David Miller (Belfast: Beyond the Pale, 1996).

24   See Liz Curtis, *Ireland the Propaganda War: The British Media and the Battle for Hearts and Minds* (London: Pluto, 1984).

25   See David Miller, *Don't Mention the War: Northern Ireland, Propaganda and the Media* (London: Pluto, 1994).

26   Literature of the 'Troubles'. This bibliography entitled 'Northern Ireland Collection' is located at the University of Ulster, Belfast and the Linenhall Library, Belfast.

vacuum but exist in tandem with other representations produced by other nations, particularly Ireland itself, that evoke different meanings and different histories. To be sure, Patrick McGee, the Irish Republican ex-prisoner, has called on Irish writers, both male and female, to 'square up to their task of writing their own accounts of the Troubles in fiction'.[27] Claiming that 'what is needed is a realistic picture', McGee suggests that writing the unadorned truth in realist fictions will help to negate the negative stereotypes and replace them with real people.[28] While acknowledging the genuine desire for understanding that no doubt lies behind McGee's demand, I am more sceptical about the ability of language to accurately reflect or transparently reveal reality. Indeed, literary realism has always relied on stereotypes, creating many new ones of its own. Further, precisely because of its claims on 'reality', realism has become one of the most effective vehicles of ideology, the most persuasive popular means of constructing 'how it is' through drawing on the recognizability of certain characters, scenes and situations. The recognizability and plausibility of fictional characters depends on their adherence to narrative conventions of plot and motive, and their similarity to characters in other fictions. Generally, realism does not change perceptions about reality, its dependence on recognizability tends to entrench received ideas. There is no access to the trauma of the Troubles in realism, just as there is no access to real Irish men and women in representations of the PIRA. Nevertheless, these images have a history that can be traced; and through charting their development, I show it is possible to follow the shifts in British and Irish perceptions as the Troubles developed.

My inclusion of works by Irish writers acknowledges a case for arguing that reader-spectator positioning affects the ways in which texts are received, and this positioning depends upon the complexity of desires, identifications and shifting allegiances that are the experience of most readers and audiences. So, while I am not dismissing this 'other voice', I maintain that, irrespective of how sophisticated the reader or audience, many Troubles texts depend upon and require

27   Patrick McGee, 'Do They Mean Us?', *Guardian*, 3 September 1997, p.13.
28   Ibid.

some kinds of stereotypes which, as the following study argues, are sometimes rather surprising. Ultimately, though, stereotypes are pleasurable things – we tend to like them because they are thrilling: a Balaclavaed Irish demon or a sexy but deadly gun-toting Irish female terrorist being repeated cases in point. Thus, just because we are often astute enough to realize that we are being confronted with a stereotype, this does not mean that the stereotype's fictional or affective force is weakened. Following Peter Sloterdijk, in *The Sublime Object of Ideology*, Zizek reminds us how 'the cynical subject is quite aware of the distance between the ideological mask and the social reality, but he none the less insists upon the mask'.[29] Zizek writes that 'cynical distance is just one way – one of many ways – to blind ourselves to the structuring power of ideological fantasy: even if we do not take things seriously, even if we keep an ironical distance, *we are still doing them*'.[30] Accordingly, as intelligent and informed subjects, we 'know that' the real male PIRA are neither demons or Hamlet and that the real female PIRA are neither deadly *femme fatales* or monstrous crones, 'but still' we believe that they are demons, *femme fatales* and crones.[31]

What follows shows how representations of the PIRA and the Troubles emerge from notions about national identity, the self and the other, and gender politics. These representations supply a 'fantasy-construction which serves as a support for [...] "reality" itself: an "illusion" which structures [...] effective, real social relations and thereby masks some insupportable, real, impossible kernel'.[32] Zizek argues that 'the function of ideology is not to offer us a point of escape from our reality but to offer us the social reality itself as an escape from some traumatic, real kernel'.[33] As this book will argue, when it comes to representations of the PIRA and the Troubles, this traumatic kernel is not only death, in terms of the bombs and dead

---

29   Slavoj Zizek, *The Sublime Object of Ideology* (London: Verso, 1989), p.29.

30   Ibid., p.33.

31   Ibid., p.18.

32   Ibid., p.45.

33   Ibid.

bodies inflicted by the Troubles, but also the British and Irish, male and female self.

Chapter 1
'The Usual Suspects': Demonic Representations of the PIRA

1.1: Signs of Evil

> The Celts! Ha! Very fashionable, the Celts, with the
> arty-crafty. Ley lines. Druids. But show them the real
> thing – an Irishman with a gun, or under a blanket in
> an H-block and they run a mile.[1]

In Howard Brenton's 1982 play, *The Romans in Britain*, a British
army officer named Chichester suggests that, for the British subject,
'the real thing' is a dangerously phallic demon. At a literal level, this
demon is 'an Irishman with a gun'. Whereas, at a metaphorical level,
this demon is an Irishman 'under a blanket' with a big penis.[2] For
Chichester, Irishmen are 'all murdering bastards' and 'the hardest
men'.[3] This sentiment is echoed within novels where the PIRA are
'wicked bastards',[4] 'evil bastards'[5] and dangerously phallic 'hard
bastards'.[6] So, contradicting Irish author Jack Holland's fictive 'editor
of the New York *Globe*', 'the Irish thing is [not] dead' but very much
alive within metonymic constructs of the PIRA.[7] These metonymic
constructs often deploy a type of psychopathology which diagnoses
the PIRA as being 'mentally deranged people'.[8] But this psychopathology only serves as a smoke screen for the real traumatic events

---

1   Howard Brenton, *The Romans in Britain* (London: Methuen, 1982), p.75.
2   Ibid., p.76.
3   Ibid., pp.75, 76.
4   Gerald Seymour, *The Journeyman Tailor* (London: Harper Collins, 1995),
     p.306.
5   Gavin Esler, *Loyalties* (London: Headline, 1990), p.22.
6   Gerald Seymour, *Harry's Game* (London: Harper Collins, 1975), p.49.
7   Jack Holland, *The Prisoner's Wife* (Dublin: Poolbeg, 1995), p.29.
8   Ambrose Clancy, *Blind Pilot* (London: Macmillan, 1981), p.104.

25

which occurred within the north of Ireland, traumatic events which, since 1968, shattered 'normal' life. A sense of what is physically and psychologically normal signals a key issue here. For instance, John Redmond observes that 'our understanding of what is ethical is' based upon 'our understanding of what is "average" or "everyday"'.[9] Therefore, it is difficult 'for us to imagine' normality such as 'humdrum actions [...] being performed by' figures who symbolize 'the epitome of evil'.[10] According to Redmond, 'for the terrorist [...] to be able to interrupt normality, he or she cannot be *of* it'.[11] Redmond's ideological positioning of 'the terrorist' parallels many British texts' ideological positioning of the PIRA whereby the Irish gunman functions at an imaginary level in order to protect the British psyche from acknowledging the reciprocity between the British self and the Irish other. This Irish other is threatening because it is a 'thing' that disrupts the 'opposition between outside and inside, between the container and the contained', between British 'good' and Irish 'evil'.[12] This Irish other is threatening because it is a 'thing' that mirrors the real extimate British self. And Brenton's text exposes this mirroring. This said, Irish authors are also more than capable of producing 'demonizing' images of the PIRA. So, although this part of the book focuses mainly upon British male subjectivity, images created by Irish authors will also be examined for the ways in which these might likewise signal problematic, self-referential projections.

The Romans in Britain is a play that utilizes history (in this case, the Roman Conquest) to allegorize British occupation of the north of Ireland and provide a commentary on the Troubles. Brenton's play manifests a politically sensitive and controversial theme. However, the play is most famous for Brenton's inclusion of a 'representation of attempted [homosexual] rape' which, according to Patricia Waugh, expresses Brenton's 'desire to shock'.[13] If Waugh is correct, Brenton's

9   John Redmond, 'Ordinary Madness', *Guardian*, 25 September 1997, p.9.
10   Ibid., p.9.
11   Ibid.
12   Dylan Evans, *An Introductory Dictionary of Lacanian Psychoanalysis* (London: Routledge, 1996), p.29.
13   Patricia Waugh, *Harvest of the Sixties: English Literature and its Background* (1960–1990) (Oxford: Oxford University Press, 1995), p.177.

desire was answered by the legal furore over the play. Indeed, this furore is advertised on the cover of the published text which states that 'the director of the first production of *The Romans in Britain* goes on trial at the Old Bailey accused by Mary Whitehouse of '"procuring an act of gross indecency"'.

In spite of the 1967 legalization of homosexuality, explicit representations of male homosexuality have remained taboo (we need only to recall the hue and cry over the British television series about the gay Manchester scene – *Queer as Folk*). Unsurprisingly, in 1982, there was outrage at Brenton's depiction of a naked Roman soldier who 'attempts to bugger' a Brit.[14] Though no doubt intended as a metaphor for colonial invasion, the sensationalism of the scene succeeded only in distracting audiences away from the allegorical point of paralleling the Romans to the British, and Britain to the north of Ireland. Interestingly, the sexual scandal (the Roman Army's anal penetration of Britain) ensures that the political scandal (the British Army's military occupation in Ireland) becomes impotent, becomes screened. There is irony here because the play's homosexual narrative was spawned from the play's political narrative which links the Romans versus the British to the British versus the PIRA. Lurking within *The Romans in Britain*'s covert text, British and Irish homosexuality, duplicity and treachery inter-connect while the real extimate enemy within is depicted as being British. John Hill makes similar observations when he writes about the 'Images of Violence' shown by 'representations of Ireland and the Irish on the cinema screen'.[15] Hill identifies a recurrence of Irish gunmen who are 'positively pathological'.[16] For Hill, because this 'pathological [trait] is closely connected to sexual abnormality [...], sexual repression, rather than "British oppression"', is shown 'to be the root of [...] the problems'. [17]

The screened politics within *The Romans in Britain* mirrors the screened politics within Troubles narratives, and an ideological gap

14   Brenton, *The Romans in Britain*, p.41.
15   John Hill, 'Images of Violence', *in Cinema and Ireland*, eds. Kevin Rockett, Luke Gibbons and John Hill (London: Croom Helm, 1987), pp.147–93 (p.147).
16   Ibid., p.166.
17   Ibid.

identified by Ronan Bennett.[18] According to Bennett in 'An Irish Answer', when depicting the Troubles, 'writers by and large, do not get involved [in politics] and the same is true of most film and television drama'.[19] For Bennett, this lack of 'involve[ment]' results in 'the Troubles' being presented 'as an appalling human tragedy, devoid of political content'.[20] Thus, 'like any bloody struggle anywhere (Vietnam, Algeria, South Africa, Angola, Peru, Bosnia), [the] bloody struggle' in the north of Ireland 'becomes nothing more than a series of repulsive and meaningless massacres' which, in turn, are 'destructive of communities and the human spirit in equal part'.[21] Not surprisingly, then, Troubles narratives charting apolitical, 'repulsive and meaningless massacres' demand apolitical perpetrators of these massacres. Here we move towards a liberal humanist gloss being superimposed onto the Troubles, an idea that is more fully explored in Chapter 2 of this book. But, as the metaphoric and the literal, as fantasy and the real, images of the PIRA as the evil extimate other answers the demand for the 'apolitical'. Thus, as highlighted by Scottish author Gavin Esler, the PIRA as fantasy are 'terrorists(s) from central casting'.[22] Such fantasy constructs highlight British attempts to create an evil other where 'the epic struggle between good and evil' is repeatedly enacted.[23]

Within Mildred Downey Broxton's novel entitled *Too Long a Sacrifice*, the epic struggle between good and evil (with the PIRA as the embodiment of evil) becomes reproduced at a literal level.[24] For instance, Broxton writes about something 'not quite human', a creature 'stood in a churchyard like a demon with antlers and blazing eyes'.[25] This creature is the evil 'horned-one', a 'hate-beast from Ancient Ireland' that usurps the mind and body of 'Tadgh' who is a

18   Ronan Bennett, 'An Irish Answer', *Guardian*, 16 July 1994, p.6.
19   Ibid., p.6.
20   Ibid.
21   Ibid.
22   Esler, *Loyalties*, p.238.
23   Philip Schlesinger, Graham Murdock, and Philip Elliott, *Televising Terrorism: Political Violence in Popular Culture* (London: Comedia, 1983), p.1.
24   Mildred Downey Broxton, *Too Long A Sacrifice* (London: Futura, 1981).
25   Ibid., p.210.

bard and a refugee from the past.[26] Demonically possessed by this personification of Satan, Tadgh is shunted from the sixth to the twentieth century and repackaged as a member of the PIRA. When this happens, Tadgh becomes an Irish gunman who is both physically and psychologically marked by an evil which, in turn, represents some magical, external and abnormal force. *Too Long A Sacrifice* was published in 1981. And the belligerent political climate within Britain at this time might have influenced Broxton's decision to screen the Troubles through fantasy.

Broxton's novel followed in the wake of major PIRA bombings in Bristol, Southampton, Coventry, Manchester, Liverpool and London. These events, quite literally, exploded what had previously been the north of Ireland's and the British Army's trauma onto the British public. According to Patrick Bishop and Eamonn Mallie, the political agenda behind these bombings sought to 'generate a gathering weariness with the problem of Northern Ireland which would translate into pressure on the British political parties to pull out'.[27] Through recourse to ancient history, myth, the supernatural, demonization, and anticipating Brenton's 'very fashionable Celts', Broxton seems to effectively displace the real politics, real trauma and, possibly, real British guilt behind these real 1978 bombings. Displacement of the political through images of evil is the keynote to this chapter and signals a process that is crucial to the construction of British male identity.

While attempting to mask the real trauma of the Troubles (bullets, bombs and dead bodies) these types of anglicized constructs of the PIRA rehearse the demand to supply the British male with an ideal identity, an impossible identity seeking masculinity and virility. Irrespective of its failure, such an identity is located within oppositions whereby masculinity and virility demands effeminacy and impotence, a sexual rather than political opponent. Even though impossible, an imaginary and ideal British identity needs positive and good attributes that are structured through an imaginary and ideal

---

26   Ibid., pp.14, 232.
27   Patrick Bishop and Eamonn Mallie, *The Provisional IRA* (London: Corgi, 1988), p.251.

negative and evil Irish other. These positive attributes include physical attractiveness, heroism, intelligence and a sense of fair play; as opposed to physical ugliness, cowardice, stupidity and mendacity. But evil comes in many forms. And the particular form imposed upon the PIRA is contingent.

Grotesque medieval gargoyles, Milton's quasi-heroic Satan, Broxton's supernatural demon, Spielberg's mischievous gremlins, Jackson's war-mongering orcs. Within film and fiction, evil plays a starring role, boasts a long and diverse career which includes performances of insanity, demonic possession, sexual deviance, and violence. Yet, as suggested by a character from David Edgar's 1976 play entitled *Destiny*, these 'demons [...] are our [Britain's] creation, [an] alter-ego, [a] dark, desire for something [...] dark and nasty in the soul'.[28] Evil as inexorable and repeatable likewise acts to side-step the political. And this manoeuvre also occurs in the work of Irish female novelists. So, within Linda Anderson's 1986 novel entitled *Cuckoo*, a character called Nick contemplates the north of Ireland and remarks that 'once something evil starts, it's easy to channel effort into serving it, but not stopping it! [...] The gunmen think they're in control. But it is'.[29] Nick is vague about what '*it*' signals and, rather esoterically, proposes an anti-Enlightenment view that 'evil' as 'human unreason' is a malicious entity, an unnameable thing.[30] The work of female novelists will be discussed more fully in Chapter 4. But here it is important to note that the inexorable and repeatable also applies to perceptions about the past because 'history' participates in human 'trauma' and the 'desire' that 'is always unrepresentable'.[31]

Not surprisingly, characterizations of the male PIRA frequently mirror these, paradoxically, unrepresentable performances of evil which include: the inhuman, Mafioso godfather, rapist, murderer, gangster, homosexual, psychopath, sadist, hardened criminal, wife beater, drunk, lout, idiot, the ugly and the impotent. As with Brenton's

28   David Edgar, *Destiny* (London: Eyre Methuen, 1976), p.59.
29   Linda Anderson, *Cuckoo* (London: Bodley Head, 1986), p.109.
30   Ibid.
31   Kaja Silverman, 'Historical Trauma and Male Subjectivity', in *Psychoanalysis and Cinema*, ed. Ann Kaplan (New York: Routledge, 1990), pp.116, 117.

and Broxton's texts, evil as demonization occurs through a process which again displaces political issues so that the bombs and bullets dispatched by the PIRA become an effect of 'normal abnormality' such as general criminality, psychopathology, international conspiracy or genetic dysfunctioning. But specific types of demonization reveal specific fears and dilemmas. These fears and dilemmas are fictionalized or allegorized at various historical points and, when discovered, serve to highlight changing perspectives about the Troubles. When specific types of demonizations occur during various historical points, these demonizations evolve as generic groups in tandem with shifting historical events. Put simply, embedded within the ostensibly apolitical fictive constructs of the evil, portrayals of male PIRA are highly political narratives about anxiety over the Troubles as well as highly fictive narratives about male identity. In a Derridaean sense, these narratives are a symptom of the desire for the 'invention' of 'the other', an impossible desire which inexorably folds back to become an invention of the self and thereby perpetuate the PIRA other as an evil embodiment of 'lack'.[32]

According to Charlotte Spivack, evil can be regarded as a deficiency.[33] This is essentially a medieval idea which conceptualizes evil as a dynamic force that progresses in stages from lack of spiritual grace to lack of physical prowess. Drawing upon ideas from the third century philosopher named Origen, Spivack claims that 'evil has no essential being but exists only negatively, like darkness, which is in reality nothing but the absence of light. In short, evil is non-being'.[34] The following examples explore these notions and supply a general overview of how repeated images of the PIRA evoke evil through lack.

Ugliness as lack occurs within Julian Romanes's 1988 novel, *The Cell*, where a character named Todd has 'a private theory that only

32   Jacques Derrida, *Acts of Literature*, ed. Derek Attridge (London: Routledge, 1992), p.342.
33   Charlotte Spivack, *The Comedy of Evil on Shakespeare's Stage* (London: Associated University Press, 1978).
34   Ibid., pp.14–15.

people with ugly names became terrorists'.[35] Ambrose Clancy depicts 'a boy' with a 'pitiless, stupid face' whose 'mouth' is 'limp, grotesque, like a stroke victim's'.[36] John Honeywood opts for intellectual lack with lumpen gunmen who are 'lame-brained' and 'low-cultured', 'paddies-in wellies'.[37] Peter Ransley favours physical lack and creates a diminutive 'five foot Irish killer'.[38] Gavin Esler supplies a metonymic role-call of the PIRA as nothing other than 'the Boxer, the Skull and the Thin Man'.[39] And Brian Moore splices male ugliness ('an adolescent boy, pitted with acne') to male effeminacy ('an almost feminine mouth with bow-shaped lips').[40] Moore provides an interesting example of how Irish writers might utilize the same negative images of republican gunmen as non-Irish writers. As noted by Patrick Magee, Moore's 1948 emigration from Ireland might well have resulted in his 'lack […] of shared experience' with the north of Ireland 'community'.[41] However, I would suggest this emigration could have also facilitated an unconscious and psychological, as well as a conscious and spatial, 'distancing' from the disturbing political issues that gained momentum from 1968 onwards.

Alan Titley observes how 'The Irish Gunman in the Popular Novel' portrays characteristics which formulate 'an almost composite picture, or rather silhouette'.[42] Titley explains the ways in which a gargoyle-type ugliness is supplied through, for instance, 'invariably bad, broken or gapped […] teeth'; a lack 'auguring ill for the skill of Irish dentistry or a crude attempt at a Freudian wish-fulfilling symbol for oral rape'.[43] In *Operation 10* (1982), Hardiman Scott complicates

35   Julian Romanes, *The Cell* (London: W.H. Allen, 1988), p.34.
36   Clancy, *Blind Pilot*, p.84.
37   John Honeywood, *The Terrorist's Woman* (London: Robert Hale, 1981), pp.116, 126, 149.
38   Peter Ransley, *The Price*, (London: Corgi, 1984), p.9
39   Esler, *Loyalties*, p.44.
40   Brian Moore, *Lies of Silence* (London: Corgi, 1984), p.9.
41   Patrick Magee, *Gangsters or Guerrillas?: Representations of Irish Republicans in 'Troubles' Fiction* (Belfast: Beyond the Pale, 2001), p.163.
42   Alan Titley, '"Rough, Rug-Headed Kerns": The Irish Gunman in the Popular Novel', *Eire-Ireland*, 15.4 (1980), 15–38 (p.25).
43   Ibid.

this notion about a wish-fulfilling symbol when British 'Super-intendent Whitaker' meditates upon 'the threat of the IRA'.[44] For Whitaker, this 'threat was like a nagging pain, a rotten tooth to be probed at constantly'.[45]

Physical ugliness as lack coincides with Jerry Palmer's notion that the appearances of thriller villains are often stained by 'de-formities'.[46] This staining implies that representations of the Irish villain impose negative physical traits which translate into an evil contagion suffered by all Catholics; a contagion which, in essence, summons a universalizing, or essentializing, akin to that deployed in representations of the female by male writers. Bearing this in mind, it is perhaps fitting that, in her 1984 novel *To Stay Alive*, the Irish and female author Linda Anderson depicts two characters parodying this type of imaginary contagion about the Irish.[47] In *To Stay Alive*, the question 'what do Catholics look like?' is answered thus: 'I can pick them out anywhere [...] their eyes are too close together, it makes them sneaky looking, so it does'.[48] Eyes also feature within Nelson De Mille's 1981 novel entitled *Cathedral*.[49] Here, De Mille evokes 'wild-eyed members of the Boston Provisional IRA' who are a group of 'wild-eyed lunatics'.[50] And, when Paul Theroux relates how during an interview in the north of Ireland he was told that 'a Catholic's eyes are too close together', it becomes apparent that the doctrine of ocular lack and Irish Catholicism is not restricted to fiction.[51] One reason why this particular myth persists might be explained through the idea that the overt myth concerning 'abnormal eyes' screens a covert myth. This covert myth relates to Oedipus and lack whereby blindness symbolizes castration. Maybe this explains why, in 1983, Julian

44   Hardiman Scott, *Operation 10* (London: Bodley Head, 1982), p.92.
45   Ibid.
46   Jerry Palmer, *Thrillers: Genesis and Structure of a Popular Genre* (London: Edward Arnold, 1978), p.21.
47   Linda Anderson, *To Stay Alive* (London: Bodley Head, 1984).
48   Ibid., p.28.
49   Nelson De Mille, *Cathedral* (London: Granada, 1981).
50   Ibid., pp.93, 200.
51   Paul Theroux, *The Kingdom by the Sea: A Journey Around the Coast of Great Britain* (London: Hamish Hamilton, 1983), p.184.

Symons's novel, *The Detling Murders*, repeated ocular lack and linked it with psychological lack vis-à-vis madness.[52] Symons's recreation of a nineteenth century detective novel presents an IRA who are 'double-eyed villains' and the 'rabid Irish' as well as a negative foil to British 'gentlemen'.[53] Other Troubles narratives supply 'idiot revolutionaries',[54] 'potato-eating Mick[s]',[55] 'shamrock waving idiots',[56] and 'potty Provos'[57] whose ubiquity creates the 'usual IRA madmen',[58] the 'criminal' and the 'mad'.[59] Interestingly, commencing in the early seventies and coinciding with the inception of 'terrorist chic', these symbols of lack can be charted chronologically from the comic to the demonic.[60]

According to Michael Seltzer, during the 1970s the lack of real heroes and real war stimulated a universal 'fascination with terrorism' which, in turn, produced the consumption of terrorism through a cultural glut of terrorist fashion, terrorist art and terrorist music.[61] In respect of British male identity, the lack of real heroes and real war might have accelerated this type of search for an ideal identity which, in turn, demanded an oppositional other: the PIRA. However, also writing in the 1970s, social historian Tim Pat Coogan claimed that 'when thinking about IRA operatives one should not visualize hardened neo-psychopaths of ice-cold nerve'.[62] On revisiting the ethos that was still reeling from the 'Swinging Sixties', the 1968 Civil Rights marches in the north of Ireland, the Student protests in France, Mexico

52   Julian Symons, *The Detling Murders* (New York: Viking, 1983).
53   Ibid., pp.110, 45, 129.
54   Susan Cheever, *A Handsome Man* (London: Weidenfeld and Nicolson, 1981), p.162.
55   De Mille, *Cathedral*, p.266.
56   Kevin Dowling, *Interface Ireland* (London: Barrie and Jenkins, 1979), p.15.
57   Lionel Shriver, *Ordinary Decent Criminals* (London: Harper Collins, 1992), p.62.
58   Peter Driscoll, *In Connection With Kilshaw* (London: Macdonald, 1974), p.34.
59   Alfred McClung Lee, *Terrorism in Northern Ireland* (New York: General Hall, 1983), p.194.
60   Michael Selzer, *Terrorist Chic: An Exploration of Violence in the Seventies* (New York: Hawthorn, 1979), pp.161–4.
61   Ibid., p.164.
62   Tim Pat Coogan, *The IRA* (London: Harper Collins, 1975), p.379.

and other major capital cities as well as, importantly, the birth of the Provisional IRA, what should be 'visualized' in terms of the Irish other? The following suggests a less sinister, more comic, Irish gunman.

Published in 1979, Kevin Dowling's novel, *Interface Ireland*, shows an awareness of the ways in which the PIRA were often the subject of ridicule when a character in the narrative refers to 'Bill and Ben the IRA men'.[63] Dowling may have 'borrowed' this pun from an early 1970s strip cartoon which is shown at (Figure 1).[64] The cartoon offers two PIRA stereotypes: one tiny and scruffy, the other huge and gormless. As an Irish author and a journalist, Dowling repeats the fantasy comic images of the PIRA that were being produced in the media at the time. But he does this to expose how such images are the product of British propaganda and how jokes about the PIRA (the quintessential Irish joke) summon the so-called 'Paddy Factor'.[65] These jokes often show incompetent bombers detonating 'own goals'.[66] Hence, laughter is employed to reinforce the opposition between the British self and Irish other. Evidently, most jokes need an other, a butt for the joke, 'some funny paddies' who offer an imaginary yet reassuring contrast to the British.[67] And although the Irish gunman in the role of buffoon still makes an appearance in later texts, these characterizations tend to be, like Dowling's, more sardonic and perceptive about how comedy can serve a political agenda. For instance, British author Ron Hutchinson's 1984 stage-play, *Rat in the Skull*, offers a scathingly witty monologue from a self-demonizing, PIRA bomber named Roche.[68] Hutchinson's bomber symbolizes the PIRA as being a gnawing presence, a 'rat' in the British 'skull' or psyche. A letter from Roche makes this clear:

63   Dowling, *Interface Ireland*, p.93.
64   *Loyalist News*, 'Bill and Ben, the IRA Men', in *Dressed to Kill: Cartoonists and the Northern Ireland Conflict*, John Darby (Belfast: Appletree, 1983), p.88.
65   Gordon Stevens, *Provo* (London: Hammersmith, 1993), p.272.
66   Tom Clancy, *Patriot Games* (London: Collins, 1987), p.73.
67   Dowling, *Interface Ireland*, p.133.
68   Ron Hutchinson, *Rat in the Skull* (London: Methuen/Royal Court, 1984).

Dear Mum, this is me in the big smoke. I've seen all the sights, the Tower, the zoo, Macdonalds, the big red buses and the bottom sides of coppers' boots from the wrong way up [...]. I was sat on my hunkers, somewhere north of the Northern Line, minding my own business, wondering whether to pick my nose or go for a slash, and a sledgehammer comes through the door, without so much as by-your-leave [...]. Your loving son [...] Michael Patrick De Valera Demon Bomber Roche.[69]

Likewise, British author Richard Burns's 1989 novel, *Why Diamond had to Die*, contains an eponymous Irish gunman whose first person narrative voice usurps the Irish joke and, paradoxically, inverts imbecility to wit.[70] 'The rain fell steadily', says Diamond: 'it was like an Irish terrorist [...] invisible in the shadows, thick in front of the lights'.[71] This said, with the words 'Diamond is dead, getting written out the script', Burns' protagonist acknowledges that his personification as an Irish other to Britishness is as contingent as his jokes.[72]

In her 1992 novel, *Ordinary Decent Criminals*, Lionel Shriver compares the north of Ireland to 'a cartoon'.[73] But cartoons need populating, need 'a greasepaint normality' of comic characters.[74] For representations of the Irish, this so-called 'normality' has a long tradition.

According to Taylor Dowling, 'in the affairs of nations [...] the perception each side has of the other [...] is crucial.'[75] For British 'affairs' with the north of Ireland, perceptions, or misperceptions, of the Irish dwell within cartoons from the nineteenth century when 'the Irishman assumed his own inimitable identity as a barbaric, stupid, less-than-human ape-man'.[76] Indeed, John Darby's study, *Dressed to Kill*, conducts an in depth exploration of 'cartoonists and the Northern Ireland conflict' which clearly demonstrates these nineteenth century

---

69   Ibid., p.7.
70   Richard Burns, *Why Diamond had to Die* (London: Bloomsbury, 1989).
71   Ibid., p.10.
72   Ibid., p.62.
73   Shriver, *Ordinary Decent Criminals*, p.210.
74   Gerald Seymour, *Field of Blood* (London: Fontana, 1986), p.314.
75   *The Troubles: The Background to the Question of Northern Ireland*, ed. Taylor Dowling (London: Thames/Macdonald Futura, 1980), p.42.
76   Ibid.

British misperceptions.[77] One hundred years later, cartoons from the early 1970s supply an intriguing continuation of this legacy.

The nineteenth century 'ape-like image of anarchy' seems to have been attributed to the Irish nation at a general level whereby 'the native inhabitants' were assigned 'major characteristics' including 'indolence, superstition, dishonesty and a propensity of violence'.[78] When the 1970s inaugurated the PIRA versus the British Army, these 'major' Irish 'characteristics' were resurrected and reconstituted with a comic gloss.

For instance, Martyn Turner's cartoon named 'Portrait of a Terrorist' is fairly typical of the of the 'Paddy O'Looney' illustrations of the PIRA by Cormac.[79] During the 1970s, these types of images supplied an Irish stereotype in terms of intellectual and physical lack that became implanted within the British psyche. Darby observes how the 'The Portrait' shows 'a young, bemused and unthreatening school-boy'.[80] This may be so. But the cartoon character's potato-shaped head, 'thick mick' expression, shin-skimming, baggy trousers and massive out-turned feet also show the British audience a portrait of a useless and moronic Irish gunman. Internalized as being the in-competent amateurs who were doomed to failure, these metonymic representations of the PIRA in their role as the inferior comic other to Britishness were also produced by the British Armed Forces: a fact made evident within the cartoon creations of a British squaddie named Carr. A cartoon which is fairly typical of Carr's submissions to *Visor*, the British Army's weekly paper, shows the benevolent and jovial attitude of a squaddie commiserating with a bungling PIRA recruit named Seamus.[81] After blowing up a petrol lorry, poor old Seamus runs out of petrol and is apprehended. But his squaddie captor is not in the least bit hostile. Instead, he places a kind hand on Seamus saying: 'Cheer up, Seamus – try to see the funny side of it'.

---

77   Darby, *Dressed to Kill*, pp.24, 25.
78   Ibid., p.24.
79   Ibid., pp.86, 91.
80   Ibid., p.72.
81   Ibid., p.88.

Another cartoon from *Visor*'s 1976 Christmas edition (Figure 2) displays a bizarre camaraderie choreographed through an Irish gunman's and British squaddie's '*danse macabre*'.[82] In this cartoon, Seamus is dressed in leprechaun garb while the protective, British squaddie wears the rather more macho battle-dress uniform and holds an artist's palate. The palate is perhaps an unintentional symbol for how these images of the PIRA emerged from the British psyche and were a screen, or a *Visor*, to the real trauma and the real politics of the north of Ireland.

Politics screened through comedy was, of course, an important cultural feature of British life in the early 1970s. Mike Yarwood joked about party politics, Les Dawson and Bernard Manning joked about sexism and racism while Jimmy Cricket and Frank Carson joked about the 'oiyrish'. This said, serious political issues mirrored this culture of comedy. For instance, the 1970s witnessed a dark period of military blunders from the British Army as well as the PIRA. Such blunders included the ghettoizing of Belfast in 'The Rape of the Falls' (1970), Operation Demetrius, internment without trial and the torture of Irish detainees (1971), and thirteen Derry civilians shot dead on 'Bloody Sunday' (1972). These incidents suggest that (through comedy) the incompetence of the British squaddie (a damaging blow for British male identity) may have been displaced onto the PIRA.

82   Ibid., pp.55, 94.

Fig 1: 'Bill and Ben the IRA Men' in Loyalist News

Fig 2: 'Seamus and British Squaddie' in *Visor*

39

After Thatcher seized the Tory party from Heath, and following successful PIRA activity such as the 1974 Guildford and Birmingham pub bombings, the PIRA were no longer considered a joke. Consequently, their status as the embodiment of evil in terms of lack began to shift from the comic to the demonic. This shift reached its zenith in the early 1980s and produced novels such as De Mille's *Cathedral*. In *Cathedral* the 'evil' PIRA leader is 'Satan', the ultimate Gothic fiend who, together with his terrorist troop, trespasses and usurps God's 'sanctuary'.[83] For De Mille, the PIRA within the cathedral are 'spooky, really spooky', are 'vampires on a castle wall [...], bloodless and lifeless', are predators 'agreeing to hunt together'.[84] A transitional text anticipating this shift is British author Gerald Seymour's 1975 novel: *Harry's Game*.[85] Like Dowling, Seymour also worked as a journalist reporting upon the north of Ireland conflict. Therefore, although British, Seymour's first-hand experience of the Troubles through his work in the media might partially explain why his fictional narrative evokes a political complexity that is often absent in other novels.

Harry's Game commences with 'the man [who] was panting slightly' and ends with the same 'man' running, his 'face hollow at the cheeks' from 'pull[ing] the air inside his lungs'.[86] With 'eyes fearful and vivid [...], he [is] shapeless [with a] grotesque breath'.[87] The man is Billy Downs, a PIRA assassin who, after shooting a British MP outside a Belgrave address, escapes back to West Belfast. En route to his wife and children, Downs stays one night in a Belfast safe-house where a girl named Theresa attempts but fails to seduce him. The death of the MP (George Danby) causes a political furore and the British government dispatches undercover agent Harry Brown to Belfast to get the killer. While Harry is in Belfast, he stays as a lodger in a guest house named Delrosa. At Delrosa, he meets, dances and has

83   De Mille, *Cathedral*, p.175.
84   Ibid., pp.447, 261.
85   Seymour, *Harry's Game*.
86   Ibid., pp.1, 311.
87   Ibid., pp.311, 312.

sex with a Catholic girl (Josephine) who unwittingly gives Harry information about Theresa's and Downs' identities. Theresa is arrested, interrogated by an RUC officer (Howard Rennie) and commits suicide. When the PIRA discover Josephine's indiscretion, she is questioned about Harry, tells them his name and address, and is punished for being a tout. Meanwhile, after an unsuccessful attempt to assassinate Rennie, Downs is ordered by his PIRA commander to kill Harry. Following a shoot-out between Downs, his PIRA accomplices, and Harry, Downs flees for home. Harry gives chase. The cat and mouse narrative concludes with Harry shooting Downs but, mistaken for a terrorist, Harry is then shot by British squaddies. Barely alive, Harry is 'finished off' by Downs's wife with his own gun.

'Hold the dawn for the dead'. Clannad's haunting refrain is the finale to the film version of *Harry's Game*.[88] And the same song also provides the chorus to a PIRA shooting within the film version of Tom Clancy's *Patriot Games*.[89] Yet, within *Harry's Game*, there is a question concerning whose death is being mourned and why. Brown the Brit versus Downs the Provo. The half-rhyming reciprocity of the doomed men's names implies that both are the same person, that being, an indistinguishable and spectral other. Linked to this idea, Joseph McMinn claims that Brown and Downs are 'two mavericks [...] who come, unconsciously, but inevitably, to have more in common with each other than their guiding organisations'.[90] The plot's main location (Belfast) suggests this may be so.

For Seymour, Belfast is 'Provo-land', an 'adventure playground par excellence for the urban terrorist', a nightmare space where Harry, a formless phantom 'who has no form in that [fantasy] world at all', conducts a 'game' in a 'theatre of war'.[91] After misrecognizing himself as the 'master of the hounds [and] the man who tracked the most wanted man in Britain', Harry finds nothing but lack.[92] This lack

88   *Harry's Game*, Dir. Lawrence Gordon Clark, Yorkshire Television, 1982.
89   *Patriot Games*, Dir. Philip Noyce, UIP/Paramount, 1992.
90   Joseph McMinn, 'Contemporary Novels on the Troubles', *Etudes Irlandaises*, 5 (1980), 113–21 (p.114).
91   Seymour, *Harry's Game*, pp.47, 62, 47, 76.
92   Ibid., pp.304, 204.

is death plus the truth that the most wanted man in Britain ('the opposition') is merely 'a boy', a 'slight body', 'shapeless', 'grotesque', 'dirty, cowed and frightened'.[93] 'Is that the terrorist?', asks Harry, 'Is that all he is? Is that the killer in all his glory?'[94] And when Harry gazes at Downs's dead body, his realization of the actual non existence of the 'evil' other evokes a horrific epiphanic moment whereby 'all the training, all the fear, all the agony, directed to killing this awkward, shapeless nonentity' brings 'nothingness': a nothingness which leaves both 'Harry Brown and Billy Downs in the awkward sack-like form that the [British] troops [...] recognise as death'.[95]

In the film version, the squaddies who misrecognize and kill Harry provide the comic, almost Shakespearean, chorus. Their roles as wisecracking 'Scousers', or 'Liverpool Oiyrish', are inherited from earlier comic versions of the PIRA. Moreover, the squaddies prompt the *jouissance* driven, 'bacchinal laughter' for the fatal moment when Harry's deadly-doppelganger-doubling with Downs is consummated.[96] And 'when the double materializes, when it becomes visible, it signifies imminent death'.[97]

As suggested, to a certain extent *Harry's Game* differs from other Troubles narratives (such as ex-soldier Alan Judd's pro-British Army novel which is aptly entitled *A Breed of Heroes*).[98] This is because Judd presents a clear opposition between evil PIRA 'snipers' and good British 'marksmen' whereas *Harry's Game* problematizes any opposition between 'Forces of Right against Forces of Evil'.[99] Thus, Harry and Downs become locked in a Manichaean-type battle whereby God mirrors Satan and Satan mirrors God. Such an idea is by no means new because, as observed by Spivack, 'throughout the early centuries of the church, the Christian formulation of evil was

93   Ibid., pp.314, 305, 312, 314.
94   Ibid., p.314.
95   Ibid., pp.318, 323.
96   Dowling, *Interface Ireland*, p.33.
97   Jean Baudrillard, *The Transparency of Evil: Essays on Extreme Phenomena*, trans. James Benedict (London: Verso, 1993), p.113.
98   Alan Judd, *A Breed of Heroes* (London: Hodder and Stoughton, 1981), p.171.
99   Seymour, *Harry's Game*, p.206.

challenged by the Manichaean doctrine of the eternal coexistence of equally substantial good and evil'.[100]

The pivotal scene for this mirroring occurs when Harry and Downs confront one another at a Republican dance hall. Here, both men experience a sense of the 'uncanny', a mutual recognition of the self as the other and the doubling which is 'the ghastly harbinger of death'.[101] Thus, Seymour writes about how:

> There was an intuitive, deep-based recognition for a moment, and Harry couldn't place it. He looked at the man, who stared straight back at him, challenging [...]. He looked away at the face that was still staring back at him, holding and returning his glance [...]. Once more he looked at the man, who still watched him [...] – then Harry rejected the suspicion of the likeness.[102]

The film version of the text summons this uncanny moment with a slow motion shot in which the men's galvanized gazes show the confusion and horror of acknowledging the self as the other. Later in the text, Harry muses about this doubling of himself and in so doing reveals a grim prescience about his own fate. For instance, we learn that 'as he [Harry] walked he set out the position, making his mind a chess board of his job [through which] he and the man he was hunting were the queens of his game'.[103] 'Now', thinks Harry, 'all the squares were grey, and the figures too. Even the two queens'.[104] Consequently, 'there would be a problem for an outsider in picking one set of pieces from another'.[105]

In contrast, the Hollywood film version of American author Tom Clancy's novel, *Patriot Games*, also shows uncanny recognitions between an Irish gunman (played by Sean Bean) and an American CIA operative (played by Harrison Ford). Yet *Patriot Games* quickly abandons these recognitions through the heroicization of the CIA

---

100 Spivack, *The Comedy of Evil on Shakespeare's Stage*, p.15.
101 Sigmund Freud, '"The Uncanny"', in *Literary Theory: An Anthology*, ed. Julie Rivkin and Michael Ryan (Malden: Massachusetts: Blackwell, 1998), pp.155–67 (p.162).
102 Seymour, *Harry's Game*, p.25.
103 Ibid., pp.167, 168.
104 Ibid.
105 Ibid.

operative and thereby preserves an image of the ideal American self. But, with Harry Brown, Seymour fails to provide an ideal British male identity because he fails to eventually divide the British self from the Irish other, the fantasy and demonic Irish other who is epitomized by lack.

At a literal level, Downs's physical lack is highlighted at the end of the narrative. Whereas, at a metaphorical level, his psychological lack is either consciously or unconsciously implied by his surname – as an echo of 'Down's Syndrome'.

Downs even admits to sexual lack. Hence, when his wife accuses him of having sex with Theresa, he pleads sexual impotence with the words: 'If I'd wanted her I couldn't have done anything about it. I was so screwed up'.[106] However, although during police interrogation Theresa corroborates Downs's excuse, Theresa's testimony portrays him as being something 'perverse', something 'abject'.[107] This becomes evident through her description of Downs's physical appearance. 'I've never seen a man like it', says Theresa, 'he had a hand like an old man's. It was tied up. Like a claw. I can't say how he was [...], it was horrible'.[108] Theresa's account of 'a hand like a claw' is reintroduced at the end of the narrative when, shot and bleeding, Downs 'claw[s] at the road surface'.[109] Some ideas from Kaja Silverman help to explain what these strange images might signify.

Writing about 'Historical Trauma and Male Subjectivity' in *Psychoanalysis and Cinema*, Silverman suggests that physical deformities such as hooks 'articulate [...] the thematics of an intolerable difference, accessible to vision, which positions its carrier as both other and inferior, and which confers upon the viewer an unwanted knowledge'.[110] For Silverman, 'hooks function much like female genitals', and are symptomatic of 'disavowal' because they 'attest to an intolerable absence or loss'.[111] Although Downs's 'intolerable

---

106   Ibid., p.178.
107   Julia Kristeva, *Powers of Horror: An Essay on Abjection*, trans. Leon S. Roudiez (New York: Columbia University Press, 1982), p.15.
108   Seymour, *Harry's Game*, p.159.
109   Ibid., p.316.
110   Silverman, *Psychoanalysis and Cinema*, p.120.
111   Ibid.

difference' is not 'visual' but imaginary, Silverman's theory coincides with Seymour's construct of Downs as an embodiment of evil through lack: a lack displayed by means of 'prosthesis'.[112] Interestingly, this symbolic deformity seems to have been inherited by PIRA demons appearing in later texts from both Britain and America. For instance, American Paul Theroux's 1976 novel entitled *The Family Arsenal* shows an Irish Republican commander named 'Sweeney' whose handshake is 'a strange clasp, without weight'.[113] This 'strange clasp' is by virtue of the fact that 'the top of Sweeney's hand was missing' to reveal 'a rounded stump and two small limp fingers, like a monster's claw'.[114] Repeating this type of image, London-born Ted Harriott's 1983 novel, *No Sanctuary*, concludes with a member of the PIRA whose 'claw-like hands' must be 'prise[ed] from 'the edge of the [confessional's] window'.[115] And, offering perhaps the most detailed description of a dextrously challenged Irish gunman, Cornish author Chris Oulds's 1986 novel, *A Kind of Sleep*, relates anatomical lack with gruesome precision.[116] 'It was his left hand', writes Oulds, 'and it lay across his dirty-jeaned thigh. Its fingers were twisted; the middle two each with an extra knuckle, and the lines of the scars on its back ran up and down over knotted tendons and caved in bone'.[117]

The uncanny, doppelgangers, evil as lack and prosthesis, all these quasi-supernatural factors serve once again to displace the political nature of the conflict in the north of Ireland. As observed by McMinn, even the characters within *Harry's Game* demonstrate apolitical attitudes. Harry and Downs are 'loners', 'indifferent to politics', 'not too bright' and 'two more sacrificial victims of a "hopeless situation"'.[118]

Years later, the media created its own version of Billy Downs with the PIRA 'Jackal' who, according to *The Sunday Times*, had a 'deathlist [...] topped by Margaret Thatcher' and was involved in a

112   Baudrillard, *The Transparency of Evil*, p.20.
113   Paul Theroux, *The Family Arsenal* (London: Penguin, 1976), p.200.
114   Ibid.
115   Ted Harriott, *No Sanctuary* (London: Secker and Warberg, 1983), p.228.
116   Chris Oulds, *A Kind of Sleep* (London: Andre Deutsch, 1986), p.4.
117   Ibid.
118   McMinn, 'Contemporary Novels on the Troubles', p.115.

'plot [...] as chilling as [...] Frederick Forsyth's work of fiction'.[119] But, as highlighted by Liz Curtis, the PIRA Jackal was, ironically, a fiction.[120] Hence, the police hunt for his whereabouts resulted in 'another wild' British 'goose chase' for the evil other.[121]

This section has charted how and why fictive constructs of the PIRA as a figure of demonic lack materialized during the mid-1970s, a period within British and Irish history when Irish republican gunman began to violently assert themselves and subvert the former metonymic constructs of 'funny paddies'. As the 1970s progressed, British desire to screen the political issues concerning the north of Ireland remained intact. However, the following sections explore how social cultural and political changes once more affected fictive constructs of the PIRA.

1.2: 'Youse Dirty Rat!': The PIRA and Gangsterism

> The Strickland story on the Shamrock Mafia caused a great sensation. [...] The Shamrock Mafia story was copied or quoted from the Tribune's early editions by every paper in Fleet Street. The news agencies sent it across the world on telex as the day's lead story from London. By midday teams of reporters and cameramen were on their way by air to Belfast. Their rooms had been reserved at the Europa hotel and they had instructions to question barmen, taxi-drivers and anyone else they could think of, about the incidence of graft and extortion within the Provisional IRA.[122]

William Everson observes how 'the activities of the [filmic] bad guys tell us far more about the changing mores of our times than [...] the

---

119 'Jackal on the Loose', *The Sunday Times*, 12 March 1989, p.2.
120 Liz Curtis, *Ireland the Propaganda War: The British Media and the Battle for Hearts and Minds* (London: Pluto, 1984), p.126.
121 Ibid.
122 Dowling, *Interface Ireland*, pp.209, 210.

good guys could ever do'.[123] In a Belfast where 'business' is 'booming',[124] or in a setting like a 'gangster film',[125] Irish bad guys tell us about the, often British, ideological mores which are buried within 1970s fictions. These fictions repeatedly screen the Irish paramilitary through the 'Mafia'.[126] Therefore, the PIRA become, for example, 'the Organisation' that conducts 'raid[s]' while 'dressed smartly in the style of managers of departments'.[127] 1970s PIRA merge with 'key Mafia figures in Italy',[128] kidnap the Pope and hold him to ransom,[129] are 'a naughty little brother [...] in [...] a family'[130] where the symbolic godfather of deadly enjoyment might be aptly named 'Valentine Hood'.[131] The PIRA 'mafia scum',[132] 'Shamrock mafia', [133] 'mafia hoods',[134] and 'common criminals',[135] are fronted by 'Mr Big in the arms business',[136] 'Mr Big' from Boston,[137] 'Michael Gun-Barrel'[138] or 'Machine-gun McNally of Kilkenny'.[139]

According to David Miller, 'the term "godfathers" in some official propaganda' summons 'the IRA' in terms of 'a criminal

123 William K. Everson, *The Bad Guys: A Pictorial History of the Movie Villain* (USA: Cadillac, 1964), p.xi.

124 Driscoll, *In Connection with Kilshaw*, p.145.

125 Benedict Kiely, *Proxopera* (London: Poolbeg, 1977), p.18.

126 Sean Herron, *The Whore Mother* (London: Jonathan Cape, 1973), p.85.

127 F.L. Green, *Odd Man Out* (North Hollywood, California: Leisure Books, 1971 (orig. 1945)), pp.7, 8, 9.

128 James Lund, *The Ultimate* (London: John Calder, 1976), p.166.

129 Jon Cleary, *Peter's Pence* (London: Collins, 1974).

130 Naomi May, *Troubles* (London: John Calder, 1976), p.183.

131 Theroux, *The Family Arsenal*.

132 James Barlow, *Both Your Houses* (London: Hamish Hamilton, 1971), p.250.

133 Dowling, *Interface Ireland*, p.209.

134 James Carrick, *With O'Leary in the Grave* (London: Heinemann, 1971), p.65.

135 May, *Troubles*, p.86.

136 Ritchie Perry, *Dead End* (London: Collins, 1977), p.28.

137 Donald Seaman, *The Bomb that could Lip-Read* (London: Hamish Hamilton: 1974), p.39.

138 Martin Waddell, *A Little Bit British* (London: Tom Stacey, 1970), p.70.

139 Chapman Pincher, *The Eye of the Tornado* (London: Sphere Books, 1978), p.35.

conspiracy similar to organised crime networks such as the Mafia'.[140] And Curtis observes how 'the word "godfathers" entered the lexicon of reporters describing the IRA in the mid-seventies'.[141] For Curtis, 'this mafia metaphor gained currency during the term of office of Labour Northern Ireland Secretary Roy Mason, whose strategy was to deal with the IRA revolt as if it were purely a criminal matter'.[142]

The 'mid-sixties' media initiation of the PIRA as 'a mafia-style organisation'[143] of 'common criminals' and 'shadowy Fagins or God-fathers'[144] coincides with novels such as *Harry's Game* where 'the representation of the IRA as an organisation turns out to be quite familiar, a criminal gang, run by godfathers, meeting in untidy rooms above chip shops'.[145] But the 1969 split between the Official IRA and the Provisional IRA together with the ensuing hostilities between the two organizations offered Mafiosi-meets-the-PIRA narratives. The split meant that Irish as well as British novels could invest in such images as the Official IRA provided a movement that could be treated with nostalgia.

This type of Mafiosi narrative occurs within Jack Higgins's novel entitled *The Savage Day* (1972).[146] Here, the 1969 historical framework allows fictive Irish gunmen to become embroiled in quasi-vendettas whereby, like Mafioso families, 'splinter groups' perpetrate revenge killings.[147] Alternatively, former journalist and, although Irish, fiercely anti-republican, Shaun Herron's *The Whore Mother* opted for a PIRA Organization which forbids those involved to abandon the Irish Cause.[148] However, as pointed out by Bill Rolston, the idea that 'you can never leave' the PIRA is 'a Mafia notion [and]

140   David Miller, *Don't Mention the War: Northern Ireland, Propaganda and the Media* (London: Pluto, 1994), p.7.
141   Curtis, *Ireland: The Propaganda War*, p.128.
142   Ibid., p.130.
143   Ibid.
144   Calvin Macnee, 'Terrorism: Telling It How It Is', *Fortnight*, 7 May 1976, [n. page]. Photocopied article supplied by Linenhall Library, Belfast.
145   McMinn, 'Contemporary Novels On The Troubles', p.113.
146   Jack Higgins, *The Savage Day* (London: William Collins, 1972).
147   Ibid., p.119.
148   Herron, *The Whore Mother*.

not a [PIRA] notion'.[149] This said, British authors John de Jorre and Brian Shakespeare gave the 1970s a 'new generation' of Irish gunman who were not 'the belted raincoats and wide brimmed trilbies' 1950s variety of Cagney gangster.[150] Among this 'new generation' of bad guys is Joseph Quaid, 'a successful businessman', Cathal Muldoon, whose business is 'a model of initiative and free enterprise', and Wally Figgis, a man 'who liked to describe himself as an entre-preneur' albeit of the 'small-scale' variety.[151] However, in spite of Quaid's, Muldoon's and Figgis's prescience about Thatcherism, to-wards the end of the narrative the Irish gunman still remains 'as bad as the bloody Mafia'.[152] As both De Jorre and Shakespeare were London-based journalists who also worked in the diplomatic service, their depiction of the PIRA are perhaps not too surprising.

However, similar metonymic PIRA types feature within Irish author Kevin Dowling's 1979 novel entitled *Interface Ireland*.[153] But, written at the end of the 1970s, Dowling's narrative announces a growing awareness that the PIRA as the Mafiosi is a British media, law and government construct. Dowling might well have gained this perspective during his work as a news-reporter in the north of Ireland. But, as *Interface Ireland*'s protagonist (Pascal) is a Belfast news-reporter, it could be suggested that Dowling has, in a similar way to British representations, displaced an ideal self into the text.

Interface Ireland shows the British media and law encouraging black propaganda about the PIRA. This results in a political con-spiracy during which Pascal and his fellow reporters are, often willingly, coerced into writing and filming the PIRA as characters who are apolitical 'thieves and gangsters' (68). For instance, the novel shows the British media and law manufacturing a 'Provisional mob' which conducts 'blackmail, extortion, and theft'; a 'Shamrock Mafia' appearing in a 'story' which 'the BBC feature in all its bulletins [...],

---

149 Jayne Steel. Interview with Bill Rolston. Belfast. July 1997.
150 John de Jorre and Brian Shakespeare, *The Patriot Game*, (London: Hodder and Stoughton, 1973), p.34.
151 Ibid., pp.31, 42–3, 109, 173.
152 Ibid., p.230.
153 Dowling, *Interface Ireland*. Further consecutive references to this novel are given after quotations in the text.

the World Service and [...] several [television] programmes' (208, 209, 210). This 'Shamrock Mafia' signals the imagined Irish 'Mobsters' who, led by 'shadowy figures' which the 'The Press' label 'Godfather figures', are 'paying off scores' with 'assassinations' and 'gangland slayings' that are fuelled by 'private vendettas' (212).

With *Interface Ireland*, the idea that, for the British, the PIRA equates with the Mafiosi is so flagrant that the earlier, more psychotic Irish stereotype becomes supplanted; the result being another instance of a metonymic lack. Put simply, the quintessential demon Irish gunman is missing and needs to be replaced. However, Dowling offers the British law as compensation for this lack. For instance, mirroring images of the psychotic Irish gunman, the security forces are 'masked figures' with 'faces [...] crushed under nylon stockings' who enjoy using torture in order to extract a suspect confession from a 'terrorist accountant' named Liam McSharry (46, 47). The British law's mirroring of the absent, psychotic PIRA becomes ratified when 'one of' the security force men 'point[s] a gun' at McSharry, dispatches 'maniacal' trigger 'clickings' then 'laugh[s]' (46).

Employed as a PIRA accountant, 'Money' is McSharry's 'job'; and his responsibilities include keeping 'lots of secrets' such as 'the structure of several firms which the Provisionals control' (47). These firms include 'retail outlets, bars and a stake in building' (47). This said, unlike Francis Ford Coppola's *The Godfather* (1972), McSharry displays none of the attributes possessed by Don Corleone's American Irish, Mafiosi lawyer/accountant named Tom Hagen. Transported from Coppola's America to Dowling's Belfast, McSharry is an 'oiyrish' coward, 'a tout', and 'a lousy informer' who betrays his PIRA godfathers (50).

At the end of the text, the idea of the PIRA being an imagined Mafiosi constructed by the British becomes ironically reinforced. This happens when a gullible 'police reporter from London' obtains dubious 'information' from an Irish source named McDowell (213). The information claims that, after 'the Provos had hired American veterans of the Vietnam war for five dollars a month', 'the Irish Godfathers sat around, smoking rich cheroots and robbing occasional banks, while the Yanks did the dangerous fighting' (213). Moreover, while McDowell dispatches these 'fictions', Pascal reflects upon 'the cynical freemasonry of veteran Belfast reporters [who] omitted to inform the police reporter [that] McDowell's imagination had already reinforced the Provisional IRA with cadres of Vietcong, Czechoslovakians, Lithuanians and Communist Frenchmen' (213). Thus, McDowell seems to be capitalizing upon British desire for a Mafiosi-PIRA. And this capitalizing reaches its zenith on the final page of the text when Pascal cynically considers how:

> The going rate for killing a British soldier – McDowell had said so – was – £500 per corpse. You got a bottle of whiskey for tearing off somebody's limbs. Every Provisional owned a luxury villa, a bar, or else a hotel. They went into battle secure in the faith that their children were stinking rich. They had bank accounts in Geneva which they filled by bullying widows. They even – it was so much worse – they even defrauded the State. It was done through the Social Security. They drew unemployment benefit to pay for planting bombs in pubs. Corruption was rife. Even tots of six got fifty pence each for taking part in a riot (213).

Ultimately, Pascal's final statement of cynicism declares that he has 'stopped believing in justice' (213). Here, a fictive Irish man voices his lack of belief in British justice, a lack caused by the British voicing belief in stories of conspiracies and godfathers. Such stories do not merely apoliticize the Troubles; they also function to desensitize the British psyche to the trauma of the real fatalities in the north of Ireland. Yet Pascal acknowledges these real fatalities. For instance, confronted with the aftermath of a bomb, he observes a colleague 'taking pictures [of] the remains of a body on a sidewalk' and reflects how 'people were frightened to learn that a human body was thirty feet of guts. They hated to know how naked they looked when badly slaughtered, like so much beef' (145). These images depict an 'abject horror', the 'entire body fall[ing] beyond the limit' as a 'corpse' which symbolizes 'the most sickening of wastes […], a boarder that has encroached upon everything […], the "I" [that] is expelled' [and] 'the abjection of self'.[154] Such an abjection of self proclaims the

---

154   Julia Kristeva, *Powers of Horror: An Essay on Abjection*, pp.3, 4, 5.

ultimate truth, '*le vrai*' of the human condition.[155] Here, *Interface Ireland* offers a fascinating yet horrific *point de caption* or fixed meaning.[156] But, like a detonated bomb, the *point de caption* explodes into nothing, 'destroys itself by definition' and 'eliminates the traces'.[157]

Dowling's abattoir lexicon, a 'slaughtered' body 'like so much beef', summons the grotesque. Indeed, the image of 'thirty feet of guts' is worthy of inclusion within a *Grand Guignol*, Gothic melo-drama. This Gothic 1970s imagery in relation to the PIRA endured. For example, in 1994 Ronan Bennett wrote about how 'the recurrent metaphor in fiction about the north' of Ireland 'is that of the charnel house, the abattoir', an imaginary space where 'the blood and the carcasses are laid out for inspection by the horrified reader'. [158] Published five years after Dowling's novel, this 'imaginary space' is reproduced within Irish author Bernard MacLaverty's novel entitled *Cal*.[159]

MacLaverty begins his novel with his protagonist (Cal) visiting the work-place of his father (Shamie). This work-place is a slaughter-house in Derry. Here, Cal listens as 'the humane killer crack[s] again' then watches 'the killing pen tip over and tumble a beast on to the floor, its legs stiff to the ceiling'.[160] Unable to stomach the slaughter, Cal 'turn[s] away' when the animal is 'immediately winched up by one of the hind shanks and its throat cut'.[161] The killing pen image forces both Cal, and perhaps the reader, to conduct an 'inspection' of death, to witness a type of horrific freeze-frame or 'essential ob-

---

155   '*Le Vrai*' is a term adopted by Julia Kristeva to problematize the notion of truth versus reality. Derek Paget, *True Stories? Documentary Drama on Radio, Screen and Stage* (Manchester: Manchester University Press, 1990), p.29.

156   '*Point de Caption*' is a term adopted by Jacques Lacan to express 'the point in the signifying chain at which "the signifier stops the otherwise endless move-ment of the signification"'. Dylan Evans, *An Introductory Dictionary of Lacanian Psychoanalysis*, p 149.

157   Reg Gadney, *Just When we are Safest* (London: Faber and Faber, 1996), p.118.

158   Bennett, *An Irish Answer*, p.8.

159   Bernard MacLaverty, *Cal* (London: Penguin, 1984).

160   Ibid., p.8.

161   Ibid.

scenity'.[162] This horrific freeze-frame anticipates the abject-horror of the human deaths endemic to the north of Ireland setting; a horror that haunts Cal, the novel's eponymous, romantic and liberal humanist hero. More will be discussed in relation to *Cal* and how both British and Irish authors sometimes evade the political through liberal humanism in Chapter 2.

A comparable horrific freeze-frame or essential obscenity occurs within *Interface Ireland* when Pascal describes a bomb explosion in which 'brutal shockwaves [...] rushed down people's ears and noses and frantic mouths'.[163] The bomb victims are 'deafened in an instant [...], their throats [...] seared [while] their lungs and stomachs explode'.[164] 'The blast', writes Dowling, 'swirled into their skulls and blew their heads off [and] their torsos were ripped from their limbs'.[165] Moreover, all this 'took less than a second [...] to happen'.[166] Highly visual and visceral, Pascal thinks about how this split-second cinematographic image contradicts the alternative reality desired by 'the public [who] preferred something nice and aesthetic [whereby] a massacre was best suggested in a safe, nostalgic way; perhaps an open family bible resting on a blackened pile of bricks'.[167] For Pascal, aesthetically pleasing 'pictures like that won prizes [whereas] the other kind of pictures were likely to make you spew'.[168] Actual newspaper photographs, such as the one that appeared on the front page of *The Guardian* on 2 January 1998, show how this aesthetically pleasing tendency has endured.[169] Taken in Belfast during the aftermath of a 1998 'New Year's Eve shooting', the photograph depicts a solitary bouquet of 'flowers left outside the Clifton Tavern' on rain-spattered steps. The photograph, then, offers 'something nice and

162 Slavoj Zizek, *Everything You Always Wanted to Know About Lacan ... But Were Afraid to Ask Hitchcock* (London: Verso, 1992), p.18.
163 Dowling, *Interface Ireland*, p.145.
164 Ibid.
165 Ibid.
166 Ibid.
167 Ibid.
168 Ibid.
169 Carlos R Lopez-Barillas, *Guardian*, 2 January 1998, p.1.

aesthetic' instead of the 'terrible, terrible thing', the real trauma of death.[170]

However, in spite of *Interface Ireland*'s grim realism in terms of death, realism in terms of the PIRA remains absent. This is because, although the novel's main narrative exposes the PIRA as Mafiosi to be a fictive construct, even Dowling's national and occupational 'credentials' do not prevent the creation of another fantasy, that being, an American Gothic alliance with Irish paramilitaries – through a character named Mick, Dowling splices a PIRA gangster to a PIRA cowboy who has a vampiric 'habit of turning up at funerals [...] smoking a large cigar' and wearing 'a pearl-grey Stetson' as well as 'a loud American suit'.[171]

Paradoxically, an 'essential' Gothic 'obscenity' lurking within fictive constructs of a Mafiosi Belfast appears to sometimes compensate for the lack of a real Mafiosi PIRA. Writing about 'representations of Belfast in recent fiction', Eamon Hughes investigates the ideology behind such images.[172]

According to Hughes, the 'representation of Belfast within the thriller genre [...] is not Belfast at all [but] simply a void, a blank space filled by novelists and film-makers with stock-properties'.[173] These stock-properties create 'an almost Gothic landscape'.[174] Within such a landscape, 'urban corruption' stands opposed to 'rural innocence'.[175] All this means that, ultimately, Belfast becomes 'a pathopolis'.[176] For Hughes, this pathopolis is 'a diseased city [...] which houses a criminal fraternity'.[177] It is 'a site of corruption, sin

170   John Mullin, 'A Shattered Peace', *Guardian*, 2 January 1998, pp.1, 2.
171   Dowling, *Interface Ireland*, p.29.
172   Eamon Hughes, 'Town of Shadows: Representations of Belfast in Recent Fiction', *Religion and Literature*, 28. 2–3 (Summer–Autumn 1996), 141–61 (p.2–3).
173   Ibid., pp.141, 145.
174   Ibid., p.145.
175   Ibid., pp.144–5.
176   Patrick Gedde's term quoted by Lewis Mumford, in *The City in History: Its Origins, Its Transformations, and Its Prospects* (London: Secker and Warberg, 1961), p.556.
177   Ibid., p.147, 145.

and nameless terrors' and a text where 'sin and criminality are inscribed [...] in the very fabric of the city'.[178] But, like representations of the PIRA, these types of appropriations of Belfast fail to supply a proper analysis of the real economic crises that underpinned the Troubles. Hence, a Belfast Gothic apoliticizes the political.

Linking the Gothic to Mafiosi Irish gunmen, and anticipating *The Godfather*'s chiaroscuro visual tone and the cinema's Mafiosi villains, films such as *Odd Man Out* (1947) evoke Belfast as a place of 'strong chiaroscuro' where earlier gangster stereotypes are collapsed into embodiments of evil Irish gunmen summoned from 'dark, ominous shadows'.[179] Indeed, *Interface Ireland* offers images of a British law who superimpose the PIRA with the Mafiosi through 'films [...] showing' a nightmare Belfast of 'monsters, dead children – and screams'.[180] However, post-1970s texts supply repeat showings of these images. For instance, lurking within *Cal*'s abattoir (Derry) city, MacLaverty supplies a Mafiosi 'thug' named Crilly.[181] Now, while Crilly could be read from the margins in terms of being a victim of economic and social deprivation, these political notions become supplanted through his 'limited [...] intellect', his lack.[182] This lack is reciprocated by an 'inadequate' and 'effete' godfather figure named Finbar Skeffington.[183] Like Crilly, Skeffington could be read from the margins; this time in terms of committed Irish Republicanism. However, Skeffington's credibility as a serious political figure is undermined when he 'first appears out of the shadows, like Dracula, to fall on his "prey"'.[184] Although this image shows Derry to be a Gothic urban space, Cal's father (Shamie) suggests that Belfast is worse. Thus, when the unemployed Cal tells Shamie that there are 'a couple

178 Ibid., pp.148, 153.

179 Hill, *Cinema and Ireland*, pp.152, 182.

180 Dowling, *Interface Ireland*, p.52.

181 Stephen Watt, 'The Politics of Bernard Mac MacLaverty's *Cal*', *Eire-Ireland*, 28.3 (1993), 130–46 (p.143).

182 Barry Sloan, 'The Wages of Paramilitary Sin', *The Honest Ulsterman*, 80 (Spring 1986), 21–31 (p.23).

183 Bill Rolston, 'Mothers Whores and Villains: Images of Women in Novels of the Northern Ireland Conflict', *Race and Class*, 31.1 (1989), 41–57 (p.42).

184 Hill, *Cinema Ireland*, p.182.

[of jobs] in Belfast', Shamie tells him: 'You're safer away from the city'.[185]

All of the above fantasy images about Belfast and the PIRA have proven to be resilient and found their way into later novels produced by British and Irish alike. So, a decade after *Interface Ireland*, Robert McLiam Wilson's fictitious character named Ripley Bogle describes Belfast as 'Belfastard!'.[186] According to Bogle, Belfast is 'a shitty city, leprous and not too pretty'.[187] And Bogle's Belfast is an ideal venue for Seymour's Irish 'Men in the Mirror called the God-fathers'.[188] So too for M.S. Power's 'part sleazy car salesman, part Mafia [IRA] boss'.[189]

Hughes links the idea of Belfast 'as a gothic locale' to Belfast as 'an imprisoning place'.[190] And when Jim Sheridan's 1994 film (*In the Name of the Father*) recuperated the Mafiosi-PIRA, the Irish god-father was relocated from a metaphorically 'imprisoning' Irish 'place' to a literally 'imprisoning' British 'place'.[191]

Shifted from the 1970s to the 1990s, and from Belfast to a British prison, Dublin-born Sheridan's PIRA godfather of enjoyment carries out an internecine revenge killing while his fellow inmates *enjoy* a performance of Coppola's *The Godfather*. While *The Godfather*'s haunting theme music resonates around the prison, the assassin *enjoys* another performance. This performance shows a British prison warder burning to death. Here, the Irish godfather's smile from behind the picture screen symbolizes a folding back that recruits an embodiment of evil in to an embodiment of Irish Mafiosi; a mirror image reflecting, perhaps, a British male audience's *jouissance*. Thus, the ultimate law of the evil Irish godfather takes pleasure from excess not lack, from 'execution' as a 'form' of punishment which, according to Zizek, is a 'form solely for the sake of form' and, therefore, 'the

185   MacLaverty, *Cal*, p.15.
186   Robert McLiam Wilson, *Ripley Bogle* (London: Pan, 1990), p.160, 161.
187   Ibid., p.161.
188   Seymour, *Field of Blood*, p.34.
189   M.S. Power, *The Killing of Yesterday's Children* (London: Chatto and Windus, 1985), Cit. Rolston, 'Mothers Whores and Villains', p.42.
190   Hughes, 'Town of Shadows', p.149.
191   *In the Name of the Father*, Dir. Jim Sheridan, Universal, 1994.

definition of the pure moral act'.[192] Bearing this last point in mind in terms of the texts discussed in this section, the 1970s PIRA as Mafiosi seem to have inaugurated British, and to some extent Irish, male identifications and projections with an ideal self as well as an ideal other. But, once again, such identifications and projections say little about the north of Ireland as a site of political conflict.

1.3: 'Reds in the Bed': The PIRA and the Communist Scare

> It is now almost a year since Airey Neave was brutally murdered [...]. How bitter that the man who wrote so clearly about one of the curses of our time should himself die because of it [...]. Although deeply English, and devoted to English things, he was not so foolish as to think that tyranny could never be established here [...]. Russia [...] now poses the main external threat to our way of life [...]. We know that once we have conquered our domestic troubles we shall be able to make a more worthy contribution to the safety of the West.[193]

1980. A new decade. But, as suggested by Margaret Thatcher, the British psyche still harboured the fear that Russia was on the verge of 'nuking' the West. The following section focuses upon how and why from the late 1960s until the present date, fictive appropriations of the PIRA have been constructed in terms of the Cold War threat, international terrorism and Irish Republicanism.

During the latter decades of the Cold War, the 'main external threat to our way of life' (the Soviet Union) was fused with the 'main' extimate 'threat to our way of life': 'Ireland and the problems facing

---

192 Zizek, *Everything You Always Wanted to Know about Lacan ... but were Afraid to ask Hitchcock*, p.95.

193 Margaret Thatcher, 'In Memory of Airey Neave: Ireland and the Problems Facing our Society', *Etudes Irlandaises*, 5 (December 1980), 145–52 (pp.145, 150–1, 151, 152).

[...] British Society'. Paralleled with Russia (the big menacing other) Britain's 'domestic' Irish enemy (the small menacing other) became implicated at a global level. Why else would Thatcher assume that a resolution of 'our domestic troubles', namely Ireland, would ensure 'safety' from the Communist Bloc?

Not surprisingly, these political concerns affected the British imagination and, as stated by Alan Titley, for 'the thriller writer [...] the IRA gunman' provided 'a replacement for', or repetition of, 'the Hun or communist agent [because] there is no need for Reds hiding around the chamber pot when Paddys begin at Holyhead'.[194]

Commencing with the inception of the PIRA, the idea of there being an internecine Soviet-Celtic plot against Britain held powerful ideological currency. This currency was boosted by both 'factual' and 'fictive' constructs. For instance, in 1984 the British media showed real news footage of the aftermath of Irish guerrilla warfare on the Grand Hotel at Brighton while in 1985 films such as *Threads* and *The War Game* showed hypothetical nightmare scenarios of the aftermaths of nuclear warfare on British cities. 1985 also produced the pro-British journalist Chapman Pincher's text named *The Secret Offensive* which rather effectively, if rather dubiously, merged the Irish enemy with the nuclear threat – and recruited CND along the way.[195] 'The CND', writes Pincher, 'assist the Communist cause'.[196] According to Pincher, 'CND delegates have been joyfully welcomed in Moscow'.[197] Moreover, says Pincher, 'the "peace" camps around' British military 'bases [offer] ideal locations for IRA terrorists [who] establish themselves in preparation for an attempt to seize the nuclear core of a weapon that could provide [...] devastating blackmail power'.[198] As for the PIRA's Grand Hotel bombing, Pincher believes this 'attempt to assassinate Margaret Thatcher [...] would have been welcome to the Politburo'.[199] Pincher's notions about 'the secret offensive' are, of

194 Titley, 'Rough, Rug-Headed Kerns', p.25.
195 Chapman Pincher, *The Secret Offensive* (London: Sidgewick and Jackson, 1985).
196 Ibid., p.262.
197 Ibid., p.263.
198 Ibid.
199 Ibid., p.287.

course, highly subjective political translations of historical events, repetitions of former highly subjective political translations of historical events spanning the late 1960s and 1970s.

The late 1960s and 1970s brought global Left wing militancy. Students marched in most major capitols of the West in protest over various issues including Vietnam and nuclear disarmament. The Red Brigade bombed Milan and Rome while, in Derry, Civil Rights protests about discrimination against Catholics attracted international media coverage and a British Right wing backlash which resulted in the Diplock Courts, internment without trial and the torture of PIRA suspects. This backlash was justified by the production, by the imagining, by the repetitions of an international communist conspiracy of spies and British traitors in dangerous league with the PIRA. The British media and MI5 Black Propaganda encouraged these repetitions, these 'spy thriller' narratives. For instance, Curtis observes how, 'on 23 October 1971, a few days after *The Sunday Times* had published details of the torture of internees, the *Daily Mirror* printed what must rank as one of the most bizarre stories of the decade'.[200] Curtis recalls the *Daily Mirror* headline in which 'huge letters on the front page announced, "IRA HIRE RED KILLERS", with the sub-headline "Czech assassin is shot by troops"'.[201] According to Curtis, these types of 'Iron Curtain', 'red scare' PIRA narratives are 'fantasy stories [which] both satisfy the popular papers' need for drama, and serve the propaganda purposes of the authorities'.[202]

As well as satisfying media need and government propaganda, these fantasy stories are symptoms of British desire to appropriate the enemy – albeit the Russians, the PIRA, or the Russians as the PIRA. Doomed to perpetual failure, such desire hysterically repeats this failure with more and more appropriations of more and more fantasy foes. So, in 1977, six years after the 'Czech assassin' fantasy, the *Daily Mirror* brandished a headline saying 'Trots hire IRA to bomb English cities' then claimed that 'British Trotskyites and Marxists [...]

---

200   Curtis, *Ireland: The Propaganda War*, p.119.
201   Ibid.
202   Ibid., pp.120, 121, 118.

spent two months forging links with wildcat IRA bombers'.[203] This 1977 'othering' of the British self coincides with the 1977 'othering' of Harold Wilson. For instance, 'manufactured intelligence' about an alliance 'between Soviet [...], other communist agencies and' the PIRA fed allegations about Harold Wilson.[204] These allegations meant that Wilson 'was [...] suspected' of being a 'Soviet agent', a communist traitor, and a political pawn for communism and the PIRA.[205] Not surprisingly, these extraordinary exposés paralleled British anxieties about the growth of militant Irish Republicanism, anxieties that we might term PIRA(noia).

When PIRA activity on the British mainland escalated, the production of Cold War narratives gained ideological momentum with the 1974 Birmingham, Guildford and Woolwich pub bombings, the 1977 assassination of SAS captain Robert Nairac, the 1978 bombings of Bristol, Coventry, Liverpool, Manchester and Southampton, and the 1979 assassinations of Airey Neave and Mountbatten. If British kudos was to remain intact, these deadly paramilitary successes had to be attributed to a formidable not to mention ubiquitous other: a domestic *and* international terror-inducing other. Hence, the Irish Republican gunman was redefined in terms of Russia and Marxist communism, a process resulting in acute British PIRA(noia) and the manufacture of outrageous myths. For example, in *Their Trade is Treachery*, Pincher recalls how, during 1974, Harold Wilson 'emerged from a meeting and said, "Now I've heard everything. I've just been told that the head of MI5 himself [Sir Roger Hollis] may have been a double agent"'.[206] In fact, Hollis was 'deeply suspected by some of his own colleagues of having been a Russian agent for nearly fifty years'.[207] Pincher

203 *Daily Mirror* article reproduced in *Big Flame*, October 1977, Cit. Curtis, *Ireland: The Propaganda War*, p.121.
204 Duncan Campbell, 'Still Dark in Paranoia Gulch', in *War and Words: The Northern Ireland Media Reader*, eds. Bill Rolston and David Miller (Belfast: Beyond the Pale, 1996), pp.191–6 (p.193).
205 Paul Foot, 'Colin Wallace and the Propaganda War', in *War and Words*, pp.158–96 (p.185).
206 Chapman Pincher, *Their Trade is Treachery* (London: Sidgewick and Jackson, 1981), p.5.
207 Ibid., p.1.

observes that Wilson's statement about Hollis is 'ironic'.[208] This is because 'Wilson had angrily called the meeting [...] to discuss false rumours, believed to have come from MI5' in the first place.[209] And, intensifying the irony, these false rumours claimed that Wilson 'and Lady Falkender were running a Communist cell in No.10!'[210] As evidenced by Troubles novels, these types of crypto-Cold War narratives are sometimes ascendants, sometimes descendants, of fictive appropriations of the PIRA.

As I have argued, many of the stereotypes attempting to seize the PIRA include a folding back to incorporate previous stereotypes albeit with, sometimes, different ideological effects. A case in point is a folding back onto comic versions of the PIRA with an early 1970s novel produced by Anglo-Irish author Martin Waddell. The novel is called, ironically, *A Little Bit British*, and the narrative submits a feisty satire of how the British media create Irish Republican 'Anarchists and Trotskyite Communists' who are 'Moscow Spawn'.[211] Here, we can forge a comic link with Waddell's narrative to Australian author Russell Braddon's equally satirical novel, *The Progress of Private Lilyworth*, which manifests 'a genial looking man from MI5 disguised as Lord Thomson of the *Sunday Times*' who is 'convinced' that an Irish Catholic nun is 'a Russian spy'.[212] On a more serious level, James Carrick created sinister PIRA 'communists'.[213] While British author James Barlow supplied a character named 'King Lamont' who claims that 'the IRA, Sinn Fein and the rest [...] are selling out to a phoney God, communism!'[214] 'Any bandit can have an audience with the Pope!' expounds Lamont: 'the doors of the Vatican are always open for the Mao-ist liberal revolutionary murderers'.[215] In the mid 1970s, fictive Irish gunmen received 'printed instructions' from the

208 Ibid., p.5.
209 Ibid.
210 Ibid.
211 Waddell, *A Little Bit British*, p.30.
212 Russell Braddon, *The Progress of Private Lilyworth* (London: Michael Joseph, 1971), p.85.
213 Carrick, *With O'Leary in the Grave*, p.59.
214 Barlow, *Both Your Houses*, p.137.
215 Ibid.

Russians about 'how to handle weapons',[216] resembled 'middle-aged Communists' or 'Whiz kid, Trotskyite, textbook revolutionar[ies]'[217] who were infiltrated by 'professional agitators and terrorists [...] financed from the Kremlin'.[218] In 1982 these repetitions made a transatlantic crossing to America for a KGB and PIRA alliance.[219] But 1987 brought the repetitions 'home' again so that a fictive British pro-PIRA lawyer could don the mantle 'Red Charlie' and indulge 'a penchant for radical causes and radical crimes'.[220] James Lund, an author boasting an enigmatic yet Disraeliesque identity, opted for a 1976 Mafiosi-cum-KGB-cum-PIRA fraternity.[221] And by 1979 this fraternity was of course repeated at a satirical level by Kevin Dowling whose 'Shamrock Mafia' are also 'red' tinted 'communist extrem-ists'.[222] Not surprisingly, Pincher contributed to these fictions. Antici-pating his so-called 'factual' accounts of communists, spies and potential nuclear annihilation, Pincher's work as an archetypal Cold War author reveals his obsession with the imaginary alliance 'between the IRA and Russia' that, claims Pincher, can be traced back 'to 1927'.[223]

Pincher's 1976 novel, *The Eye of the Tornado*, charts a KGB attempt to 'Klobber Great Britain' through 'a political coup' against a female Tory prime minister named 'Mrs Fletcher'.[224] Here, we have a prophetic gesture towards the then newly elected Conservative leader of the opposition: Margaret Thatcher. Moreover, Pincher's narrative offers a contrast to Chris Mullin's later 1982 novel entitled *A Very British Coup*.[225] This is because Pincher's imagining of a 'quick putsch' is not inspired by an autocratic Right wing establishment or

216   Seaman, *The Bomb That Could Lip-Read*, p.71.
217   Driscoll, *In Connection with Kilshaw*, pp.172, 18.
218   Perry, *Dead End*, p.72.
219   George V. Higgins, *The Patriot Game* (London: Martin Secker and Warburg, 1982), p.140.
220   Clancy, *Patriot Games*, p.122.
221   Lund, *The Ultimate*, p.208.
222   Dowling, *Interface Ireland*, p.54.
223   Pincher, *The Eye of the Tornado*, p.26.
224   Ibid., pp.25, 98.
225   Chris Mullin, *A Very British Coup* (London: Hodder and Stoughton, 1982).

conspiracy but rather by far Left Marxism.[226] Pincher supplies a paranoid vision of a Britain that is 'a soft target [...] riddled with reds', a Britain that is chock-a-block with KGB-led 'trade union militants', 'nuclear disarmers', 'dissident students' 'atomic traitors', and, of course, a British traitor.[227] This traitor is called Nigel Cunningham-Smith, a man who 'could have been a left-winger since his student days, covering his intentions, like Philby did, with [...] right-wing camouflage'.[228]

The KGB coup envisioned by Pincher is performed by Irish gunmen who hijack the KSV *Mallard*, a ship carrying primed Polaris nuclear warheads. But, for Pincher, the idea of Britain being held to deadly, nuclear ransom is not enough in terms of demonization. Thus, he also makes his paramilitaries politically incorrect. So, after demonstrating a ludicrously archaic, male-chauvinist 'contempt for petticoat rule', the gunmen refuse to 'deal with [...] a government headed by a woman'.[229] All this exacerbates the panic about the potential detonation of the stolen warheads and enables the coup to take place. 'They gave Mrs Fletcher twenty-four hours to stand down', writes Pincher: 'twenty-four hours to [...] eliminate the "monstrous regiment of women"'.[230] Eventually, all ends well. A loyal and heroic Captain (Thomas Parrington) wins a bold nuclear stand-off, the KGB capitulates to Britain and, contemplating 'divine intervention', Mrs Fletcher 'thank[s] the Almighty in her prayers'.[231] Through this narrative, Pincher supplies his reader as well as himself with all the essential motifs for a Cold War thriller: left wing anarchy, the Soviet other, a nuclear threat, traitors and, crucially, the PIRA.

Pincher's novel comfortingly preserves the notion of 'orbital war' and therefore denies the late-1970s increasing perception of 'war' signalling 'two different things: on the one hand a total but virtual war (an orbital war); on the other hand a multiplicity of real

226   Pincher, *The Eye of the Tornado*, p.101.
227   Ibid., pp.101, 105, 85, 80.
228   Ibid., p.102.
229   Ibid., pp.67, 88.
230   Ibid., p.87.
231   Ibid., p.198.

wars at ground level'.[232] These 'real wars at ground level', for instance the 'war' in the north of Ireland, inflict the shock of a too proximate real, a too proximate enemy, a too proximate confrontation with real dead bodies. Therefore, repeating the idea of the PIRA being KGB accomplices to the nuclear threat, Pincher feeds the, inherently British, desire for an unequivocal yet virtual external enemy and an orbital war. This is, perhaps, a suitable role for an author whose novel declares that he is a 'world-renowned British defense correspondent'. Put simply, Pincher creates a fantasy mediated in a text where 'the card-carriers conditioned to respond like robots to the Lenin dictum [display] the ugly face of Communism'.[233] This 'ugly face' repeats both the literal and metaphorical contagion of disfigurement exhibited by early representations of the PIRA and equates with the communist contagion imagined by Pincher's PM. 'I always thought', muses Mrs Fletcher, that 'Communism was a mental disease. More's the pity it's not certifiable'.[234] Her desire to contain madness echoes Michel Foucault's theory about 'The Birth of the Asylum' which suggests that during the late eighteenth and early nineteenth centuries it was believed that 'Catholicism frequently provoke[d] madness'.[235] Communism *and* Catholicism, this explains why Pincher's Irish gunmen are both literally and metaphorically adrift in a 'Ship of Fools'.[236]

Ugliness, madness and contagion. Pincher's depiction of his very-British PIRA hijackers, who are merely political puppets of the KGB, once more signals an hysterical folding back to several other Irish stereotypes. Comic 'oiyrishness', demonic Irishness and Mafia Irishness, all lurk beneath the creation of an, ultimately, incompetent Marxist Irishness. For instance, a character named Delaney, 'a Marxist by proxy rather than intellectual persuasion', possesses 'several decaying teeth' and is 'ferret-faced [...] with a nose that made him look as though he had caught a chill when the priest christened

232 Baudrillard, *The Transparency of Evil*, p.27.
233 Pincher, *The Eye of the Tornado*, p.86.
234 Ibid., p.87.
235 *The Foucault Reader: An Introduction to Foucault's Thought*, ed. Paul Rabinow (London: Penguin, 1984), p.146.
236 Michel Foucault, *Madness and Civilisation: A History of Insanity in the Age of Reason*, trans. Richard Howard (London: Tavistock, 1971), p.7.

him'.[237] And Pincher's decision to spell the 'oiyrish' dialogue phonetically intensifies Delaney's 'thick mick' characterization. So, when asked if he is able to 'align [...] Marxism with [his] faith', Delaney replies: 'Me mother wouldn't tink so, God rest her soul'.[238] Delaney's naive, almost child-like attitude towards politics also implies intellectual bankruptcy. 'Call me "Pat"', quips Delaney: 'We Marxists approve of nicknames'.[239]

Acting as a demonic, gangster-like foil to Delaney's comic 'paddy' role is 'Machine-gun' McNally of Kilkenny, one of the hardest and most fanatically anti-British of all IRA hard-liners'.[240] McNally is 'inhuman', an 'animal', a psychopath who could 'murther his mother if he was ordered to' and would 'be havin' no hesitation in 'shootin' the children taken as hostages.[241] Comic, demonic, gangsters, and lumpen auxiliaries to the Soviet state, Delaney and McNally are, paradoxically, everything in terms of the Irish stereotype but, ultimately, nothing more than another British fantasy.

The political insignificance of Pincher's Irish gunmen is highlighted when a fictive British MP explains how 'the eye of the tornado is a CIA expression for any vortex round which a major KGB operation involving violence is planned'.[242] But Delaney and McNally (a buffoon and a psychopath) are unlikely victors in the overthrowing of a nation, are failed appropriations of the real PIRA, are false perpetrators of a fantasy coup, are misrecognitions of the 'eye of the tornado [who] look like the IRA but may not be'.[243]

Pincher's adoption of the Cold War thriller genre can be discussed in terms of Schlesinger's and others observations about 'the secret service thriller [which] places "terrorism" firmly within a political context [such as] the Cold War'.[244] Originating 'during the

237   Pincher, *The Eye of the Tornado*, p.15, 14.
238   Ibid., pp.15, 14.
239   Ibid., p.35.
240   Ibid.
241   Ibid., pp.49, 79, 10.
242   Ibid., p.54.
243   Ibid., p.76.
244   Schlesinger, Murdock and Elliott, *Televising Terrorism*, p.80. Further consecutive references to this edition are given after quotations in the text.

Edwardian era' the secret service thriller 'emerged when the security of Britain was [...] seen as [being] under attack from external enemies [...] and alien forces' such as 'the Soviet Union [and] Irish republicans' (81). The British heroes in these narratives 'were [...] upper class gentlemen who [personified] everything that was best about the British way of life' (81). Such gentlemen 'were [either] amateurs serving their country out of love and duty [or] full-time members of the newly formed intelligence and security services' (81). But, importantly, 'all were gentlemen [with] no formal training' except for 'the skills and qualities [...] acquired on the playing fields of the public schools' (81).

Representations of British gentlemen thwarting external Soviet enemies and alien terrorist forces of course remained within fiction as 'ideological baggage packed in the heyday of Empire' (81). However, Kim Philby's 1963 'defection to Moscow' triggered psychological shock-waves about there being an enemy within the British establishment and, consequently, a 'declin[e]' in the 'ideological fortunes of the gentleman' together with a rise in 'the professionalization of the "secret state" within the thriller' (81). Pincher's Philbyesque traitor (Cunningham-Smith) is an early symptom of this shift in British attitudes which, eventually, paved the way for a new 'tough, abrasive, unsentimental', albeit still gentlemanly, 'professionalism' epitomized by James Bond (81). But this refashioning of the British male ideal still required a powerful communist, or Irish crypto-communist, rival who was utterly different and utterly other to Britishness.

Writing in 1964, before the dissolution of the Communist Bloc, William K. Everson suggests that 'now [...] the cold war seems to be thawing again, perhaps [...] the "Reds" [...] have missed their chance for movie immortality'.[245] But, according to Palmer, at this same historical point the Russians still supply an essential ingredient for thriller fiction, especially James Bond thrillers where SMERSH provide 'collective villains' for the virile and masculine British hero who always triumphs over the 'foreign power'.[246] For Michael Selzer,

---

245 Everson, *Bad Guys*, p.139.
246 Palmer, *Thrillers: Genesis and Structure of a Popular Genre*, pp.7, 8, 17.

Bond is 'no example of prissy propriety'.[247] However, Bond's 'villains [are] kept obscure [and are] almost blank screens onto which the' male audience may 'project his wildest imaginings [while] the story unfolds from the perspective of the hero [...] with whom the' same male audience 'is tacitly encouraged to identify'. [248]

Repeated through various actors, Bond's contribution towards ideal British masculinity has been mediated through Sean Connery with a gentlemanly-cum-rugged Scottishness, George Lazenby with a gentlemanly-cum-GI Americaness, Roger Moore with a gentlemanly-cum-archly-camp Englishness, and, ironically, Pierce Brosnan with a no-holds-barred apotheosis of heroic Anglo-Irishness. Brosnan's status as the 1990s Anglo-Irish Bond is rendered doubly ironic by his former roles. These roles include, 'a top secret' communist 'agent with a nuclear bomb' in *The Fourth Protocol* (1987) and a ruthless PIRA gunman in *The Long Good Friday* (1979). More recently, of course, we have come full circle with English actor Daniel Craig – but maybe his earlier performance as a gangster in the 2004 film titled *Layer Cake* makes him a little bit Irish too?

If Bond signals a post-Philby reorientation of the quest for a 'pure' British male ideal, it is not surprising that versions of Bond occur as repetitions within Troubles texts. But, created from an international potpourri of the Scottish, the American, the English, the Irish and, as implicated through Fleming's narrative formula, the Russian, the possibility of locating an authentic British masculinity within these already hybrid identifications becomes even more problematic and illusory. If Bond is not, in fact, a symbol of pure Britishness, this may account for the reason why British identifications with Fleming's hero supplied by Troubles texts appear to slide between the PIRA antagonist and his non-Irish rival. For instance, in 1975, David Martin's Irish gunman 'find[s] [him]self picturing scenes from a Bond spectacular'.[249] While, in 1977, helplessly embroiled in Irish terrorism as well as Russian and international arms dealing, Ritchie Perry's hero voices a desire for assistance from

247   Selzer, *Terrorist Chic*, p.152.
248   Ibid.
249   David Martin, *The Task* (London: Secker and Warburg, 1975), p.8.

'James Bond'.[250] Ted Harriott shows a British colonel telling a sergeant that 'according to [a] newspaper' the sergeant is 'the British Army's version of James Bond'.[251] But, as the story-line unfolds, an Irish gunman fantasizes about an 'American woman [whom] perhaps [...] would appear in the doorway, hold him at gun-point [...] and [...] turn him over to the police'.[252] At this point, Harriott tells his reader how this gunman 'almost laughed aloud at the image of a plump matron with her blue-rinsed hair pointing a gun and wheezing asthmatically through a James Bond act'.[253] Interestingly, this fantasy of a plump American matron might signal an acknowledgement from Harriott that British male identifications with a pure masculine image are as illusory as 'a James Bond act'. The recognition of such an acknowledgement could explain why, in 1984, even the female and Irish author Linda Anderson portrayed a British soldier in the north of Ireland who 'felt queasy when he received his yellow card [and] licence to kill'.[254] It might also explain why, in 1988, Anthony Melville-Ross showed an SAS man admitting a misidentification of the self as 'being so damn smart [...] like [...] James Bond'.[255] And why, in 1989, Richard Burns subverted Bond through parody.[256] During Burns's narrative, a comic Irish gunman (Jack Diamond) is instructed to 'memorise [an] address [then] destroy the paper'.[257] Diamond's riposte to the request suggests that the situation is 'just like James Bond'; which is why he asks: 'Should I eat' the message?[258] If an acknowledgement of British misidentification did occur within British and male-authored fiction and, in the case of Anderson, even female-authored Irish fiction, it is little wonder that, by 1990, Gavin Esler's Irishman named Dunlop exhibits confusion over a multiple-choice, impossibly macho, persona that offers identifications with an

250   Perry, *Dead End*, p.44.
251   Ted Harriott, *No Sanctuary*, p.221.
252   Ibid., p.70.
253   Ibid.
254   Anderson, *To Stay Alive*, p.19.
255   Anthony Melville-Ross, *Shaw's War* (London: Michael Joseph), 1988), p.107.
256   Burns, *Why Diamond had to Die*.
257   Ibid., p.33.
258   Ibid.

'Action Man soldier, maybe in the SAS, maybe the real James Bond'.[259]

Maybe in the SAS. Maybe the real James Bond. Through fiction, an important reciprocity between these two images of British action-men can be located. Like Bond, representations of the SAS are symptomatic of the desire for images of ideal male Britishness which could account for the 1990s spate of so-called 'Big Boys' Books' published by ex-SAS operatives such as Andy McNab,[260] Chris Ryan,[261] Terence Strong,[262] and James Rennie.[263] The fly-cover blurb to Rennie's 'faction' novel displays this type of imaginary machismo. 'If Ian Fleming's James Bond exists anywhere today,' declares Rennie, 'he is to be found within the ranks of 14 Company [where] every single day of each year for the past twenty-one years, Operators have been deployed [...] against [...] terrorism in Northern Ireland'.

All these dogged yet in the end failed attempts to preserve a pure British, albeit quasi-Irish, Bond hero are a ramification of the late 1980s and 1990s nostalgia for the Communist Bloc. This nostalgia is expressed in British, and former investigative journalist, Gordon Stevens's 1993 novel entitled *Provo*.[264] In *Provo*, Stephens implies how the removal of the Berlin Wall deprives the British self of the communist other, a lack seeking compensation through an Irish Re-publican other. The anxiety suffered by Stevens's fictive British Army officer makes this clear. 'Now that the Berlin Wall had come down,' muses the officer: 'Germany was reunited and, [with] the Soviet empire totally disintegrated into republics, the whole thrill and tension of exercises under the noses of the enemy had evaporated'.[265] Germany is 'no longer a soldier's posting', laments the officer: 'Nowhere was any more. Except Northern Ireland'.[266]

259   Esler, *Loyalties*, p.188.
260   Andy McNab, *Immediate Action* (London: Bantam, 1995).
261   Chris Ryan, *Stand By, Stand By* (London: Century, 1996).
262   Terence Strong, *Whisper Who Dares* (Bath: Chivers, 1983).
263   James Rennie, *The Operators: Inside 14 Intelligence Company – The Army's Top Secret Elite* (London: Century, 1996).
264   Gordon Stevens, *Provo.*
265   Ibid., pp.262, 263.
266   Ibid., p.263.

This said, as late as 1991, Frederick Forsyth's novel entitled *The Deceiver* persisted with Communist Bloc fantasies through a series of four spy thriller adventures: three involving communist spies and one involving the PIRA.[267] Yet, in spite of Forsyth's Cold War repetitions, his awareness of his plot's anachronistic subject matter, and perhaps his own status as 'author-cum-deceiver', becomes apparent. This happens when a fictive British Intelligence officer states how 'we cannot dwell in the past, chewing over the Cold War all over again'.[268] 'The point is', says the officer, 'there are other menaces that threaten our country and which are on the increase'.[269] These menaces include the 'proliferation of high-tech weaponry to highly unstable tyrants in the Third World [...] and of course terrorism'.[270]

The absence of Russia as a formidable shadowy foe created an ideological gap, a negation of the psychological difference between the British self and Soviet other which included the economic, material difference between Marxism and Capitalism. If 'Marxism is a mirror to Capitalism', when the mirror image 'evaporates', when identity 'disintegrates', nostalgic and comforting repetitions ensue.[271] This is why the late 1980s saw various Cold War fictions resurrected and rewritten as the 'red' PIRA other whom, it could be argued, symbolizes 'the return of the repressed'.[272] The repressed is the Communist Bloc, the surrogate object of desire stimulating 'the return' of a McCarthyesque reds-in-the-bed PIRA(noia) through 'fear' about 'the Provos [and] extreme Marxism' as well as the fantasy that 'hoards of Russian, Chinese, Libyan and Kurdish revolutionaries [...] lurk under every Falls Road floorboard'.[273] As suggested by Baudrillard, these types of repetitions take place because 'without the Other

267   Frederick Forsyth, *The Deceiver* (London: Transworld, 1991).
268   Ibid., p.223.
269   Ibid.
270   Ibid.
271   Jean Baudrillard, *Selected Writings*, ed. Mark Poster (Oxford: Polity, 1988), p.4.
272   Jean Baudrillard, *The Transparency of Evil*, p.97.
273   *Fortnight*, 9 January 1976, p.14. Photocopied article supplied by the Linenhall Library, Belfast.

as mirror, as reflecting surface, consciousness of self is threatened'.[274] Thus 'consciousness of self' becomes problematic when the self, the 'subject', is 'purged of the other' and then 'doomed to self-metastasis, to pure repetition'.[275] Without the evil communist enemy, British male identity confronts the self as 'pure repetition' and British masculinity as a neutral, or neutered, 'hell of the Same'.[276]

Deprived of the Cold War, the desire for the preservation of British masculinity eventually necessitated a shift of focus from the Communist Bloc. In both fact and fiction, SMERSH was usurped and repeated as international terrorism (the latter still thriving as an ideological obsession in 2006) and a tendency to convert all that was left-wing into communism or Irish Republicanism while Bond was usurped and repeated by the SAS-type hero. Hence, in 1988, James Adams, Robin Morgan and Anthony Bambridge produced *Ambush: The War Between the SAS and the IRA* and announced that 'since the ending of the Cold War [...] there was no longer any real need for the James Bond type of secret agent'.[277]

With 1990s Hollywood films such as *Patriot Games*, *Blown Away*,[278] and *The Jackal*,[279] the Cold War becomes repeated in terms of international terrorism and America – a prophetic cinematic trend made real with the destruction of the Twin Towers. But these 1990s films did, of course, anticipate the wrong enemy within: Ireland as opposed to Islam. In *Blown Away*, a maverick and deranged PIRA bomber, a repetition of the 1970s Irish demon, rampages through a pyrotechnic thriller but is finally thwarted by a 'good' Irish American 'cop'. Played by Tommy Lee Jones, the bomber is 'too crazy for the IRA', a 'sick freak' who arrives in the US 'to create a new country called chaos and a new government called anarchy'. *Patriot Games* shows the PIRA being flown across from Ireland for military training 'in a North African training camp' then terrorizing the US before a

274 Ibid., p.122.
275 Ibid.
276 Ibid.
277 James Adams, Robin Morgan and Anthony Bambridge, *Ambush: The War Between the SAS and the IRA* (London: Pan, 1988), p.49.
278 *Blown Away*, Dir. Stephen Hopkins, MGM, 1992.
279 *The Jackal*, Dir. Michael Caton-Jones, Universal, 1997.

secret service, action man hero, played by Harrison Ford, saves the day. The plot, observes Geoffrey Macnab, results from 'the Soviet Union [being] out of commission [and] Hollywood' being compelled to 'find new territories for its secret service' as well as 'fresh roles for Harrison Ford'.[280] According to Macnab, *Patriot Games* is an 'attempt [...] to move beyond the Cold War and the *Temple of Doom*'.[281] But, with the PIRA acting out the Soviet versus America fantasy, this 1990s attempt to 'move beyond' only produces another repetition. With *The Jackal*, Hollywood supplies a 'cliché-ridden thriller [that] follows a conventional hero-versus-villain format' through a ludicrous narrative which recruits Russian gangsterism and the Irish para-military.[282] Here, the PIRA gunman is pitted against a Russian hit-man whose mastery of a dizzying number of disguises must surely be symptomatic of the hysterical search for the real yet frustratingly illusive Cold War villain.

During the late 1980s and 1990s, Troubles novels also repeated the Cold War through international terrorism. For instance, com-mencing in Portugal then travelling to 'Merrie England', 1987 produced Julian Romanes's *The Cell* which appropriated the Mafiosi, the PLO, the Russians and the PIRA to produce a terrorist 'cell from hell'.[283] One year later, Anthony Melville-Ross published *Shaw's War* and dispatched a plot in which two renegade British SAS officers (Harry Shaw and Bill Townsend) cross the Atlantic because 'be it American or Russian, the brain of the octopus supplying arms to the IRA war was in the United states and must be attacked there'.[284] Shaw criticizes the 'American Seals' for causing 'a monumental mess [in] their attempt to rescue the Iranian hostages' as well for not doing 'all that well during the invasion of Granada'.[285] Thus, Shaw articulates a desire for an identity that is not merely an ideal foil to the PIRA but also an ideal foil to the American military elite. Bearing in mind that

280   Geoffrey Macnab, *Sight and Sound*, July 1992, p.56.
281   Ibid., p.56.
282   David Tse, *Sight and Sound*, February 1998, p.47.
283   Romanes, *The Cell*, p.101.
284   Melville-Ross, *Shaw's War*, p.75.
285   Ibid., p.41.

the text's author is a British ex-submariner, Shaw's desire could once again be a British displacement.

Shaw's War reads like a roll-call of international demons, the PIRA, NORAID, Gaddafi, Arafat, Zionism, Hitler, the Russians and the Iranians are all implicated in 'a covering up' which is, finally, 'all very British, don't you know'.[286] Obsessed with the notion that the real other to Britishness is the PIRA, Shaw threatens to 'crucify whoever suggests that we're up against commie agitators or Soviet spies'.[287] The British self against the manifold other is problematized when Shaw announces: 'I know who I am'.[288] But Shaw's ostensible lack of 'an identity crisis' is a fiction. This is because his own identity is, paradoxically, entirely founded upon lack, founded upon not being American, or Irish, or Russian and, perhaps, founded upon not being Melville-Ross. James Daniel's 1996 SAS-cum-PIRA-cum-international terrorism novel might be perceived in the same terms.[289] So too, Chris Ryan's 1996 faction.[290] Daniel's Royal Military Academy at Sandhurst background and Ryan's SAS career suggest this may be so.

During the late 1990s, Cold War narratives and the PIRA still made headline news. 'Traitor in jail plot to betray MI5 to IRA', declares Chester Stern in his denunciation of 'traitor Michael Bettaney' who, it is claimed, not only tried to 'betray former MI5 colleagues working undercover in Ireland to the IRA,' but is also guilty of 'selling secrets to the Russians'.[291] Likewise, Neil Sears comments upon British traitor John Symonds.[292] According to Sears, Symonds was 'trained by the KGB in the arts of seduction, and equipped with a mouth-full of precious metal'.[293] And Symonds's political 'outing', writes Sears, 'could have come straight from a

---

286   Ibid., pp.37, 42, 52, 272, 274, 231.
287   Ibid., p.144.
288   Ibid., p.247.
289   James Daniel, *They Told Me You Were Dead* (London: Pan, 1996).
290   Chris Ryan, *Stand By, Stand By*.
291   Chester Stern, 'Traitor in jail plot to betray MI5 men to IRA', *Daily Mail*, 14 June 1998, p.13.
292   John Sears, *Daily Mail*, 13 September 1999, p.6.
293   Ibid., p.6.

James Bond novel'.[294] In the same week, 'Traitor Granny' Melitta Norwood became exposed as a KGB spy.[295] For *The Sunday Times*, Norwood is 'on a par with such celebrated spies as Burgess, Maclean, Philby, Blunt and Cairncross'.[296] Ultimately, Bettaney, Symonds and Norwood repeat the Cold War threat of the evil of communism in terms of 'nuclear risk'.[297] Moreover, these three political renegades must surely have boosted the ratings for the then new 'BBC series' entitled *The Spying Game*.[298]

Still psychologically immersed in the Cold War, Pincher writes, 'the cold war may be over but our fascination with the undercover war between East and West lives on' (a fascination still thriving today).[299] According to Pincher in the *Daily Mail* (1999), 'espionage and its associated skulduggeries have always commanded intense interest [...] because, as entertainment, espionage has everything going for it'.[300] This 'everything', says Pincher, contains 'secrecy, treachery, bribery, blackmail, violence, vanity and often sex, all being played for enormous stakes, especially when nuclear weapons were involved'.[301] Undoubtedly, Pincher may well have a point. But, surely, the biggest stake in Cold War narratives is often British male identity, especially when these narratives include the PIRA.

294 Ibid., p.6.
295 David Hughes and James Clarke, 'Traitor Granny may still be Sent for Trial', *Daily Mail*, 13 September 1999, p.1.
296 Editorial, *The Sunday Times*, 12 September 1999, p.5.
297 Sears, *Daily Mail*, p.6.
298 Ibid., p.6.
299 Chapman Pincher, 'Sex, lies and secrets – why we love the spying game', *Daily Mail*, 13 September 1999, p.10.
300 Ibid.
301 Ibid.

1.4: 'I know how rumours start': Homosexuality and the Irish Gunman

> THIRD SOLDIER: I don't want you talking about this.
> SECOND SOLDIER: Did I say a word?
> THIRD SOLDIER: I don't want to hear a word.
> SECOND SOLDIER: If that's your attitude.
> THIRD SOLDIER: Marcus Clavius. I do not want to hear, one night out drinking, back home, years from now, on a lovely evening, surrounded by admirers, sons. I do not want to hear [about] me not getting it up a British arseful of piles. Right?
> SECOND SOLDIER: Right.
> THIRD SOLDIER: I know how rumours start.[302]

As mentioned in section 1.1, the media attention given to the explicit and sensationalist homosexual rape scene within *The Romans in Britain* depoliticizes the text's political metaphor which is itself disguised through allegory and inversion. But the Roman soldier's paranoia concerning 'rumours' about 'not getting it up' offers a double inversion. Firstly, an inversion of British occupation in the north of Ireland in terms of the Roman occupation of Britain. Secondly, an inversion of British paranoia. This paranoia relates to 'rumours' about the British male 'getting it up' an Irish male 'arse'; a paranoia (or PIRA(noia)) screened through Roman paranoia caused by 'rumours' about 'not getting it up a' British male 'arse'. Para-doxically, *The Romans in Britain* implies that the extimate enemy within the enemy is British. The traitors are, and always have been, British. And abject homosexuality is, likewise, British.

Homosexuality and politics, especially the politics of Cold War treachery, summon a rumour-ridden period of Britain's political past, namely, the communist outings of the Philby, Maclean and Cairn-cross. This period also summons the doubly damning communist-homosexual outings, the so-called 'pinko' outings, of Burgess and Blunt. 'Shame' and 'guilt' are keywords here: shame and guilt about

302 Brenton, *The Romans in Britain*, p.42.

treachery is yoked to shame and guilt about sexual deviancy which, in turn, subverts ideal images of British male identity. In the novel entitled *Both Your Houses*, British author James Barlow's 1971 image of a British army officer illustrates this idea.[303] This becomes evident through the officer's outraged and indignant reaction towards a suggestion that his troops should 'search' an IRA suspect by 'hav[ing] a feel of his balls'.[304] Such a reaction is, I would suggest, symptomatic of shame and guilt or, to put this idea another way, 'methinks he doth protest too much?'[305]

Not surprisingly, Pincher's writings reveal hostility towards and denunciation of Cold War spies. His attitude emphasizes the embarrassment caused to male patriotism and virility by the discovery and exposure of communist-homosexuals. In his aptly entitled 1981 book, *Their Trade is Treachery*, Pincher's account of these events shows how a psychologically painful blow to Britishness reached its apotheosis with Burgess and Blunt, the infamously homosexual 'two' from the 'Ring of Five' British spies.[306] 'Guy Burgess', writes Pincher, 'was dishevelled [...] and a pouncing homosexual [whereas] contrary to the popular belief [...] Anthony Blunt' was not 'second division' to Philby and Maclean but 'one of the most damaging spies ever to operate in Britain'.[307] According to Pincher, Blunt was 'a sanctimonious hypocrite' and a 'cowardly' communist whose 'treachery [could] have hanged him a hundred times over'.[308] Pincher's 'case histories' of Burgess and Blunt utilize a dual (and negative) perception of homosexuality with the 'pouncingly' fey Burgess, and the 'cowardly' abject Blunt.[309] And Pincher's fictive texts appropriate these homosexual histories. Indeed, within *The Eye of The Tornado* these histories coincide with paranoia about the KGB and 'the blackmail hook' which is 'usually [repeated] through the homosexual

303   Barlow, *Both Your Houses.*
304   Ibid., p.19.
305   Ibid.
306   Pincher, *Their Trade is Treachery*, p.19.
307   Ibid., pp.118, 106.
308   Ibid., pp.107, 106.
309   Ibid., p.292.

action photograph, [the] hoary old [blackmail] trick [that] still work[s] [because] the Russians [are] past-masters at sneak photography'.[310]

For Kaja Silverman, the production of 'histor[ies]' relates to 'trauma' and 'male subjectivity' in terms of a 'desire [that] is always both absent and unrepresentable'.[311] Bearing these issues in mind, the following section shows how British histories of homophobia are an inversion whereby the trauma of repressed homoerotic desire is mediated, or 'outed', in terms of an imaginary contagion, that being Irishness and the PIRA.

Writing in *Cinema and Ireland*, John Hill observes how 'homosexuality' is often shown as being 'a form of castrated masculinity'.[312] Indeed, fey or abject homosexuality in relation to fear of a lack of British machismo is repeated by Troubles texts where even 'the Pope [...] prefers to take on the homosexuals [because] they're not so popular as the Communists'.[313] Within these types of texts, British histories of sexual and political deviance conceal both the 'trauma' and 'desire' of the real, repressed homosexuality which 'is always both absent and unrepresentable' yet becomes present and representable through displacement on to Irishness.[314] Put simply, British masculinity cannot bear to acknowledge an unconscious desire to, quite literally, bugger the PIRA.

Displacement enables the homosexual identifications which block ideal perceptions about British masculinity to be transferred on to the PIRA who are, in turn, appropriated by the Burgess-Blunt factor. These displacements occur in various ways. The most elementary route again involves a folding back to former PIRA stereotypes which produces comic Irish homosexuals, demonic Irish homosexuals, Mafiosi Irish homosexuals and communist Irish homosexuals. Indeed such stereotypes insist that 'even the IRA must go gay sometimes'.[315]

310 Pincher, *The Eye of the Tornado*, p.105.
311 Silverman, *Psychoanalysis and Cinema*, pp.116, 117.
312 Hill, *Cinema and Ireland*, p.188.
313 Lund, *The Ultimate*, p.182.
314 Silverman, *Psychoanalysis and Cinema*, p.119.
315 Robert Charles, *The Hour of the Wolf* (London: Robert Hale, 1974), p.51.

In 1979, Andrew Lane created not one but two fey Irishmen (Corrigan and Maginnis).[316] Corrigan is 'a latent homosexual' who lives with his 'big, but not tough [...] boyfriend [in] a flat [...] decorated in a flamboyant, feminine style'.[317] Maginnis is 'an ageing repressed queer [with] a little mouse-like prick'.[318] He supplies the perfect foil to Lane's hero who is 'all man!': a fact observed by Maginnis's sexually frustrated wife when she tears 'open [the hero's] zipper and his member [springs] out at her like an angry lion from its cage'.[319]

1981 brought a trans-Atlantic crossing of this theme with American author Ambrose Clancy's *Blind Pilot* in which a 'BBC situation comedy [is] devoted to jokes about homosexuals, women and the Irish'.[320] Clancy also supplies an Irish gunman who is in league with 'commie stuff [and] want[s] [an] alliance' with the IRA but 'sound[s] just like [an] Englishman'.[321] Here, Irish duplicity connects with English duplicity and manifests a contagion of spies and lies.

Alternatively, with Rupert Holloway's 1982 novel, *The Terrorist Conspiracy*, the 'Paddy's move on [from] the age [of] cowboy gunmen [to] the age of the Technocratic Terrorist [in] London-derry'![322] But the 'Londonderry Gay world' unsettles the heterosexual British hero (Captain Robert Hallam) who 'disliked and distrusted homosexuals at the best of times, let alone in the middle of a mission'.[323] Hallam's desire to find a 'master' PIRA terrorist involves visits to a 'Gay Club' where 'cheap scent' emanates from a male Irishness that is 'giggly,' 'childlike' and 'gay beefcake'.[324] And when Hallam embarks upon a bogus relationship with a homosexual named the Collector, he finds himself 'treading a shaky tightrope [...],

316 Andrew Lane, *The Ulsterman* (London: New English Library, 1979).
317 Ibid., pp.74, 125.
318 Ibid., pp.23, 25.
319 Ibid., p.24.
320 Clancy, *Blind Pilot*, p.63.
321 Ibid., pp.120, 63, 120.
322 Rupert Holloway, *The Terrorist Conspiracy* (Lewes: The Book Guild, 1982), p.10.
323 Ibid., pp.57, 56.
324 Ibid., pp.57, 59.

frequently flirting [...] but always pulling back' until, eventually, the Collector is brutally murdered gangster-style.[325] Hallam discovers the Collector's 'naked body [...] criss-crossed with razor slashes'.[326] Holloway's gruesome and sadistic account of the body reveals that 'his eyes had been burnt with cigarettes [and] there was blood everywhere'.[327] 'His teeth had been knocked out', writes Holloway, 'his fingernails pulled out [and] the body had been brutally nailed through the arms and legs to the floor with six-inch nails – crucified!'[328]

An additional narrative thread in the novel supplies shades of a true Cold War tradition. When Hallam discovers that his British adjutant is also gay and, because of sexual blackmail, a traitor. However, as stated on the novel's back cover, when Hallam finally confronts the Master Irish terrorist, 'he look[s] in the [terrorist's] eyes' and finds them 'intensely hypnotic and beguiling'. Hypnotic and beguiling? Although Hallam is not meant to be homosexual and the text seems to punish homosexuality, this fictive British hero's seduction by the Irish other implies otherwise. Moreover, if *The Terrorist Conspiracy* really does mirror its author's 'active service [as] a captain' with the British army 'in Londonderry', macho British military life evidently provides some bizarre experiences not to mention a fascination for homosexual Irishness (back cover).

1982 also produced Hardiman Scott's *Operation 10*, a novel in which Margaret Thatcher is kidnapped by a ring of five Iraqi-abetted PIRA activists who, in one way or another, all signal some kind of lack (an echo of earlier images discussed in section 1.1).[329] Scott's paramilitaries are: a sexually frustrated Irishwoman, a resentful British Army Sergeant, a puritanical and 'severely dyspeptic' Irishman, 'a vicious[ly] psychopath' Irishman and a fey 'practising gay' Irishman named Terry O'Donovan.[330] Fey and gay, O'Donovan is like 'a typical

325   Ibid., p.57.
326   Ibid., pp.59, 61.
327   Ibid.
328   Ibid.
329   Scott, *Operation 10*.
330   Ibid., pp.7, 90, 147, 108, 171.

London businessman [but] walk[s] in a manner [...] not completely masculine'.[331] As far as Scott's British Superintendent Whitaker is concerned, O'Donovan is 'a queer bomber'.[332] 'The adjective [queer] was chosen advisedly', writes Scott, because, for Whitaker, 'there was nothing that would ever make him describe a man who distributed lethal explosives as "gay"'.[333] With this logic, O'Donovan is rendered aesthetically drab rather than aesthetically gay; an Irish homosexual who lives 'in sleazy hotels', a 'bleedin' poncey Provo git' whom Whitaker nicknames 'Peachblossom'.[334] Finally, though, he still mirrors 'a typical London businessman', still mirrors a mincing Britishness.

Quasi-homosexual godfather figures occur throughout the 1970s and 1980s in British male and, maybe surprisingly, in some Irish male authored texts – which might say more about taboos concerning masculinity than actual political issues relating to the north of Ireland. In 1977, the PIRA commander-cum-godfather from Gerald Seymour's *Harry's Game* is described as a 'bugger', 'a miserable sod', and a 'boring nagging whore of man'.[335] Whereas in 1984 MacLaverty's *Cal* supplied a novella in which the PIRA commander-cum-godfather (Finbar Skeffington) exudes latent homosexuality.[336] Skeffington is a father-fixated, middle-aged bachelor who co-ordinates the paramilitary violence of his young male recruits through a regime embracing the 'puritanical', 'sexually repressed' and 'fanatical'.[337] John Hill cites 'teetotalism', disapproval of 'the use of the word "fucking"' and the 'quoting' of Patrick Pearse as further evidence for this Irish godfather's homosexual status.[338] As Pearse 'was signatory to the 1916 "Proclamation of the Republic", [a] prophet of Irish Nationalism [and] a key figure in the 1916 Easter Rising', the implicit analogy of Pearse to Skeffington effectively disparages 'an iconic symbol of Irish

---

331   Ibid., pp.172, 179.
332   Ibid., p.179.
333   Ibid.
334   Ibid., pp.184, 185.
335   Seymour, *Harry's Game*, pp.268, 269.
336   MacLaverty, *Cal*.
337   Hill, *Cinema and Ireland*, p.182.
338   Ibid., p.182.

Republicanism'.[339] Thus, Pearse's military and political image is blurred with a 'closet' homosexual 'Provo' image.[340]

Issues of class also play an important ideological role in MacLaverty's novel. Skeffington is not 'working class'.[341] He represents bourgeois Irishness because, following the occupation chosen by Pearse, he is a school-teacher. However, like Burgess and Blunt, Skeffington also 'represents [the] bourgeois' homosexual and, ultimately, Britishness.[342] Perhaps, then, with Skeffington, at either a conscious or unconscious level, we have an, albeit implicit, 'British' PIRA villain penned by an Irish author? Further credence might be given to this notion through the legendary status of the early IRA godfather (Pearse); a status which usually omits any reference to homosexuality and hybrid nationality, the latter caused by virtue of him being 'the son of an Irish mother and an English father'.[343] But, within Pearse's poetry, the courtly, Anglo-Irish, homosexual self becomes evident. 'There is fragrance in your kiss', writes Pearse, 'That I have not found yet / In the kisses of women / Or in the honey of their bodies'.[344]

We can develop these ideas from a chronological perspective by recalling how, in section 1.2, I highlighted the way in which Rolston locates abject PIRA godfathers within Troubles fiction.[345] In his article entitled 'Mothers, Whores and Villains', Rolston cites John Broderick's *The Fugitives* (1976) as a text exemplifying this trend.[346] So

---

339   Tim Pat Coogan, *Michael Collins: A Biography* (London: Arrow, 1991), p.29.

340   Esler, *Loyalties*, p.115.

341   Watt, 'The Politics of Bernard MacLaverty's *Cal*', p.143.

342   Ibid., p.143.

343   Coogan, *Michael Collins*, p.29.

344   Taken from 'A Mhic Bhig na gCleas' ('Little Lad of the Tricks'). This outing of Pearse's self 'appalled' his fellow Republicans. According to Ruth Dudley Edwards 'Pearse found boys physically attractive [but] homosexuality was so aberrant as to be almost beyond comprehension'. Ruth Dudley Edwards, *Patrick Pearse: The Triumph of Failure* (London: Victor Gollancz, 1977), pp.127, 52, 53, 127.

345   Rolston, 'Mothers, Whores and Villains', pp.42, 43.

346   John Broderick, *The Fugitives* (London: Pan, 1976).

too M.S. Power's *The Killing of Yesterday's Children* (1985).[347] However, whereas Power's godfather is dogged by 'homosexual repression', Broderick's godfather 'is a misogynist whose repressed homosexual tendencies lead him', like Skeffington, 'to believe in the cleansing power of blood sacrifices'.[348] Continuing this hybrid and homophobic legacy, 1996 brought British author Chris Petit's *The Psalm Killer* and an Irish godfather named McKeague, 'a violent homosexual who surround(s) himself with a cohort of youths'.[349] Alternatively, British author James Daniel portrays an Irish schoolboy who 'let[s]' another schoolboy 'put his hand in his pocket [...] and start gently rubbing [...] his shaft'; a homoerotic experience which pre-empts a heterosexual experience and an Irish paramilitary career where 'sex' and the ability 'to kill [...] ruled his every action [because] the two were synonymous'.[350] It is interesting to consider how and why Daniel might have originally discovered a psychological connection between homosexuality and death. Perhaps from his training at the Royal Military Academy, Sandhurst.

The above examples show how the Burgess-and-Blunt factor signals repeated histories of guilt and shame that become displaced onto Irishness, especially in terms of repressed homoerotic desire; a theme which Neil Jordan eventually glamorized and eroticized with *The Crying Game*'s images of transvestism.[351] These histories of homosexuality are also metaphorically or literally repeated to suggest that upper-class, homosexual and traitor impaired Britishness occurs through contagion with Irish republicanism. British author Donald Seaman's 1974 novel, *The Bomb That Could Lip-Read*, and American author Tom Clancy's 1987 novel, *Patriot Games*, offer interesting textual pivots to this theme.

Seaman's narrative presents the Russians (again) and the Irish involved in a political '*flagrante delicto*' against the British upon

---

347   M.S. Power, *The Killing of Yesterday's Children* (London: Chatto and Windus, 1985).
348   Rolston, 'Mothers, Whores and Villains', pp.42, 43.
349   Chris Petit, *The Psalm Killer* (London: Macmillan, 1997), p.97.
350   Daniel, *They Told Me You Were Dead*, pp.14, 16, 17.
351   *The Crying Game*, Dir. Neil Jordan, Palace/Channel 4 Films, 1993.

whom a PIRA gunman named Kelly inflicts a metaphorical sodo-mization, a violently necrophiliac anal fuck.[352] This happens when Kelly 'turn[s] [an] old [British] man's body into a booby-trap'.[353] Here, using a substance he describes as 'lovely stuff', Kelly 'ram[s] [...] explosive up the anus of the corpse'.[354] 'It's like stuffing the Christmas turkey', says Kelly: 'nothing to it'.[355] After dressing the corpse as 'a British Colonel', Kelly 'poke[s] [a] pencil into the body again [then] force[s] a [...] detonator into the anus' and dispatches a 'human mine'; a 'booby' trap for the British Army which contains 'an elite' team of 'unsung' bomb disposal 'heroes'.[356] According to Seaman, these heroes 'wear a badge [depicting] a burning grenade'.[357] The badge is called 'The Flaming Arse-hole' and symbolizes 'a most coveted honour'.[358] So, while the PIRA degrade a potentially deadly British 'arse-hole', the British 'honour' another pseudo-macho 'arse-hole' and attempt to displace the abject, the inescapable unconscious homoerotic drive, into something heroic, something elite.

Patriot Games commences *'just like some Chicago gangster movie'* with gun-toting Irish republicans who receive 'training in Soviet military camps'.[359] Clancy's accumulation of Mafiosi, com-munist and Irish republican narratives also recruits homosexuality. Yet, offering a direct inversion to *The Bomb that could Lip-Read*, *Patriot Games* replaces the metaphorical Irish buggering of the British with the literal British buggering of the Irish, specifically, the sodomizing of a proletariat Irish paramilitary demon named Sean Miller. While serving time in a British prison, Miller is 'brutally sodomiz[ed]' by a 'vicious' robber and discovered 'face down on the floor of his cell, his pants gone'.[360] Clancy explains the British robber's motive for the rape as being 'a way to atone for [...]

352   Seaman, The *Bomb that could Lip-Read*, p.16.
353   Ibid., p.76.
354   Ibid.
355   Ibid.
356   Ibid., pp.76, 77, 78.
357   Ibid., p.88.
358   Ibid.
359   Clancy, *Patriot Games*, pp.5, 223.
360   Ibid., p.200.

crimes'.[361] Here, Clancy might be suggesting that guilt can sometimes act as the catalyst which triggers homoerotic desire. Fair enough, but there remains a question about why British guilt over British crime should receive atonement through the homosexual rape of an Irish republican? Even though the British rapist 'little regretted' his crimes 'in any case', the notion of displacement could supply a partial answer.[362] This is because the prisoner's denial over guilt for robbery might have facilitated a psychological repression which, in turn, might have triggered another, deeper, psychological repression – guilt caused by British homoerotic desire for the Irish other. If so, Clancy suggests that homosexual desire can be mediated through denial and displacement.

Although in the novel Clancy describes Miller as being a 'small young man', in the film version of the text Miller is played by a physically powerful British actor named Sean Bean. It seems odd that a hale and hearty Yorkshireman (well known for heroic British performances in roles such as Sharpe and Boromir) should be chosen for the role of a diminutive Irish gunman. But the casting of Bean might imply that, once again, the British male subject has acknow-ledged an othering of the self, acknowledged 'the rage of Caliban seeing his face in the mirror' and, 'surprised' by the reflected image, asked: is that 'Me?'[363]

Miller is the villain of the narrative yet, paradoxically, his status as sexual victim connects the proletariat Irish with masculinity, the 'rough-trade' guaranteeing the opposition to British homosexuality which after the rape connects with upper-class effeminacy. This upper-class effeminacy is epitomized by a character named Dennis Cooley, a British Communist and Irish republican conspirator who is a 'harmless-looking little poof', 'a real wimp', 'a bloody cipher', 'a zero' from 'a Marxist background'.[364]

Unlike the examples from Seaman and Clancy, repetitions of Burgess and Blunt (displaced as Britishness contaminated with

---

361 Ibid.
362 Ibid.
363 Esler, *Loyalties*, p.124.
364 Clancy, *Patriot Games*, pp.501, 506, 411, 412.

Irishness) can, like early representations of the PIRA, embrace a comic or satirical tone through images of innocuously fey gays. At a political level, this has the effect of unravelling and exposing the more 'serious' characterizations. Thus, in 1971, Russell Braddon offered a slapstick British Army and espionage romp which includes 'a dirty old [homosexual] corporal'.[365] Whereas in 1989 Richard Burns created a character named 'Lord Pellon' who informs a spoof PIRA gunman that '68 was a revelation [...], had I been born thirty years earlier I might have become a Soviet agent like Philby and Blunt'.[366] Pellon's 'urbanity' is 'shocking'.[367] 'Too rich, and too English, to take part in riots', his communist activities favour 'money launder[ing]'.[368] With Pellon, we glimpse an important issue whereby the group most frequently othered as homosexual are the effete English Aristocracy. And when it comes to othering and outing abject homosexuality, British authors supply a wealth of examples. In 1971 Clifford Hanley created a fastidious 'English poof' named Brian who is a 'girlish and evil' member of a communist inspired PIRA team.[369] Not surprisingly, Brian's sexual lack is eventually punished through physical lack when his foot is amputated. However, fusing communism with the Mafiosi and Irish republicanism, in 1976 James Lund wrote about 'ugly rumblings' concerning 'too many unmarried Tory MPs [who] were reputed to have strange sexual predilections'.[370] In 1977 Ritchie Perry opposed a similarly eclectic enemy with a British operative from the 'sceptred isle['s] [...] Special Responsibilities [...] department'.[371] But the operative (Austen) is 'a brutal, homosexual psychopath', 'a homicidal maniac', and 'a natural killer' suffering from 'periodic attacks of megalomania'.[372]

1981 saw American authors repeating this trend with Ambrose Clancy's depiction of an upper class, mother-fixated, British aristocrat

365   Braddon, *The Progress of Private Lilyworth*, p.15.
366   Burns, *Why Diamond had to Die*, p.169.
367   Ibid., p.168.
368   Ibid., p.169.
369   Clifford Hanley, *Prissy* (London: Collins, 1978), pp.95, 114.
370   Lund, *The Ultimate*, p.47.
371   Perry, *Dead End*, p.31.
372   Ibid., pp.44, 47, 44, 47.

named Robert Crenshaw who is contaminated by Irish republicanism as well as fantasies about 'love and shaded rooms in the heat of the afternoon, where', Crenshaw imagines, 'perfect bodies tanned except for the cream white of buttocks lay entwined, languorous, making the gentle fierce moves to pleasure, oblivion, peace'.[373]

In 1978, ex-British Army officer (Clive Egleton) published a novel entitled *The Mill's Bomb*.[374] The novel is a spy-cum-PIRA fiction where the 'shadowy world of [British] Intelligence' meets the shadowy world of Irish Republicanism (45). Here, Egleton repeats the ring of five Cold War and homosexual histories yet splices these histories on to a crypto-Troubles plot so that British and Irish duplicity once more interlink. Edward James Mills, an ex-SIS agent, is Egleton's main protagonist. The back cover of Egleton's novel explains that, after being released from ten years imprisonment for his alleged part in the 1964 theft of 'one million dollars worth of Bearer Bonds [that] were destined for the Russians', Mills is determined to 'find out the truth' about what really happened. Mills's quest for truth involves navigating the Machiavellian dealings of upper class British and communist traitors. These traitors fraternize with Irish Republicanism and are the puppet-masters of two PIRA gunmen (Farren and Rooney) who are dispatched from Dublin to secure 'two hundred Kalashnikov AK47s' (136). Farren and Rooney are truly the rough trade, stereotypical demonic 'paddies' who are completely out of their depth throughout their doomed involvement with the upper-class godfathers of British espionage. Hence, just prior to a panic attack over the possibility of 'cracking up', Farren's internal monologue states that 'Rooney wasn't a man, simply a machine, a child-like psychopathic gunman who was surely destined for a padded cell when the shooting stopped and the politicians no longer had any use for him' (90). Ironically, Thurston, a traitor within 'a trio of senior British Civil Servants', compounds Farren's and Rooney's 'thick mick' status (41). 'If Farren and Rooney hadn't bungled it', muses Thurston, 'things might have been different' (219).

373   Clancy, *Blind Pilot*, p.258, 268, 269.
374   Clive Egleton, *The Mills Bomb* (London: Hodder and Stoughton, 1978). Further consecutive references to this novel are given after quotations in the text.

Egleton's fiction repeats a fictive past which shows how 'it all began back in 1964 with a professor Yuki Kiktev [...], a missile expert who was working on [...] H-Bombs from outer space' (24). Russians, British traitors, nuclear bombs and the PIRA. Not surprisingly, Egleton evokes a sense of paranoia looming large. For instance, a character named Morris Gilchrist muses over the 'British hero Edward James Mills' and considers a 'suggestion that Mills was not the only rotten apple in the barrel' (45). And although the idea 'seemed ludicrous at first', Gilchrist 'remember[s] that Philby had been the third man in the Burgess-Maclean affair' (45).

The Mills Bomb supplies narrative circularity as well as narrative repetition. This is established with an opening epigraph. The epigraph alludes to a 1951 statement from Cyril Connolly which, at the end of the novel, is appropriated by a fictive British policeman named Harper. The statement reads thus:

> What was it Cyril Connolly had written back in '51? 'After the third man, the fourth man, after the fourth the fifth man, who is the fifth man, always beside you?' (222).

Coupling real British traitors ('Burgess, Philby, and Maclean') with a fictive British traitor ('and now Thurston'), Harper asks: 'Who was the fifth man then? Richard Ingold or Matthew Quarry? Or was there a sixth?' (222). It is worth noting that at this point in the novel, both Farren and Rooney are dead. Therefore, all that remains is British paranoia *about* treachery fused with British desire *for* traitors, a paranoia and desire also directed at British homosexuality in respect of 'a fag' named Ollenshaw (208).

When Mills is informed about Ollenshaw's sexual preferences, his dizzying mind-swings from passionate denial to reluctant acceptance are symptomatic of the desire to displace British lack of machismo in terms of homosexuality from conscious British identifications. 'Ollenshaw a fairy?', thinks Mills, 'it wouldn't be the first time a dead man had been pilloried by malicious, unfounded gossip' (208, 209). 'Liddell was wrong', decides Mills, 'Or was he?' (208, 209). However, Mills equivocal attitude towards Ollenshaw becomes unequivocal when suspicions about homosexuality deepen. When this happens 'Mills frown[s], suddenly remembering how Ollenshaw had been in the habit of clapping an arm around his shoulders and giving him a hug' (208, 209). Ultimately, though, because Mills is the heterosexual hero who kills Farren and Rooney, Egleton ensures that the British male reader's ego is left in reasonable tact.

Published in 1996, British author Reg Gadney's *Just When We Are Safest* offers another British hero, an M15 agent named Rosslyn who is embroiled in a hunt for a PIRA bomber.[375] However, the novel's fly-leaf announces how Rosslyn's investigations gradually reveal 'not only terrorism but the rivalries and corruption within the [British] Secret Services'. Here, once more, a mixture of Britishness and Irishness evokes a hybrid otherness which, in turn, is admitted by Rosslyn's statement claiming that 'we're all a little bit Irish, aren't we'.[376] When a British character named Patrick Coker is introduced to the plot, this otherness signals homosexuality and Irish Republicanism. Coker is an abject 'habitué of gay clubs in Dusseldorf'.[377] And his 'ignominious departure' from the British army because of 'drug abuse' accompanies a bygone 'relationship with an East German agent'.[378] Stood in his 'English garden', Coker first appears as 'a small powerful man [...] holding a machete'.[379] 'Not what you'd expect to see in an English country garden', muses Rosslyn, 'this bouncer with his glinting heavy slasher, with the muscles of a bodybuilder pumped full of steroids'.[380] It is interesting to speculate upon what type of man Rosslyn does 'expect to see in an English country garden'. Maybe a British and aristocratic effete? More importantly, though, Rosslyn's surprise could be founded upon the surprise of his own homoerotic desire for Coker's 'penis'. After all, Gadney's hero appears to be rather in awe of the unmistakably phallic symbol presented by Coker's 'glinting heavy slasher'.

---

375 Gadney, *Just When We Are Safest.*
376 Ibid., p.196.
377 Ibid., p.152.
378 Ibid.
379 Ibid., p.195.
380 Ibid.

Perhaps the most outrageous displacement of the Burgess and Blunt factor occurs within Jack Higgins's 1995 novel entitled *Angel of Death*.[381] According to Kevin Toolis, this novel 'charts muddy betrayal'.[382] This muddy betrayal is perpetrated by an upper class homosexual couple (Tom Curry and Rupert Lang) who are both Cambridge educated, Marxist, and infatuated with the north of Ireland.[383] Curry is 'Anglo-Irish', a 'Professor of Political Philosophy [and] a major in [...] Russian Military Intelligence'.[384] Whereas Lang is 'an apparently effete aristocrat'.[385] Their 'homosexual relationship which lasted throughout their period at university' is rekindled when, twenty years later, they hatch a scheme whereby, with assistance from the KGB, 'a civil war' in the north of Ireland will bring 'a new state entirely [...] which is Marxist-Leninist'.[386] Identifying with 'Burgess, Philby and Maclean', Curry and Lang dismiss the PIRA as being an organization of 'nasty young louts' and reject Irish republicanism because 'Communism is the answer'.[387] Sean Dillon provides the opposition to Curry, Lang and the KGB; he is 'the big IRA gunman that turned sides [...], an ex-IRA enforcer now working for [...] British intelligence'.[388] Dillon, of course, thwarts the British Marxist coup showing that, maybe, the only way to counter the threat of indigenous, homosexual-communism and British treachery is to appropriate 'big IRA gunmen'.

Since the 1980s, British fascination with the British Intelligence Services and the SAS has not stopped the production of homoerotic otherings but, in tandem with these otherings, the SAS has also encouraged the production of powerful and exciting PIRA opponents. But the SAS inaugurated a more brutal, 'queer-bashing' machismo as a male ideal. Hence, the very British yet rather camp and ageing

---

381 Jack Higgins, *Angel of Death* (London: Penguin, 1995).
382 Kevin Toolis, 'The Troubles with Harry', *Observer Review*, 17 March 1996, p.6.
383 Higgins, *Angel of Death*, p.33.
384 Ibid.
385 Ibid.
386 Ibid., pp.33, 63.
387 Ibid., pp.42, 59, 66.
388 Ibid., pp.100, 98.

Roger Moore could no longer be tolerated in the role of James Bond (an SAS prototype) and was, paradoxically, supplanted by Pierce Brosnan, a young and macho Irishman (a PIRA prototype).

The spate of autobiographical-cum-fictive books written by ex-members of the SAS often display a rampant homophobia. Take, for instance, Chris Ryans's disapprobation of his 'poncified major' and 'poofters'.[389] But Ryan's vitriol could mask a traumatic denial of homoerotic desire for the potent yet rough trade Irish who supply the SAS with an ideal macho enemy.

John Newsinger observes how SAS authors offer images of displacement whereby 'killing' substitutes for 'the sexual act' through 'fantasy'.[390] Quoting from Michael Asher's 1990 faction entitled *Shoot to Kill*, Newsinger highlights this idea:

> The corporal 'told us to pick up the weapon, to feel the balance and weight of the thing and to touch the smooth slumbering surface of the gun-metal [...]. He taught us to cock the mechanism, to peel the working parts back and feel them wheeling in perfect harmony – the superb precision of the killing machine'.[391]

Newsinger describes this extract as being 'a pretty straightforward simulation of masturbation' but, I suggest, the extract might also be a pretty straightforward simulation of a homoerotic act.[392] However, like Brenton's Roman soldier, the British male psyche might not '*want you talking about this*' because '*you know how rumours start*'.

There are, perhaps, some Troubles novels (and films) that depict a more delicate handling of homosexual desire whereby genuine desire is prohibited by, for instance, cultural taboos or political loyalties. A gay reading of these types of texts might highlight the need for acknowledgement and acceptance of sexual diversity. For instance, in Neil Jordan's *Michael Collins*, a genuine homoerotic desire between Harry Boland and Michael Collins does seem to

389   Ryan, *Stand By, Stand By*, pp.23, 62.
390   John Newsinger, 'Our Boys in the North', *Irish Studies Review*, 16 (1996), 34–7 (p.35).
391   Ibid.
392   Ibid.

exist.[393] So too between the PIRA gunman (Martin Fallon) and his male comrade within the film version of Jack Higgins's *A Prayer for the Dying*.[394] Moreover, an analysis of fictive constructs through which homosexual desire is mediated across enemy boundaries would certainly offer an intriguing study. Indeed, such a study might choose to examine how film is more able to portray homoerotic desire in a more sensitive and discreet manner than the written word. However, as discussed, when screened through British paranoia and the PIRA positive images of homosexuality are few and far between.

1.5: 'Let the Devil take the hindmost': From the SAS to Thatcherism

> On an afternoon in London in 1980, black clad members of the Regiment scaled the walls of the Iranian Embassy in Princes Gate and killed all but one of the terrorist gang holding twenty hostages inside. In eleven minutes relayed to television screens across the world by the picket of international camera crews that had gathered in the early days of the siege, the SAS emerged from its self-imposed shadow to spawn a hundred books and thousands of newspaper articles on its history and its talents.[395]

In 1988, British journalists James Adams, Robin Morgan and Anthony Bambridge published *Ambush: The War between the SAS and the IRA*. The book claims that, historically, the PIRA have suffered 'a deeply paranoid fear of [...] the SAS'.[396] For these three British writers, the PIRA are 'blood-crazed psychopaths' and 'mad dogs' like 'Mafia [...]

---

393   *Michael Collins*, Dir Neil Jordan, Warner Brothers, 1996.
394   *A Prayer for the Dying*, Dir. Mike Hodges, Samuel Goldwyn, 1987.
395   Adams, Morgan and Bambridge, *Ambush: The War Between the SAS and the IRA*, p.56.
396   Ibid., p.73.

godfathers'.[397] Indeed, claim Adams and others, 'twenty-five years' after fighting 'communist guerrillas [...] in Malaya [...], an assessment of 'that conflict' would conveniently transfer from the Malayan jungle to [...] South Armagh'.[398] Here, once more, depending upon the political ethos at the particular time, the ubiquitous Irish gunman slides from one dominant construct to another and turns up as 'his' mirror-image, in this case the SAS.

Ambush insists that during the mid-1970s the PIRA were inept adversaries for the SAS. In order to qualify this idea, the authors recall the 1975 Balcombe Street Siege; an event in which PIRA gunmen took a British couple (John and Sheila Matthews) hostage. But, according to Adams and others, the 'terrorists' were afraid that 'the police were planning to send in the SAS' and, therefore, 'could hardly surrender fast enough'.[399] Hence, the gunmen 'came out shaking like leaves in their true colours for all the world to see'.[400]

The SAS's 1980 storming of the Iranian Embassy also signalled an event 'for all the world to see'. This event was captured on a live broadcast which, in turn, was hysterically repeated so that British audiences could witness again and again the British military's professional elite acting like superheroes. However, black clad and Balaclavaed, the SAS looked just like an Irish Republican para-military. So, from here on, the PIRA needed to be reconstructed as a *para*military professional elite, a worthy opponent for the SAS, a serious threat demanding a counterforce of British heroism which, in turn, became an index of Thatcher's own virility. This may well explain why Adams and others supplant their depiction of a cowardly 1975 Balcombe Street PIRA with a more formidable, politically potent variety of Irish gunman. As a British enemy for the late 1980s onwards, this Irish gunman became 'more proficient, more deadly and certainly more dangerously armed'.[401] From this historical point in time, the PIRA are, seemingly, 'bent on murder', 'dictated by com-

---

397   Ibid., pp.125, 89, 35, 107.
398   Ibid., p.47.
399   Ibid., p.46.
400   Ibid.
401   Ibid., p.183.

92

mon sense and realism' not to mention 'cunning'.[402] Put simply, the PIRA became 'the most ruthless terrorist army in the world' and 'the best terrorist group in the world'.[403] This quasi-British image of the PIRA and quasi-Irish image of the SAS endured. So much so that, over a decade later, Gordon Steven's *Provo* displayed confusion over the identity of 'men' wearing 'black Balaclavas with eye-holes cut in them' who could be either 'SAS [...] or IRA'. [404]

SAS professionals versus PIRA professionals. Two years after the Iranian Embassy Siege, the Falkland's War generated a further mythologization of the SAS. John Newsinger writes about how the 'the Falkland's War prompted a revival of popular militarism in Britain', whereby 'Thatcher's victory over the Argentinean junta became the cornerstone of her political ascendancy, and' the ensuing image of 'military prowess that made' this British conquest 'possible has been celebrated ever since'.[405] 'Kill-and-tell stories [...] by former members of the Special Air Service', observes Newsinger, 'have been best sellers' and, subsequently, 'the new popular militarism' manifested 'the contemporary celebration of British military prowess'.[406] This celebration was 'not only an important element in the construction of Conservative political hegemony in the 1980s and early 1990s, but [it is] also something that offers useful insights into the construction of [British] masculinity, of a particular macho-warrior variety'.[407] And, recalling the 2003 war in Iraq, this 'macho-warrior' formulation of British masculinity seems to have been inherited by Tony Blair's alliance with George Bush.

Nostalgia for the Iranian Embassy Siege and the Falkland's War preserved the SAS's professional 'sameness' to the PIRA whose subsequent big successes preserved the worthy enemy, repeated the SAS's Iranian and Argentinean other with the Irish other. And the current PIRA cease-fire might well rekindle this nostalgia.

---

402   Ibid., pp.viii, 7, 31.
403   Ibid., pp.21, 31.
404   Stevens, *Provo*, p.65.
405   Newsinger, 'Our Boys in the North', p.34.
406   Ibid., p.34.
407   Ibid., p.34.

From 1980 onwards, these Irish successes included the 1982 Hyde Park and Regents Park bombings, the 1983 Harrod's bombing and kidnapping of *Shergar*, and the 1984 Brighton bombing. PIRA successes of course continued with the 1988 Deal Barracks and Ballygawney bus bombings, the 1990 assassination of Ian Gow, the 1991 mortar bombing of Downing Street, the bombing of Warrington and the Baltic Exchange, the 1997 Canary Wharf bombing and the Grand National bomb hoax. Bearing such issues in mind, this section examines the ways in which mythologies of professionalism, the Iranian Embassy Siege and the Falkland's War are keenly relevant to political and fictive representations of the SAS in respect of accumulative repetitions of the PIRA.

Melville-Ross's 1988 SAS versus IRA narrative, *Shaw's War*, shows how fiction hysterically repeats SAS and PIRA macho militarism. For instance, during the novel Melville-Ross's hero (Shaw) recalls his involvement in the Iranian Embassy siege, his advancement 'towards an enemy position in the Falklands' then the PIRA bombing of 'military bandsmen', 'Harrods' and 'a Brighton Hotel'.[408] The consecutive ordering of these historic events allows Shaw to supplant the Iranian enemy with the Argentinean enemy and the Argentinean enemy with the Irish. This process displays the hero's desire to compensate for the absent trauma and *jouissance* of siege and war with a compulsive, psychological repetition of death through the PIRA. The following extract from *Shaw's War* makes this clear.

> He thought of military bandsmen tossed like ragdolls from an exploding bandstand in London. He thought of dying soldiers and screaming horses which, seconds before, had been a ceremonial parade in a London street. He thought of the carnage amongst police and civilians at Harrods and of the so nearly *successful* attempted massacre of the British Cabinet at a Brighton hotel [my italics].[409]

After this graphic, and obsessional, anaphoric repetition of death, Shaw's SAS accomplice fuses the Argentinean other with the Irish other and repeats both enemies for the narrative events in which

408 Melville-Ross, *Shaw's War*, pp.11, 89.
409 Ibid., p.90.

Shaw's highly professional and individual war is enacted in a thriller world 'like the Falklands and Ulster' wars all over 'again'.[410] Interestingly, *Shaw's War* is relevant to ideas from Jerry Palmer.

According to Palmer, the thriller text contains 'three worlds' which belong to 'the bureaucrat/programmer', 'the professional/improviser' and the 'amateur/incompetent'.[411] For Palmer, the 'bureaucrat/programmer' often typifies 'collective villains' who, like SMERSH for James Bond, perform the role of evil other for the heroic 'professional/improviser'.[412] Although the bureaucratic villain can also be a professional/improviser, the hero' is 'never bureaucratic'.[413] As for the 'incompetent amateur[s]', their 'textual space', or ideological sphere, is occupied by the villain or the 'ectopic' girl.[414] These ideas relate to narratives concerning the SAS and the PIRA whereby the SAS becomes the professional/improviser, the 'good little Sassman'.[415] Such narratives also portray the good little Sassman as being 'a thoroughly well-trained professional killer'.[416] Whereas the PIRA becomes the bureaucratic/programmer who is sometimes plagued by 'paddies' displaying an amateur incompetence. Even though both the SAS and the PIRA are in reality collective forces, individualizations of the fictive SAS hero against the fictive villainous collective PIRA establish this opposition. 'There is no such thing as a typical SAS guy', writes ex-SAS operative Chris Ryan in 1996: 'they are all individuals, all very different'.[417]

Blurring fact with fiction, *Standby, Standby* is Ryan's 'graphic account' and 'thriller' narrative of his SAS 'career'.[418] From his active service in the Gulf War to his 'personal hatred of the IRA' and his heroic adventures in conflict with 'South American' drug barons and the PIRA, Ryan's ideal, self-referential hero is no bureaucrat/pro-

410   Ibid., p.92.
411   Palmer, *Thrillers: Genesis and Structure of a Popular Genre*, p.10.
412   Ibid., p.8.
413   Ibid., pp.12, 14.
414   Ibid., pp.10, 14.
415   Melville-Ross, *Shaw's War*, p.69.
416   Tom Gibson, *A Wild Hope* (London: Robert Hale, 1983), pp.206, 207.
417   Ryan, *Stand By, Stand By*, p.158.
418   Ibid., back cover

grammer (back cover).[419] *Stand By, Stand By* shunts the action from Ulster to Colombia, repeats the Cold War's Soviet villains with Irish villains and James Bond with Sharp – an SAS man. The choice of the name Sharp is, I think, important. This is because the name implies that Ryan's hero is not merely physically and phallically piercing but also intellectually 'sharp', the latter being something that is not always associated with brute masculine strength. Accordingly, Sharp is an all-round intelligent but macho professional while his enemies are 'professional terrorists' who, after forming a 'collective' with Colombian drug barons, are defeated by Sharp and his team.[420] Moreover, this SAS victory is enacted in a terrain befitting 'Robinson fucking Crusoe' and therefore a terrain equating the SAS with Defoe's archetypal improviser.[421]

Anticipating Ryan's work, the preface to Terence Strong's 1983 novel, *Whisper Who Dares*, states that 'the IRA and the SAS [are] each in its own way a mysterious and deadly organisation'.[422] Here, echoing British perceptions about the invincibility of the SAS, Strong promises that his narrative will show an SAS 'beyond our wildest imagination', an SAS 'fundamentally opposed' and 'pitted against' the PIRA enemy (preface). But the preface is misleading because, invested with a 'sixth sense professionalism' and 'superprofessionalism', Strong's highly individualized four-man SAS team fight no less than sixty Irish gunmen who, in spite of being trained to 'Green Beret standard' by American quasi-Mafiosi Mercenaries, are easily defeated (357, 462, 144). As a result, although Strong claims that his professional SAS face an equally professional IRA, he actually depicts the PIRA as being an organization of comically inept 'paddies', a 'rag tag army of fanatical misfits' which includes a token demon whose 'eyebrows [...] meet in the middle' (420, 483).

In his struggle to make this fiction appear credible, Strong appropriates real Irish republicans (such as Martin McGuinness, Billy

---

419 Ibid.
420 Ibid., p.220.
421 Ibid.
422 Terence Strong, *Whisper Who Dares* (Bath: Chivers, 1983), preface. Further consecutive references to this novel are given after quotations in the text.

McKee and Gerry Adams) to create an Irish leadership that flounders within a SMERSH-type communist bureaucracy. This leadership is plagued by an internal rift between the 'Chief of Staff ' (Billy McKee) and Gerry Adams who, we are told, 'had been recently promoted from a Belfast commander to the PIRA General Headquarters Staff' (58, 59, 474, 469). Strong shows McGuinness contemplating how 'things [might] change [with] a fist of steel [and] the fiery Communist, Gerry Adams, in control' (310). Here, folding back to earlier fantasy images of the Irish gunman, the communist enemy to Britain is repeated then compounded through McKee's anxiety about the PIRA 'slipping into the hands of the Communists from its bruised young roots up to the very top branches' (475). In addition, mirroring the shift from fears about the Cold War to fears about international terrorism, Adams's status as a communist/bureaucratic/programmer includes a fierce global fanaticism with IRA godfather overtones – the latter summoning yet another metonymic folding back. And so, during a fictive political tirade, Adams advocates kindling 'fire in the bellies of the kids' and the creation of 'a common bond with every freedom fighter in the world today' (475). 'We have powerful allies willing to give us everything we want', rants the fictive Adams, 'that means we'll get all the money and equipment we [...] need, and the biggest fuckin' propaganda and misinformation *organisation* in the world behind our cause' [my italics] (475).

Although fictions where the SAS triumph over the PIRA concoct ideal masculine wars, because the 'masked men in Balaclavas' evoke the ultimate masculine image, these imaginary victories, paradoxically, just establish the SAS as an other 'other'.[423] Therefore, the PIRA gunman is finally and successfully incorporated into the body of the male Brit which, in turn, establishes an impossible double-bind identity. However, irrespective of this impossible double-bind identity, the 'action man' feats of the real SAS might account for why every British Prime Minister 'discovers the SAS'.[424] Identification is the keyword here. Every British Prime Minister identifies *with* then *reproduces* the SAS as the ideal image of British virility. In this way,

---

423   Schlesinger, Murdock and Elliott, *Televising Terrorism*, p.70.
424   Strong, *Whisper Who Dares*, p.171.

the Iranian Embassy Siege and the Falklands War provided a mirror image for Thatcher. These events also contributed towards her phallic status and perpetuated the repetition of British fictions such as the 1992 film *Who Dares Wins*.

Announcing the SAS motto in its title, *Who Dares Wins* shows an SAS siege against 'home grown terrorists led by Moscow', the communist other.[425] The SAS hero is played by the actor named Lewis Collins whose performance is a repetition of his utterly British and macho role in the television series about an SAS-type partnership: *The Professionals*. In respect of *The Professionals*, Schlesinger and others imply how repetition is especially evident within an episode broad-casted 'just four months after the Iranian Embassy Siege [that] featured a group of masked agents [...] storming a building almost exactly like the Iranian Embassy'.[426] British patriotism is of course continually nourished by these fictions which, in turn, are continually nourished by the media.

According to Patricia Waugh, the Falklands conflict manifested 'new heights of vulgar jingoism' from the British tabloid press which transformed Thatcher 'into the new Bodicea'.[427] But Waugh moderates her observation about the media's creation of an iconic Iron Lady by claiming that The Falklands War 'secured a highly questionable victory' for Thatcher 'with the sinking of the enemy cruiser *General Belgrano*'.[428] 'Highly questionable' or not, the annihilation of the symbolically male enemy cruiser ratified Thatcher's hard, phallic persona. And fictions repeating the PIRA likewise repeat the Falklands War, professional British soldiering and, by implication, Thatcher's 'victory'.

Published in 1990, Jonathan Kebbe's Troubles novel, *The Armalite Maiden*, shows a Derry based British officer named Major Roy Draycott, a 'professional soldier [who] went nuts during the Falklands' because he 'wanted to be over there assaulting the beaches'.[429]

425 Schlesinger, Murdock, and Elliott, *Televising Terrorism*, p.75.
426 Ibid., p.73.
427 Waugh, *Harvest of the Sixties*, p.174.
428 Ibid., p.174.
429 Jonathan Kebbe, *The Armalite Maiden* (London: Heinemann, 1990), p.9.

His desire for military conflict, which is perhaps an unconscious desire for death, parallels Thatcher's 'gung ho' attitude towards the Falklands.[430] This becomes evident when Draycott announces: 'I want our boys to walk tall again, I want the Bogside and Creggan to shit themselves when we leave Base'.[431] I'm talking about the British Army', insists Draycott: 'the men who swept ashore in the Falklands and made the world sit up'.[432] In order to make the world sit up, Draycott's soldiers must exude absolute machismo which means 'no more poncing around Derry like celebrities!'.[433] Draycott's violent obsession with the Falklands is repeated through a violent obsession with the PIRA as well as, it might be argued, an implied folding back to displaced British homosexuality found within earlier Troubles novels. This displaced homosexuality is expressed through Draycott's violent, crypto-sexual, anal vocabulary such as 'I want the Bogside and Creggan to shit themselves when we leave base'. So too through his denial about not wanting a regiment of 'boys [...] poncing around'.

Likewise, Gerald Seymour's 1985 Troubles novel entitled *Field of Blood* shows a Belfast-based 'Scots Guard lieutenant' making a comparison between the Ulster conflict and the Falklands.[434] 'What do you say this place is? Bally what?', asks the Guard, who then adds: 'I'd say the British army is half scared to death. When we were in the Falklands [...] we *dominated* the Argies'.[435] This comparison between the Falklands and Ulster is repeated by another soldier in Seymour's novel who thinks about how 'Turf Lodge is the enemy – just like Longdon and Tumbledown were the enemy'.[436] But the soldier acknowledges an important difference between the Falklands and Belfast, that being, within the north of Ireland 'you won't see any bloody white flags because we don't have any Argie conscripts

430   'When Auntie Met the Iron Lady', *Auntie: The Inside Story of the BBC*, Prod. Jeremy Bennett, BBC1, 1987.
431   Kebbe, *The Armalite Maiden*, pp.48, 49.
432   Ibid.
433   Ibid.
434   Seymour, *Field of Blood*, pp.338, 339.
435   Ibid.
436   Ibid., p.339.

here'.[437] 'Here', the PIRA enemy territory functions to create more than just a replacement for an Argentinean landscape. The Irish gunman in Turf Lodge is not a conscript. Instead, he is the mis-recognized reflection in the mirror, the voluntary recruit, and the doppelganger to the professional British soldier. Crucially, he is no longer the comic 'paddy' imagined in the early 1970s.

For Newsinger, in addition to reclaiming the Malvinas Islands, the SAS conformed to 'marketisation' and was transformed into 'a valuable export'.[438] Having conformed to marketization, the SAS eventually symbolized the values embraced by ferocious Thatcherite capitalism, values mirrored, paradoxically, by fictive PIRA gunman. During the 1980s, these values underwent an ideological shift where-by 1970s perceptions about negative greedy acquisitiveness became transformed into positive heroic Toryism. Evidence for the earlier negative attitude towards ferocious capitalism is shown within Gerald Seymour's 1975 novel entitled *Harry's Game* which evokes a 'Chief of Staff' who is 'a hard man with few feelings that did not involve the end product'.[439] Seymour's PIRA boss is 'like some cost-effectiveness expert, or a time-and-motion superman [who] demand[s] value for effort'.[440] The one-dimensional relentlessness of Seymour's auto-maton is foregrounded in the film version of the novel where actor Tony Rohr exudes a monotoned, quasi-homoerotic gloss.

Seymour's Irish godfather reflects the cultural and political ethos contemporary to *Harry's Game*, an ethos preparing for the inception of a rampant Thatcherism. Not yet firmly established and therefore not yet ideologically sanctioned or condemned, in 1975 Thatcherism was too new a concept for ideal identifications and too new a concept for ridicule. But, nevertheless, it had to be taken seriously.

The success of the Chief-of-Staff in *Harry's Game* is credited to his associations with Britishness, in particular his status as a former member of the British Army where 'he had risen to corporal in the

---

437   Ibid.
438   John Newsinger, *Dangerous Men: The SAS and Popular Culture* (London: Pluto, 1997), p.160.
439   Seymour, *Harry's Game*, p.189.
440   Ibid., p.189.

parachute regiment'.[441] At least three main elements construct his persona. Firstly, he is a ruthless entrepreneur. Secondly, he is a ruthless militarist. And, thirdly, he is a ruthless professional. The latter becomes crucial to the representation of the PIRA in the1980s.

Thatcherism prompted an evolution in the cultural and ideological meanings evoked by the word 'professional', or 'professionalism'. Prior to this political period, the term 'professional' was not the counterpart of the term 'elite'. Professionals were to a large extent part of the British work force's rank and file which included school teachers, civil servants and nurses. The 1980s gradually 'promoted' professionalism to a status that evolved, like the SAS, into 'a convenient myth'.[442] This myth sought 'to rehabilitate for the eighties', while at the same time benefit, 'the very perpetrators of the change from the national ethos of amateurism and public-spiritedness to one of hard-nosed professionalized acquisitiveness'.[443] Even 'the Arts Council published its [...] 1985 [...] report under the title of '"A Great British Success Story"'.[444] Likewise, during the 1997 'peace-talks' over the north of Ireland, Gerry Adams and Martin McGuinness seem to have internalized this aspect of Britishness; as displayed by their Irish republican version of 'professionalized acquisitiveness'.[445] And, like many election-vote-seeking British parliamentary candidates, Adams and McGuinness appeared in an election video that was 'the most sophisticated [or professional] in structure, given the demands of mainstream culture'.[446]

Professionalism, professionalized acquisitiveness and Great British, or Irish, success stories. Linked to these ideas, the authors of *Ambush* claim that 'it took nearly forty years for the veil to be lifted' from the SAS: 'the Regiment [who] must [always] engage in the

441   Ibid.
442   Waugh, *The Harvest of the Sixties*, p.161.
443   Ibid.
444   Ibid.
445   John Roberts, 'Sinn Fein and Video: Notes on a Political Pedagogy', *Screen*, 29.2, (Spring 1988), 94–7 (p.96).
446   Ibid.

unrelenting pursuit of excellence'.[447] However, SAS excellence not only symbolizes the creation of an imaginary masculine, virile and male Britishness but also symbolizes the excellence prescribed by professionalism, a macho professionalism that, during the 1980s, was the forerunner of the creation of an equally imaginary, masculine, virile and male Britishness named 'entrepreneurism'. So, 'who dares wins' became 'devil take the hind most'. Macho SAS-professionalism became macho entrepreneur-professionalism, an accumulative process whereby the supreme PIRA professional was enabled to summon either or both identities. Later, during the late 1990s, a photograph that appeared on the front page of the *Guardian* (1998) suggested that New Labour Britain had crossed the Irish sea and continued this 'devil take the hind most' capitalist model – the picture showed a signpost in Crossmaglen. The sign, we are told, used to announce the PIRA message 'Sniper at Work' but now announces: 'Sniper: Job Seeking'.[448] Not surprisingly, then, novels about the Troubles repeated these social and political shifts.

In Paul Theroux's 1977 novel entitled *The Family Arsenal*, a PIRA 'barbarian with taste' steals 'an old master'.[449] Theroux's narrative seems to have anticipated a more enterprising PIRA, the forerunners of the real PIRA 'crime bosses' who twenty years later were accused of a scam which involved them receiving a 'share in a £3 million reward for the return of Old Masters they helped steal'.[450] Unlike earlier Troubles fictions, such as James Barlow's 'pre-yuppie' 1974 novel in which the Irish gunman's demonization is intensified *because* he 'has money', 'a good business', 'a Cortina GT', and 'smart clothes', later novels depicted gunmen who are a parody of consumerism, a displacement of British Tory values that were, by the 1990s, starting to become unpopular and therefore ripe for ridicule.[451] Demonic yuppie to comic yuppie. This of course signals another

447   Adams, Morgan and Bambridge, *Ambush: The War Between the SAS and the IRA*, pp.56, 57.
448   Paul McErlane, *Guardian*, 13 April 1998, p.1.
449   Theroux, *The Family Arsenal*, p.47.
450   William Lowther, 'IRA to share in £3m US art theft reward', *Mail on Sunday*, 21 September 1997, p.1.
451   Barlow, *Both Your Houses*, pp.80, 154.

metonymic folding back that is repeated in Richard Burns's 1989 novel, *Why Diamond Had To Die*.[452] Here, we can recall Burns's comic Irish gunman (Diamond) who dispatches an attitude that parallels a risible *laissez faire* 'buy-now-pay-later' Britishness.[453] Consequently, when faced with imminent danger, Diamond quips: 'If I was going to die – literally – or not – I might as well die beyond my means'.[454] Consequently, Diamond reaches for his 'credit cards' instead of a gun.[455] In order to develop these notions, a chronological overview of various Troubles texts from British authors shows how Thatcherism was gradually annexed to earlier PIRA figures.

In section 1.2, I showed how De Jorre and Shakespeare's 1973 novel, *The Patriot Game*, supplied 'a new generation' of the PIRA which included 'efficient ruthlessness' and 'free enterprise' that was of the 'small-scale entrepreneur' class.[456] 1974 was a prolific year for the PIRA proto-yuppie. Peter Driscoll supplied a bizarre communist-capitalist, a 'Whiz kid, Trotskyite', and a 'market for goods sold by the IRA'.[457] Robert Charles opted for empire building with 'terror incorporated'.[458] And Donald Seaman retreated to comic ineptitude with an Irish gunman whose 'innate Irish genius for mismanagement' needs assistance from a 'Mr Big'.[459] Seaman's PIRA organization contains an employee who 'sound[s] [...] like a car salesman rather than a man planning homicide'.[460] Moreover, the narrative shows the PIRA embroiled within a cut-and-thrust, market force universe where 'an international mart in spies [are] graded, like professional footballers, with an appropriate transfer value'.[461] 'If caught', these

452   Burns, *Why Diamond had to Die*.
453   Ibid., pp.82, 83.
454   Ibid.
455   Ibid., p.83.
456   De Jorre and Shakespeare, *The Patriot Game*, pp.31, 56, 109, 173.
457   Driscoll, *In Connection With Kilshaw*, pp.18, 128.
458   Charles, *The Hour of the Wolf*, p.32.
459   Seaman, *The Bomb that could Lip-Read*, pp.68, 39.
460   Ibid., p.150.
461   Ibid., p.141.

spies, like all failed professionals, 'will eventually be returned to the exchange system'.[462]

1976 saw a minor shift from these negative images of Irish professionalism when James Lund created a successful Irish gunman who is involved in 'Commie big business'.[463] This shift was continued in 1977 with Ritchie Perry's PIRA gunmen who are affiliated to a seemingly incompatible communist-capitalist association and a set of values whereby 'professional was the key word [because] it not only denoted expertise [but also] monetary rewards for services rendered'.[464] Shades of Mafiosi business nonce are included within Perry's narrative, especially through a character termed 'the money man, the Provisionals equivalent of Meyer Lansky [whose] sole concern is finance'.[465]

1979 saw an acceleration of 'excellent Provo material'.[466] So, by 1981, American authors had also begun to borrow entrepreneurial themes for Troubles fictions. Cue Ambrose Clancy who created a PIRA activist who chats about the financial rewards of gun-running.[467] 'Any money in it?', enquires one of Clancy's Irishman, 'You want in?' asks another.[468] However, Clancy's erstwhile and entrepreneurial PIRA still symbolize a dismal archetype to Thatcherism because, ultimately, they have 'settled for meaningless work that paid them bread and circuses, cars and jogging shoes, marijuana and subscriptions to magazines and museums'.[469] But, in 1982, Rupert Holloway acknowledged a PIRA rebirth when a British Army Officer declares 'the days of the Cowboy gunman are over for good – now we're in the age of the Technocratic Terrorist', a 'master terrorist' who is 'a professional killer', 'a highly skilled pro', and 'a top trade pro'.[470] Finally, published in 1990, a satirical residue of capitalist

462   Ibid.
463   Lund, *The Ultimate*, p.78.
464   Perry, *Dead End*, p.75.
465   Ibid., p.126.
466   Lane, *The Ulsterman*, p.84.
467   Clancy, *Blind Pilot*, p.51.
468   Ibid., p.51.
469   Ibid., p.143.
470   Holloway, *The Terrorist Conspiracy*, pp.10, 11, 130, 166.

ideals is evident within Gavin Esler's *Loyalties*.[471] After suggesting that 'any interview' with the high-ranking Republican paramilitary named P.J. O'Neill 'might appeal to the Euro-Yuppie after a hard day at the office', Esler summons Irish capitalists and an economic universe where 'business was business, even for the IRA' who, like all typically Thatcherite businessmen, fret about 'a gap in the market for bombers'.[472]

Professionals yet bunglers, 'dodgy' homosexuals yet Kray-twin-style killers, Mafiosi gangsters yet traitors, ruthless entrepreneurs yet criminals, everything the PIRA formerly symbolized through the 'wildest' British 'imagination' is, during the film entitled *The Long Good Friday* (1979), explicitly returned back to Britishness, especially Englishness.[473] Within this state-of-Britain film, the PIRA have a crucial background and defining role whereby the British director John Mackenzie repeats generic PIRA stereotypes to construct an Anglo-Irish scenario for Englishness, a prophetic discourse considering that in 1979 rampant Thatcherism had not yet reached its apotheosis. Thatcherism was of course supposed to have vanquished the threat of socialism, and therefore Mackenzie's PIRA emerge as highly politicized, highly organized, highly professional foils to Englishness, an efficient, clean-cut, motivated force resembling Thatcher's yuppies, the precursors of the model that would be adopted by New Labour. With *The Long Good Friday*, Mackenzie transfers the catalogue of earlier PIRA traits into the London criminal underground where a seriously dangerous Irish other lurks as the unconscious beneath a seriously dangerous English self. Before discussing the film in more detail, there follows a brief summary of the plot.

The Long Good Friday tells the story of a London gangland entrepreneur's ultimately doomed 'hands across the ocean' business deal with the Italian-American Mafiosi.[474] The London gangster-cum-entrepreneur (Harold Shand) is performed by actor Bob Hoskins.

471   Esler, *Loyalties*.
472   Ibid., pp.10, 11, 130, 166.
473   *The Long Good Friday*, Dir. John Mackenzie, Writer Barrie Keeffe, Handmade Films, 1979.
474   Barrie Keeffe, *The Long Good Friday* (London: Handmade, 1984), p.9.

Shand is patriotic, working-class, and married to a middle-class woman (Victoria) played by Helen Mirren. Mackenzie's patriotic, if criminal, protagonist wants to 'expand [his] illicit empire' with an 'East End [Docklands] development funded by' British and American 'organised crime'.[475] But a series of violent assaults against Shand's organization gradually thwarts the Anglo-Mafiosi business alliance. These events include bombs and several murders together with the murder of Shand's homosexual associate (Colin). After rounding up all the London gangland bosses and locking them in an abattoir (a charnel house motif so endemic to Troubles novels set in the north of Ireland), Shand interrogates the bosses to see if he can find out who is to blame for the mayhem which is 'like fucking Belfast on a bad night'. Although he is at first unaware of his ironic analogy of London to Belfast, Shand eventually discovers the truth. Harris, another associate, has been paying money to the PIRA in return for an Irish workforce that never strikes. The deceased Colin and Shand's right hand man (Jeff) are also implicated. At the end of the film, Shand discovers that while Colin was delivering protection money in Belfast, three of the PIRA's top men were killed. So, the PIRA suspect that Shand himself is guilty of treachery and enact 'revenge'. Instead of realizing his entrepreneurial dream of a Dockland empire, Mackenzie's bull-dog Brit learns that his own organization is riddled with traitors and the Italian-American deal is ruined. The film ends with Shand being kidnapped by the PIRA and, presumably, executed.

Looking back on reviews of *The Long Good Friday*, it seems evident that Mackenzie's film was regarded as being a seminal British gangster thriller, or state-of-Britain on the cusp of the 1980s film. For instance, Jeremy Clarke observes how the film depicts the 'London Docklands before the 1980s when the yuppies moved in and Canary wharf', quite literally, 'went up'.[476] This is the location where, in true entrepreneurial style, Shand plans a deal that is 'going to be worth [...] billions [...] in 1988' – at the beginning of the film 'a detailed model

475   [n.a.], [n.t.] http://www.shef.ac.uk/city/showroom/1996/september/long_good_ friday.html (6 September 1999).
476   Clarke, Jeremy, 'The Long Good Friday'. http://www.festive.demon.co.uk/ reviews/lastminute.com (6 September 1999).

of the River Thames' shows his 'dream [...] as envisioned by an artist [...] like a Costa Brava resort'.[477]

Shand's perception of the PIRA is characteristic in the sense that his catalogue of representations of the Irish ranges from comic 'pig-eyed Micks!' to demonic and communist 'red-necked terrorist scum'. Such metonymic stereotypes are of course phantoms. Nevertheless, Shand believes in the existence of these phantoms whom he threatens to 'annihilate' and 'crush [...] like beetles'. Echoing Shand's other associates, Jeff corrects his boss's misrecognition. 'You can't wipe them out', says Jeff: 'bring out the tanks and flame throwers [...], they'll just pour back'. 'But It's my manor', persists Shand, only to be informed that 'the British Army's been diving about' in the north of Ireland 'with shit flying at them for the last ten years'. Indeed, Jeff is flabbergasted that Shand is 'not impressed' by the PIRA and tells him that he 'won't stop them [because] to them you're nothing – nothing [except] the shit on their shoes'.

According to Hill, although *The Long Good Friday* 'portray[s] the IRA as apparent victors', the film 'only do[es] so by invoking the ancient stereotype of the inexplicably violent and demonic Irish'.[478] For Hill, Mackenzie portrays the PIRA as being merely 'an obscure and shadowy presence [that] appear[s] as if from nowhere [and] take[s] off with Harold as their prisoner'.[479] Owen O'Brion, a Sinn Fein press officer, offers similar criticisms.[480] 'In the *Long Good Friday*', claims O'Brion, because the PIRA 'blow up the entrepreneur's [capitalist] enterprise', the 'Irish' are depicted as being 'anti-capitalist not Richard Bransons'.[481]

Hill and O'Brion underestimate Mackenzie's Thatcherite Irish paramilitaries whose 'greater expertise' causes 'bloody havoc' in Britain and cannot be defeated.[482] There is nothing obscure or anti-capitalist about an Irishness that dispatches bombs and a ferocious

477   Keeffe, *The Long Good Friday*, p.1.
478   Hill, *Cinema and Ireland*, p.174.
479   Ibid.
480   Jayne Steel, Interview with Owen O'Brion, Belfast, July 1997.
481   Ibid.
482   Keffee, *The Long Good Friday*, p.vi.

moral law or, for that matter, an Irishness that depicts ruthless and efficient professional entrepreneurs.

In the prologue to his screenplay, Barrie Keeffe notes how the film was originally named *The Last Thriller*, a title that hints at the film's apotheosis of the extimate Irish enemy.[483] Another contingent title, *The Paddy Factor*, was also considered then rejected, a decision that is symptomatic of the elimination of the comic, 'paddy factor', Irishman.[484] Since the inception of the PIRA, the loss of the 'thick mick' stereotype has summoned an hysterical search for the real demonic PIRA which, reaching its zenith with *The Long Good Friday*, finally becomes unravelled into an hysterical denial of demonic Britishness. During the closing scene of the film, Shand 'looks ahead into the driver's [...] mirror and to his horror sees [...] the smiling eyes of the Irish boss he thought had been shot'.[485] Thus, ultimately, Mackenzie and Keeffe offer a filmic metaphor for the British 'horror' that is experienced through an encounter with the self – the PIRA face in the mirror.

---

483 Ibid., p.v.
484 Ibid., p.vii.
485 Ibid., p.45.

Chapter 2
To Kill Or Not To Kill?: *Hamlet* and the PIRA[1]

2.1: The Universal Dilemma

> He smiled grimly to himself. Concentrate. Don't let your attention wander. That's the way to get yourself killed. Maybe that would be better than killing? He was surprised at the suddenness of the thought. He squinted again along the length of the rifle as he considered this question and his response to it. It was a question which had come into his head off and on during the last few months. Not about getting killed. He wasn't into getting killed. No way. If it happened it wouldn't be by choice. He surveyed the scene before and below him. Nothing had changed. Was it right to kill?[2]

Gerry Adams's 1996 autobiography, *Before the Dawn*, contains a short story, a fiction through which Adams attempts 'to capture [...] something of the harsh reality of the campaign launched by the IRA'.[3] The story's hero (Sean) is an Irish Republican sniper who, lurking in a Belfast attic, contemplates universal as well as ethical issues. To kill or not to kill? To be or not to be? Murder or suicide? These two, very different, questions prompt Sean's philosophising about morality. 'Was it right to kill?', Sean asks.[4] He replies thus:

> No, he told himself, it wasn't right to kill. But there was no choice. Of course there was a choice. No one forced him to do what he was doing. He could leave

---

1 William Shakespeare, *Hamlet* (London: Penguin, 1980).
2 Gerry Adams, *Before the Dawn: An Autobiography* (London: William Heine-mann, 1996), p.170.
3 Ibid., p.168.
4 Ibid., p.170.

now. Leave? What good will it do, staying there? No one would know and no one could complain. He'd have done his best.[5]

Here, like Hamlet, Sean considers universal, ethical and moral issues about the rights and wrongs of killing. His internal monologue as a split subject humanizes the PIRA sniper for a general readership – after all, most people do occasionally give themselves a pep-talk. This general readership includes the British. And, as Adams is no doubt aware, Sean gainsays how most British readers would usually perceive a PIRA sniper. Sean is *not* a 'thick mick stereotype', is *not* demonic, is *not* an unscrupulous and violent psychopath. On the contrary, even though Adams's young PIRA hero is politically committed to the Irish Republican Cause, he is articulate, humane, and principled enough to debate the rights and wrongs of assassination. Not surprisingly, this humanization of the PIRA created a furore in the British Press. Hence, on 26 December 1996, the *Daily Mail* reproduced a large extract from Adams's short story.[6] A feature article by David Sparrow, together with a photograph of a stereotypically balaclavaed PIRA activist, accompany the extract.

Sparrow condemns the way in which 'Adams [attempts] to justify killing men wearing British Army uniforms' and implies that Adams *is* Sean who, in turn, is visually manifested through the photograph.[7] 'Adams takes up the account', writes Sparrow: 'from imagination or memory only he can say'.[8] Indeed, Sparrow reminds us that 'there have always been strong rumours of [Adams's] IRA past'.[9]

Adams's humanization of the PIRA succeeds through the depiction of a standard dilemma that has been central to literature, fiction and film since William Shakespeare's drama: *Hamlet*. This dilemma hinges upon 'action' as well as responsibilities, duties and issues of moral conscience: all of which problematize Sean's decision about whether or not to, in the words of Hamlet, 'take arms against a

5   Ibid.
6   Andrew Sparrow, 'Faces that damn Mr Adams (And Shames Labour MPs)', *Daily Mail*, 26 September 1996, pp.6–7.
7   Ibid., p.6.
8   Ibid.
9   Ibid.

sea of troubles'. Hamlet's questions are Sean's questions and Adams enhances his fictitious hero's image by posing such a Shakespearean dilemma.

A few pages after Sean's fictive PIRA mission, Adams presents the reader with a series of photographs. The first photograph portrays Adams with maternal figures: 'Ma, Gerry and Margaret', the latter being Adams's sister. Elsewhere in the text, he writes about 1971 and the mass internment of Republican fathers whose sons were then 'taunt[ed]', or haunted, by Loyalists who chanted: 'Where's your daddy gone?'[10] He also writes about his experiences of 'lying low in a billet reading *My Oedipus Complex* by Frank O'Connor' together with his time spent in 'Cage 6 [of] the Kesh [prison]'.[11] Adams recalls how those in Cage 6 were tormented by a 'hut ghost' named 'Harvey' and 'a plan to poison Republicans in jail'.[12] In spite of these events, though, he found that the Kesh 'was in many ways a relief' from the larger, metaphorical prison named Belfast.[13] Throughout the text, Adams's talent for eccentricity is also apparent. For instance, he claims to have often duped the British Army and that his 'crazy behaviour' caused 'alarm' amongst prison warders.[14] All this might suggest that Adams's autobiography contains several important themes and motifs reminiscent of *Hamlet*. After all, like *Hamlet*, Adams' provides a story about an oath-bound assassin who is a split subject navigating a moral choice about killing. He also suggests close identification with the mother and '*My Oedipus Complex*'. Ghosts. Feigned madness. Wronged fathers. Poison. A story-within-a-story. A prison-within-a-prison. All in all, Adams's self-portrayal, or fictional self-portrayal, summons a doppelganger of Hamlet: a doppelganger repeating Hamlet's 'abstract and brief chronicles of the time'.

It could be argued that Adams's identifications of himself and the PIRA with Britishness with regard to Hamlet signal a conscious and deliberate ploy used ironically in order to highlight the difference

---

10   Adams, *Before the Dawn*, p.153.
11   Ibid., pp.210, 234.
12   Ibid., pp.243, 222.
13   Ibid., p.222.
14   Ibid., p.196.

between hard facts and academic fiction. 'For many people', writes Adams, 'the issue of force is an academic one, since they rarely find themselves in situations where they have serious choices of this kind to make'.[15] For Adams, 'there are those who are against all violence as a matter of both principle and practice, but for the majority it is a measure of last resort'.[16] Here we have a fundamental difference between latter-day British appropriations of Shakespeare's Hamlet and Adams's 'Irish' Hamlet. Sean is *not* an archetypal and metonymic image of liberal humanism, is *not* a universally tragic figure whose action results from a psychologically damaging 'fatal flaw'. However, in a broader sense, Adams's Hamlet disrupts 'the smooth surface' of Shakespeare's play and challenges 'an "orthodox" [British] inter-pretation'.[17] Indeed questions about how and why the PIRA are (in various different ways) imagined as being Hamlet figures signal the keynote of this chapter.

Hamlet, I argue, is the Ur-text of modern Britain as well as the dilemma of political action. Therefore, Sean's action performs an implicit political agenda which attempts to make British readers acknowledge that sometimes, if the cause is just, a man can suspend his moral conscience and kill without being punished. Consequently, the story of Sean the sniper gets a 'happy ending'. Sean escapes leaving his victim (the dead British officer) 'staring unseeing at the clear Irish sky' with an 'expression' on his face that is both 'curious' and 'surprised'.[18]

An important aspect of Sean's dilemma can be examined in terms of 'choice' and, specifically, whether or not Sean has any 'serious choices'.[19] After all, 'the big decisions are generally made by others'.[20] However, Sean's musings from the Belfast attic do suggest 'free choice' or moral choice.[21] Even though the law forbids his

15   Ibid., p.172.
16   Ibid.
17   Terence Hawkes, *That Shakespeherian Rag: Essays on a Critical Process* (London: Methuen, 1986), p.110.
18   Adams, *Before the Dawn*, p.171.
19   Ibid., p.170.
20   Ibid.
21   Slavoj Zizek, *The Sublime Object of Ideology* (London: Verso, 1989), p.166.

involvement with the PIRA, he has *chosen* to join the movement, *chosen* to become an assassin. But Sean's subject position is ideologically complex. This is because, although subject *to* British law, Sean does not recognize himself or his 'community' as being subjects *of* British law.[22] The community to whom he gives an oath of allegiance is, quite literally, 'outlawed' and choosing 'the right thing' means it is 'necessary to kill' those serving in the British Army who, Sean thinks, 'have no compulsion about killing' either.[23] For Zizek, the subject 'is never actually in a position to choose: he is always treated *as if he had already chosen*'.[24] So, in a province subjected to British rule, Sean's 'free choice' to oppose the British is therefore a 'paradox' because he has 'freely chosen the wrong side' *as if he had already chosen* the subject position of the enemy.[25]

All this said, Adams's text does imply that an ideological economy embracing both political force and physical force does not always have to suffer a punitive expenditure. 'God made the Catholics [...] but the Armalite made them equal', observes Adams.[26] His statement suggests that ballot-box democracy (legal action) is compatible with the Armalite (illegal action). And those who insist that the Armalite is 'just as just' as political democracy would agree. Hence, Patrick Bishop and Eamonn Mallie write about how 'the decision to run [Bobby] Sands in the Fermanagh and south Tyrone by-election [was] accompanied by deep misgivings on the part of Gerry Adams, Martin McGuinness and Danny Morrison'.[27] These misgivings arose

22   Ibid., p.165.
23   Adams, *Before the Dawn*, p.170.
24   Slavoj Zizek, *The Sublime Object of Ideology*, p.165.
25   Ibid., p.166. Zizek's Lacano-Althusserian critique suggests how in fact humanist ideology claims that the liberal state is based on choice when, in fact, it is not. Hence, as demonstrated with the row over British citizenship with Mohammed al Fayed, a person cannot simply choose to be a British subject. Likewise, as demonstrated with the row over elected members of Sinn Fein who cannot take their seats in Parliament because every MP has to 'freely' pledge allegiance to the Queen, a person simply cannot choose not to be a British subject either.
26   Ibid., p.186.
27   Patrick Bishop and Eamonn Mallie, *The Provisional IRA* (London: Corgi, 1987), p.377.

because the three men 'were concerned that their candidate might not *win* [my italics]'.[28] At a meeting debating this issue, Morrison is reported to have asked: 'Who here really believes that we can win the war through the ballot-box? [...] But will anyone here object if with a ballot paper in this hand and an Armalite in this hand we take power in Ireland?'[29]

In 1981, after sixty-five days on hunger strike, Sands died in Long Kesh prison. His death created a symbolic father (an Irish King Hamlet) commemorated as a forefather who must be avenged. Together with his nine doomed comrades and the 'rebel' Irishmen executed during the 1916 Easter Rising, Sands functions as a 'good' father within whom the law of the PIRA father is enshrined for the PIRA sons. Indeed, a photograph that appeared in a 1988 edition of *Fortnight* makes this clear.[30] The photograph shows Adams in the foreground with the smiling and spectral presence of a mural depicting Sands in the background. An accompanying caption to the photograph ('Adams lives in the shadows cast by the past') does not gainsay this notion. Further, Bill Rolston's in depth studies concerning the north of Ireland's murals also imply how symbolic PIRA fathers are not forgotten. To note one of many examples illustrated in Rolston's work, a mural of Sands is embellished with the declaration that 'you cannot put a rope around the neck of an idea': a philosophically Hamletian yet defiantly Irish Republican sentiment.[31] To be sure, as the symbolic power of the dead cannot die, a more fitting caption for both the photograph and the mural might have been 'Remember me'.

Adams's subtext repeats the structure of many British fictions, both academic and popular, as a symptom. These fictions attempt to transcend the political specificities of the north of Ireland through the narrative of a 'tragedy', a 'tragedy' that offers 'universal' appeal with the depiction of a 'normal', 'civilized' human subject who is torn

28   Ibid.
29   Ibid., p.378.
30   Frankie Quinn, *Fortnight*, March/April 1998, p.18.
31   Bill Rolston, *Drawing Support: Political Murals in Northern Ireland* (Belfast: Beyond the Pale, 1992), p.27.

between moral issues such as duty, conscience, injustice and revenge. The following examples make this apparent.

As early as 1947, British author and screenwriter F.L. Green published *Odd Man Out* and created an Irish gunman named Johnny who, after being wounded in a raid, finds himself alone, an outcast, a maverick.[32] At this point in the story, Johnny supplies an eloquent internal monologue through which he philosophizes about how 'an immortal soul [is] a glorious thing [which resides] in its raiment of flesh and bone'.[33] But philosophizing descends into despair when Johnny 'remember[s] that [he has] killed a man'.[34] Moreover, because 'the facts of [this] sin [are] sordid [and] evil [he is] horrified by the fact that soon [his] body would die [leaving the soul [...] to venture forth on [a] perilous passage'.[35] In fact, shortly afterwards, we learn that Johnny's 'soul cried out in horror, because the body was dying and the great burden of sin prevented the soul from taking flight across the territory beyond life'.[36] Johnny is clearly plagued by a moral conscience, his soul is 'lost, threatened with extinction'.[37] And this Christian subtext with regard to sin is a key theme within *Hamlet*. Like King Hamlet, Johnny is condemned to 'fast in fires, till the foul crimes done in [his] days of nature are purged away'.[38]

However, published not long after the birth of the PIRA (1969), Jack Higgins's novel entitled *The Violent Enemy* supplies us with Sean Rogan – one of the first Irish, paramilitary Prince Hamlets.[39] Higgins's is an interesting figure in terms of Troubles fiction. Although born in England, he spent much of his childhood in Belfast during the 1930s before leaving Ireland for America. His hybrid nationality and his first-hand experience of the older republican movement, as opposed to the PIRA, might have some bearing on his

32   F.L. Green, *Odd Man Out* (North Hollywood, California: Leisure Books, 1971 (orig. 1947)).
33   Ibid., p.156.
34   Ibid., p.157.
35   Ibid., p.155.
36   Ibid., p.167.
37   Ibid.
38   Shakespeare, *Hamlet*, I. 5. 11.
39   Jack Higgins, *The Violent Enemy* (London: Hodder and Stoughton, 1969).

115

depictions of both (with a more flagrant moral high ground, and a paramilitary with a conscience, often being attributed to older republican figures). And, of course, a gunman with a conscience is compatible with Hamlet, an idea that can be located within *The Violent Enemy* where the hero, Rogan, is a convicted gunman whose pen-picture evokes what Marvin Rosenberg terms a 'power Hamlet'.[40] Higgins's protagonist is 'a giant [with] brains and brawn, [a] dangerous man [...] that's Sean Rogan'.[41] But Rogan is also a 'sweet Hamlet'. For instance, his face shows 'skin [...] stretched tightly over high Celtic cheek-bones, a stubble of beard covering [...] hollow cheeks and strong pointed chin'.[42] His 'eyes [are] grey like water over a stone or smoke through trees on an autumn day, calm and expressionless, holding their own secrets'.[43] But the 'face' belonging to Higgins's enigmatic hero reveals something else, that being, the Hamletian demeanour 'of a soldier, or a scholar perhaps [but] certainly no criminal'.[44]

Higgins's other novels suggest that this author does seem to have a penchant for Irish Hamlets. In 1995, his novel entitled *Angel of Death* produced Sean Dillon, an ex-Irish republican gunman who has 'a remarkable', not to mention Hamletian, 'talent for acting'.[45] So, in spite of having been 'the most feared enforcer [...] the IRA [...] ever had [...]', Dillon 'went to the Royal Academy of Dramatic Art [...] then joined the National Theatre'.[46] Furthermore, Dillon only 'joined the IRA' when his 'father [...] was shot dead by paratroops' but then left because his moral conscience could not tolerate 'fifty thousand

---

40 'Sweet Hamlet' versus 'power Hamlet' are terms used by Marvin Rosenberg to describe two types of twentieth century Hamlets. John Gielgud's performances of 'sweetness-thought-fragility-inwardness' represent 'sweet Hamlets' whereas Laurence Olivier's performance of 'power-strength-activity-forcefulness' represents a 'power Hamlet'. Marvin Rosenberg, *The Masks of Hamlet* (Cranbury, NJ: Associated University Press, 1992), p.94.

41 Higgins, *The Violent Enemy*, p.10.

42 Ibid.

43 Ibid.

44 Ibid.

45 Jack Higgins, *Angel of Death* (London: Signet, 1996), p.13.

46 Ibid.

ordinary people [being] maimed or injured'.[47] In fact, Dillon is so 'disenchanted with the glorious [Irish] cause' that he atones for his sins by altruistically flying 'medical supplies for children [...] into Bosnia'.[48] He even rescues 'the Royal Family from a dreadful scandal involving the Duke of Windsor's involvement with the Nazis' and assists the British against a PIRA-cum-communist plot.[49] With his moral conscience repaired, Dillon is indeed 'a man who can look in the mirror and not be afraid'.[50] These redeeming qualities mean that, like Rogan, Dillon survives the text. But his survival is dependent upon his partial Anglicization.

Alternatively, Higgins does sometimes permit his Irish Hamlets a fittingly, princely and tragic fate. Cue his equally sentimentalized and romanticized Hamlet that is found within *A Prayer for the Dying* (1973).[51] So too within *The Savage Day* (1977).[52]

In *The Savage Day*, shortly before his own heroic death, a young IRA recruit named Binnie becomes conscience-stricken when he is traumatized by the death of a British soldier. Binnie displays this moral aspect of his nature in his face which has 'the skin [...] drawn [so] tightly over [the] cheekbones [that], skull-like', he is akin to 'Death himself'.[53] Here, the capitalization of 'Death' imposes a further universalization, a renaissance *momento mori* motif. 'I didn't look,' says the remorse-stricken and tearful Binnie to his comrade, 'I couldn't. Is he dead? [...] Oh my God'.[54]

In *A Prayer for the Dying*, Higgins supplies an ex-PIRA gunman named Martin Fallon who is similarly racked by a Hamletian moral conscience then, like Binnie, suffers a tragic and heroic fate. This happens at the end of the narrative when Fallon rescues da Costa (an ex-SAS English Priest) and da Costa's niece (a blind girl named Anna) from a homosexual English Gangster (Meehan). Fallon bears

47   Ibid., pp.13, 186.
48   Ibid., pp.13, 189.
49   Ibid., p.13.
50   Ibid., p.187.
51   Jack Higgins, *A Prayer for the Dying* (London: Pan, 1981).
52   Jack Higgins, *The Savage Day* (London: Pan, 1977).
53   Ibid., p.189.
54   Ibid.

close resemblances to Hamlet. For instance, his father is dead: 'killed at Arnhem fighting for the English'.[55] Fallon is 'mad', 'a bloody lunatic', 'a man of genius' who is 'marked by life' (187, 153). He is also 'a fine human being – committing, for his own dark reasons, a kind of personal suicide' (130). And he is a philosopher as well as a scholar, a fact noted by Meehan who, with 'genuine astonishment in his voice', says to Fallon: 'Heidegger? [...] You've read Heidegger?' (13). Added to all of this, Fallon is well acquainted with music and literature. To be sure, as 'a doctor of music' he is able to evade the British law by posing as a church-organ tuner who 'expertly' checks 'the swell organ' then gives the police 'a masterly performance' (131, 77).

As well as his musical knowledge, Fallon's literary knowledge includes Shakespeare. 'You know what Shakespeare said', quips Fallon while declaring his intention to murder Meehan's brother, 'a good deed in a naughty world' (159). Yet, paradoxically, he becomes Anglicized through his own aesthetic wisdom. This happens when da Costa confronts Fallon about his violent past and asks: 'how could you do what you've done [...] with so much music in you?' (130). At this point, Fallon identifies with an English renaissance scholar and soldier when he announces that 'Sir Philip Sidney was reputed to be the most perfect of all knights of the court of Elizabeth Tudor' (130). 'He composed music', claims Fallon, 'and wrote poetry like an angel' (130). But Fallon gives his tribute to Sidney an ironic twist by observing that 'in [Sidney's] lighter moments, he and Sir Walter Raleigh herded Irishmen together into convenient spots and butchered them like cattle' (130).

The fantasy constructions of Irish Hamlets explored here displace the PIRA on to Hamlet and thereby to some extent Anglicize as well as apoliticize the Irish republican gunman. Perhaps surprisingly, a clear example of this fantasy occurs in Irish author Jack Holland's *The Prisoner's Wife* where the heroine (Nora) displaces her imprisoned PIRA husband on to a romantic intellectual named Michael whom she recalls standing 'with a cloak thrown over his shoulders [and] reciting

---

55   Higgins, *A Prayer for the Dying*, p.130. Further consecutive references to this novel are given after quotations in the text.

bits of Hamlet'.[56] So, in contrast to the Irish demons from the sections in Chapter 2 of this study, fictions portraying 'tragic' PIRA gunmen often succeed because the inner conflict of the protagonists persuade the reader or audience of their essential humanity. As stated rather sardonically by the Canadian novelist, Lionel Shriver, 'the Infatuated Troubles Writer [...] gets everything wrong with feeling'.[57]

Shriver's allusion to 'feeling' complements Eve Patten's observations about how characters portrayed as being 'misguided idealists' appear within 'a series of slim novels set against the violence of the seventies and early eighties'.[58] According to Patten, these novels 'established a determinist formula which repeatedly located a well-meaning individual within a debilitating and ultimately damaging political context'.[59] This 'determinist formula', claims Patten, results in a 'fictional essentialism', a phenomenon that serves to 'reinforce for an international readership a compulsive literary stereotype [thus] extracting the lyrical moment from tragic inevitability'.[60] For Patten, there exists 'a novelistic obligation to offer a consensual (and usually apolitical) liberal humanist comment [which has] tended to universalize rather than particularize the situation' within the north of Ireland.[61] Interestingly, Patten's allegations are directed at, primarily, Irish writers. So, quoting 'the critic J.T. Leerson', she blames Irish portrayals of the Irish self upon 'the destinatory vector towards an English audience'.[62]

Although Patten's observations are persuasive, they fail to reveal how the universalizing 'determinist formula' she describes was in fact established by Shakespeare and his critics. Moreover, this formula locates its most famous exemplar in Hamlet which, in turn, and for

---

56   Jack Holland, *The Prisoner's Wife* (Dublin: Poolbeg, 1995), p.113.
57   Lionel Shriver, *Ordinary Decent Criminals* (London: Harper Collins, 1992), pp.425, 426.
58   Eve Patten, 'Fiction in Conflict: Northern Ireland's Prodigal Novelists', in *Peripheral Visions: Images of Nationhood in Contemporary British Fiction*, ed. Ian A. Bell (Cardiff: University of Wales Press, 1995), pp.128–48 (p.128).
59   Ibid., p.131.
60   Ibid., pp.129, 132.
61   Ibid., pp.131, 132.
62   Ibid.

different reasons, emerges within British as well as Irish representations of the Irish Republican gunman. Consequently, many of these representations, either consciously or unconsciously, replay the key dilemmas, plot and characters of *Hamlet*, albeit with significant and interesting variations. Not surprisingly, political or ideological implications accumulate from the repetition of this formula. After all, for many people Shakespeare symbolizes the quintessential English dramatist while Hamlet symbolizes his main character. In consequence, and as implied through the fictions so far discussed, it appears that many appropriations of the PIRA as Hamlet Anglicize the Irish gunman through the universalizing process facilitated by, typically renaissance, generic themes, techniques and dilemmas. Because *Hamlet* is so well-known (especially in terms of British literary heritage), the text provides an ideal intertext (or symbol) for the universalizing symbol of all these values. Put simply, these Hamletized Troubles fictions suggest that if the PIRA are shown to be 'socially acceptable' they must transcend the debilitating and dehumanizing context of their damaging political context and become fully human, or, ironically, sometimes partly, sometimes fully British. At this point it is important to stress that I am not suggesting that British or Irish writers *intentionally* construct representations of the PIRA as Hamlet; although this may be the case in some instances where the heroes are either SAS, RUC or British Army.[63] But what I am suggesting is that, whether or not these representations are constructed at a conscious or unconscious level, the PIRA as Hamlet

---

63   Anthony Melville-Ross's *Shaw's War*, Andrew Lane's *The Ulsterman*, and Donald Seaman's, *The Bomb That could Lip-Read* are explicit examples of this trend. Ross's hero (Shaw) is a maverick SAS revenger: 'the Prince of Denmark type'. Lane's hero (Boggs) is a maverick RUC revenger who recites from *Hamlet*: '"Alas! poor Yorick," quoted Boggs sadly. " I knew him, Horatio; a fellow of infinite jest, of most excellent fancy."' Seaman's revenging Army hero is required to deal with 'all the slings and arrows of outrageous military fortune'. Anthony Melville-Ross, *Shaw's War* (London: Michael Joseph, 1988), p.23. Andrew Lane, *The Ulsterman* (London: New English Library, 1979), p.163. Donald Seaman, *The Bomb that could Lip-Read* (London: Hamilton, 1974), p.32.

symbolizes an ideologically mediated fantasy concerning desire, guilt and moral dilemmas.

Both Hamlet and PIRA enact the epitome of 'criminal' acts, namely revenge killing. These acts replay ethical, political, and legal impasses which structure a universal philosophy about humanity. But, as I have emphasized throughout this chapter, to universalize the localized is a political step which, according to Angela McRobbie, 'is a very dangerous thing to do'.[64] Ultimately, if the United Kingdom's 'real' domestic or *local* 'problem' (the north of Ireland) is depicted (not to mention displaced) in terms of a universal 'fantasy', Britain cannot be blamed for failing to resolve political violence but can be *excused* for not 'realising a solution' to a *universal* human predicament. If, as claimed by Tom Paulin, the English literary canon usurps Irish writing, it follows that possibly the most famous character in English literature (Hamlet) functions to usurp the Irish rebel while at the same time ousting Irish folk-heroes, such as Cuchulain, who are a symbol of Irish masculinity.[65]

British law has of course its role to play here. Law is a social structure that is dependent upon crime for its existence – law cannot exist without crime and law is crucial to Britishness. When the crime is, like Shakespeare's portrayal of Claudius's murder of Hamlet's father, 'murder most foul', there follows 'a sweep to revenge'. But a problem arises when the revenger, such as Hamlet or the PIRA, seeks retribution from the law, be this through Claudius or Britain. This is because a situation is prompted whereby revenge against the tyrant and a redoubling of the law becomes manifested. Many Troubles texts by British authors show how this Hamletian-type revenge is padded (or 'paddied') in fiction so that revenge equates with terrorism; and terrorism is always *wrong* because it is illegal and against the law. In Shakespeare's play, the ethical dilemma is resolved with Hamlet's death. Whereas in some Troubles texts claiming to 'report' the Republican 'cause aright', the Irish gunman succumbs to the 'fell

---

64   Angela McRobbie, *Postmodernism and Popular Culture* (London: Routledge, 1994), p 127.

65   Tom Paulin, *Ireland and the English Crisis* (Newcastle-upon-Tyne: Bloodaxe Books, 1984), p.15.

sergeant Death'.[66] Such deadly resolutions are based upon a fundamentally *English* morality. So in moments where the ethical dilemma is structured in fiction, the English psyche feels justified for its identification with the PIRA, especially if the fictions show the terrible cost of revenge at the expense, or moral economy, of the law. Bullets and bombs against Britain must be ethically outlawed. Fittingly then, not to mention coincidently, for Rosenberg, Hamlet can be performed 'like an unpredictable bomb urgent to go off'.[67] Whether or not Troubles texts choose to portray a literal bomb explosion, conditioned to self-destruct, Hamletian Irish paramilitaries are created as the metaphorical bomb whose detonation, albeit physical or psychological, the British psyche experiences by proxy. This said, Seamus Deane suggests that explanations about these Irish stereotypes might cause a change in British perceptions about the PIRA.[68]

According to Deane, 'if you can show how and why a stereotype works and is adopted [...] people will begin to change [because] the moment it is seen as a political fact or a social fact, and not a fact of nature, it begins to change'.[69] Whether or not an awareness of the political or social fact constructing Irish Hamlets would 'change people' is, maybe, debatable. After all, surely most 'people' are not oblivious to the fact that stereotypes *are* stereotypes or 'archetypes'.[70] However, Deane observes how 'all the basic stories are synchronic [but] all the analyses of them are diachronic, that is, they are shaped by their moment in history'.[71] He also observes that 'the demon which inspires the artist is often the exaggerated form of things which are

---

66   The fly-cover to Aly Renwick's text, *Last Night Another Soldier...*, is a prime example of this self-validating tendency displayed by Troubles' authors: 'Aly Renwick [...] helped set up Information on Ireland and edited the first publication of *British Soldiers Speak Out On Ireland. Aly Renwick, Last Night Another Soldier ...* (London: Barbed Wire, 1989).
67   Rosenberg, *The Masks of Hamlet*, p.135.
68   'The Arts and Ideology: Jennifer Fitzgerald talks to Seamus Deane, Joan Fowler and Frank McGuinness', *Crane Bag of Irish Studies*, 9.2 (1885), 60–9.
69   Ibid., p.65.
70   Ibid.
71   Ibid., p.66.

troubling the society as a whole'.[72] Here, Deane acknowledges that stereotypes such as Hamlet do not exist in some transcendental, Platonic sense. Like the PIRA, Hamlet is appropriated in many different ways and for many different social, political and psychological reasons. And constructs of the Irish gunman are often based on Ernest Jones's psychoanalytical model.[73]

Displaced onto the Irish gunman by the unconscious of British (and sometimes Irish) authors, these types of active and dynamic repressing forces are galvanized by moral and ideological taboos as well as sexual desire in terms of both the state law and the paternal law. So, when the PIRA are screened through Hamlet and Oedipus they signify far more than generalized, character studies of fictive constructs. Here we can recall Deane's observations and relate them to *Hamlet*, the PIRA, and the Oedipus myth: a triadic construct that furnishes 'archetype[s] [and] basic synchronic stories'. These stories contribute to 'analyses [which] are diachronic [...], shaped by their moment in history'. Such a moment in history is, of course, provided by ideology and the political events from the north of Ireland which, in turn, are psychologized through Hamletized and Anglicized PIRA figures.

As the following two sections explore more closely, these notions are relevant to British and Irish authors of the PIRA because, inevitably, fictive characters include the 'real' author, a subject who has 'an unconscious as well as a conscious [and] imagination springs at least as fully from the former as from the latter'.[74] Through identifying Hamlet with Shakespeare and every conscience-ridden male subject compelled to negotiate and continue negotiating the Oedipus Complex, Jones suggests that Hamlet is Shakespeare, that Hamlet is a symptom of 'the personality of Shakespeare himself'.[75] But every subject is also compelled to negotiate an ideological conscience. 'Thus conscience does make cowards of us all', especially

---

72   Ibid., p.68.
73   Ernest Jones, *Hamlet and Oedipus* (London: W.W. Norton, 1976).
74   Jones, *Hamlet and Oedipus*, p.19.
75   Ibid.

authors of the PIRA who, like Shakespeare, are 'the ghost[s] behind and within' their characters'.[76]

2.2: 'Imagine *Hamlet* in Irish':[77] *Jig* and the Maternal Thing

> He blinked, rubbed his eyes, focused on Celestine's face, trying to associate what he saw there with the woman who'd whispered *Trust me*, *trust me* on the sofa downstairs. He had thought that if she was capable of sexual treachery, what else could she bring herself to do? There were no limits, no boundaries. Anything was possible.[78]

Lacan's Hamlet marks a departure away from Freud, Jones and Olivier. This departure summons a foregrounding of Gertrude, the mother figure who becomes the key to the problem of Hamlet's desire that is bound up with the desire of the Other. As suggested, a Freudian reading of *Hamlet* tends to concentrate upon a question of guilt over an unconscious Oedipal rivalry between King Hamlet and Hamlet who then psychologically navigates an unconscious identification with Claudius. Thus, in Freud's *Hamlet* Gertrude is a relatively minor character. But, for Lacan, Gertrude plays a more important role. In his essay entitled 'Desire and the Interpretation of Desire in *Hamlet*', Lacan suggests that Hamlet's inability to act can be explained through Gertrude's failure to *choose* between King Hamlet and Claudius. After all, Hamlet should not have a dilemma about avenging King Hamlet, the good monarch and symbolic father, and killing Claudius, the bad usurper and real father of sexual enjoyment. Yet Hamlet is faced with a more complex dilemma which is caused by Gertrude who not only seems to like Claudius but also refuses to articulate her unequivocal

---

76   Gary Taylor, *Reinventing Shakespeare* (London: Vintage, 1991), p.243.
77   Campbell Armstrong, *Jig* (London: Hodder and Stoughton, 1987), p.563.
78   Ibid., p.65.

124

desire for either husband. The question of Gertrude's desire relates to Freud's question '*was will das weib*?', 'what does a woman want?'.[79] Lacan rephrases this question as '*che vuoi*?': 'what does the (m)other want from me?'.[80] 'Today's lecture', writes Freud, 'deals with a subject which has a claim second almost to no other [...], the riddle of the nature of femininity [...], women [...] *are* themselves this riddle'.[81]

Hamlet is presented with a number of questions about Gertrude's desire and what does the (m)other want from me? Does she want him to kill Claudius? Does she want him to be Claudius? Does she really enjoy sex with Claudius? Does she want to, as Prince Hamlet says, continue 'honeying and making love / Over the nasty sty?'. For Lacan, the answer to the latter question might be 'yes'. Rosalind Minsky explains why. 'In an attempt to find out what women really want', claims Minsky, Lacan 'develops the concept of *jouissance* to suggest a form of sexual pleasure peculiar and specific to women'.[82] Following Lacan, Zizek's observations about Hamlet's 'doubt as to his mother's desire' compound these ideas.[83] 'What does she really want?', asks Zizek, 'what if she really *enjoys* her filthy promiscuous relationship with his uncle?'.[84] Ultimately, the questions concerning Gertude's desire frustrate Hamlet's interpellation to revenge which is made by the paternal law of his dead father. And, of course, his father's dictate about not harming Gertrude further complicates matters.

Linked to Hamlet's dilemma over Gertrude's desire, Lacan claims that the subject's desire is always the desire of the Other. The subject does not desire the other but, instead, desires to be desired by the Other. Accordingly, for Lacan, Gertrude 'becomes one of the

---

79   Zizek, *The Sublime Object of Ideology*, p.112.
80   Jacques Lacan, 'Desire and the Interpretation of Desire in *Hamlet*', *Yale French Studies: Literature and Psychoanalysis*, 55/56 (1977), 11–52 (p.13).
81   Sigmund Freud quoted by Shoshana Felman, in *What Does A Woman Want?: Reading And Sexual Difference* (London: Johns Hopkins, 1993), p.69.
82   Rosalind Minsky, in *Knowing Women: Feminism And Knowledge*, ed. Helen Crowley and Susan Himmelweit (Cambridge: Polity, 1992), pp.186–204 (p.200).
83   Zizek, *The Sublime Object of Ideology*, p.120.
84   Ibid.

innermost elements in Hamlet's drama [which is] the drama of Hamlet as the man who has lost the way of his desire'; a drama 'dominated by the Mother as Other'.[85]

Drawing closely upon Lacan's *Hamlet*, this chapter develops the above ideas concerning the Mother as Other with recourse to the previous chapter's issues concerning how certain British represent-ations of the PIRA might rely upon Shakespeare's *Hamlet* as a subtext. As suggested earlier, such representations display the ways in which Shakespeare's subtext can be manipulated to produce sig-nificant differences that have political and ideological implications. Like British representations of the Freudian Irish gunman, British representations of the Lacanian Irish gunman may sometimes offer self-conscious treatments, or re-workings, of the Hamletian theme whereby a well-meaning and inherently moral individual is trapped within a damaging and determining political context or ideological structure. This is not, of course, to imply that Shakespeare's texts cannot be effectively appropriated and refashioned by non-British cultures (including Irish) for completely different and diverse social and political agendas.[86] Here, though, through a detailed reading of a single text, I want to focus upon how British authors might create exemplary as well as an exceptional representations of Irish Hamlets which do not merely or unconsciously reproduce the same formula as Shakespeare but, instead, alter the formula in significant ways re-sulting in a strange hybrid, an impossible beast: an Irish, yet quintessentially British, Hamlet. The novel to be discussed, *Jig*, is by Scottish author Campbell Armstrong. And the impossible beast, the metonymic Hamletian hybrid, is evoked by Armstrong's character named Padraic Finn.

> How can we sit around and talk English if we're supposed to be an independent country? English is a barbaric tongue, Jig, a mishmash. It doesn't have the

---

85   Lacan, 'Desire and the Interpretation of Desire in *Hamlet*', p.12.
86   Caribbean writers have of course rewritten *The Tempest* from a postcolonial perpective. Feminists have rewritten *Hamlet*. And *The Merchant of Venice* has also been treated to a less anti-Semetic approach.

sweetness of the Gaelic. Have you ever imagined what it would have sounded like if Bill Shakespeare has written in the Gaelic? Imagine *Hamlet* in Irish.[87]

Now, it goes without saying, that an Irish *Hamlet* written in either 'the Gaelic' or the English language could signal a politically disruptive rewriting of the text. Here, though, although Finn articulates a desire to have *Hamlet* 'written in the Gaelic', he does not suggest any displacement of the play's British authorial voice, that being, Shakespeare's. But he cannot have a Gaelic 'Bill Shakespeare', cannot have a Gaelic *Hamlet* as Shakespeare's *Hamlet*. And why should an Irish Republican desire a Gaelic *Hamlet*? Put simply, what is Armstrong's British representation of Irishness trying to say? Irrespective of Finn's opinion about the English language being 'a barbaric tongue', Armstrong portrays an Irish gunman who appears to desire the civilizing, universal and apolitical morality embedded within English culture through Shakespeare's *Hamlet*. And this desire is, arguably, a displacement of British values on to the PIRA.

Like Shakespeare's Hamlet, Armstrong's Irish Hamlet (a character named Jig) is also an eponymous hero. And Jig's 'teacher' (Finn) is a re-working of King Hamlet (109). Finn represents Jig's historical and mythical Irish Republican fathers such as *Padraic* Pearse and *Finn* McCool. He is the paternal figure who interpellates Jig and sends him from Ireland to America with an injunction to enact revenge. This revenge is for money that has been stolen from Finn's organization. Moreover, paralleling King Hamlet and Hamlet, Jig and Finn share the same first name, Patrick and Padraic. This said, although Armstrong makes interesting borrowings from *Hamlet*, especially with motifs such as 'a lot of dying' and 'treacheries', his text does not doggedly reproduce Shakespeare's plot (85, 73). For instance, Jig is a man of action not procrastination, albeit a doomed one. He is a young man of 'steel', of 'backbone and guts', with 'a chill dedication to the cause': someone who does not kill 'indiscriminately' but with 'elegance' (67, 357).

---

87   Armstrong, *Jig*, p.65. Further consecutive references to this novel are given after quotations in the text.

Armstrong manipulates Shakespeare's plot to displace the central conflict away from the rivalry of King Hamlet versus Claudius or King Hamlet versus Hamlet in terms of the phantasmagorical prize of the mother's body. Instead, Armstrong shows the central conflict orbiting around a mother figure, or a Mother Ireland figure (Celestine), and the question concerning 'what does the (m)other want from me?'. As the narrative unfolds, Jig's inner turmoil shifts from his desire to gain revenge for the stolen money and Finn's paternal approval to the maternal Thing whose desire is unfathomable and must be determined, to the maternal Thing whose desire is determining because it determines the fate of the protagonist.

Jig commences with a ship named the *Connie O'Mara* that is sailing from America to Ireland with a 'Courier' who has substantial funds for a break-away PIRA organization named the 'Association of the Wolfe'. Finn is the leader of this break-away group, and Jig is Finn's crack assassin, 'a natural marksman' who Finn has 'moulded' and possesses 'a strong affection for' (109). The older man's fondness for Jig is compounded when he considers that 'along the way' both Jig and himself 'came to understand and maybe even love one another a little bit too' (110). And Finn's 'love' is indeed reciprocated, a fact made evident throughout the narrative when Jig yearns to be Finn's 'own bloody hero', desires 'Finn's faith in him [to be] completely justified', regards Finn as being 'indestructible and immortal', doesn't 'want Finn to be disappointed in him', and can't 'bear the idea of Finn thinking badly of him' (492, 494, 529, 389).

Before reaching Ireland, the ship's captain sees 'the ghostly shape of a white yacht' that emerges 'out of the black like some kind of spirit' (15). The yacht contains Irish Loyalist paramilitaries who hijack the *Connie O'Mara*, murder O'Reilly, poison the Courier and take the money. All this is easily achieved because the crew of the *Connie O'Mara* is riddled with traitors. Thus we have at the beginning of the plot some important tropes from *Hamlet*: a ghost, treachery, murder and poisoning.

One of the traitors, Seamus Houlihan, a loyalist paramilitary whose namesake immediately evokes an Irish mother, Kathleen Ni Houlihan, functions throughout the novel's subplot in much the same way as the PIRA demons explored earlier in this study. Houlihan is a 'fanatic', a 'thug' and a 'monster': a Loyalist mirror to the demon PIRA prototype and an other to the English ego ideal (474). He travels to America, has no compunction about bombing church-goers within 'a Presbyterian church in White Plains, New York' or machine-gunning a bus-load of school children (477). Together with his ac-complices, Houlihan acts on orders from a man named 'the Reverend Ivor McInnes who, apart from the fact that he 'has a pronounced [...] Liverpool accent', supplies a fairly accurate caricature of the Reverend Ian Paisley (411,114). McInnes also travels to America and, under the pretence of researching for a book, orchestrates Houlihan's atrocities against exclusively Protestant targets. He does this in order to discredit the Irish Republican paramilitaries and 'outrage Ameri-cans enough [to] send some troops over [to Ireland] to wipe out the IRA' (572). Aged 'about fifty', McInnes is 'big [with] a large craggy face that [is] handsome' (146). Like Houlihan, he is 'the worst kind of monster' (573). But he is also a 'megalomaniac' with a 'roguish charm which, as a political tool, could be extremely useful', especially when embellished with a smile that displays 'strong white teeth' (253, 146, 148). In fact, McInnes smiles a great deal and, in turn, incites 'a lot of smiling' from his adoring congregation (393). He is 'clever and [...] cunning' and licentious then, at the end of the novel, revealed to be married to Jig's 'bigamous stepmother': Celestine (253, 587). Thus, McInnes offers a parallel to *Hamlet*'s Claudius, epitomizes a 'smiling, damned villain'.

Like Hamlet, Jig is aged 'about thirty', an 'only child' and, according to the *Sunday Telegraph*, evokes 'humanity', 'compassion' and accomplishes 'a tragic stature' through death (118, 140–41, front inside cover). Therefore, in some respects, Armstrong's ill-fated hero satisfies a liberal humanist and British formula which attempts to transcend the particularities of the Irish struggle through a narrative that has universal appeal. But, in a similar way to the examples discussed in 2.1, the *Hamlet* subtext provides Armstrong's characters and plot with significant and interesting variations of this liberal humanist formula. And this is especially apparent when the *Hamlet* subtext accords with a Lacanian approach.

Jig's real name is Patrick Cairney. He is introduced during a scene in which he enjoys sex with a young woman named Rhiannon who is a nurse; a fittingly maternal sexual partner for a quasi-Oedipal protagonist. We learn that although Jig is posing as an archaeology student, he is actually an Irish Republican assassin of Irish-American extraction who acts on behalf of the Association of the Wolfe. Thus, prior to his revenge mission, Jig is already a man of action. He is a courtier, Rhiannon's lover; a soldier, an Irish paramilitary; and a scholar, a university student. Moreover, his codename (Jig) summons a 'lunatic fellow' with an antic Irish disposition (90). Indeed, when he is sent to America on Finn's mission to retrieve the stolen money and enact revenge upon those responsible, he assumes the antic disposition of a drunken vagrant in order to disguise his real identity (116). However, summoning moral dispositions, Finn and Jig both desire 'an end to the *atrocious* image the IRA had made for itself' (65). But even though Jig has a strong emotional attachment to Finn, he nevertheless perceives in him 'a kind of madness', 'a needle-sharp single-minded-ness', 'a manic light' and, perhaps, the 'kind of madness' which acts as a mirror image to an ideal Hamletian self (65).

Jig's mission involves seeking out the identities of an anonymous group of wealthy American men. These men are called the 'Fund-raisers' and, although they have previously supplied financial aid to Finn's organization, the group is now suspected of harbouring a traitor who is believed to be responsible for the theft of the missing money (44). Unbeknown to Jig, his own father (senator Harry Cairney) is a member of the Fund-raisers. Together with his accomplices, Cairney senior is horrified by the 'sense of treachery' prompted by the rumour-ed accusations of there being 'a traitor in the ranks' (45, 46). Moreover, in spite of his old age and ill-heath, the senator is married to a beautiful and much younger woman (Celestine). At the end of the novel he learns that the marriage is bigamous.

Celestine's physical attributes summon images of a young Gertrude. Her 'yellow hair', 'blue eyes' and 'rather gaunt [...] almost stark [...] beauty' rehearse a renaissance lady who plays 'baroque' music 'on her piano' (42, 51). And when Jig meets Celestine he is plunged into 'the abyss of some terrifying, filthy enjoyment' where the question 'what does the [step] mother want from me?' propels him into a fatal journey through desire.[88] This fatal journey commences when Jig visits his father and, late one night, Celestine visits Jig in his bedroom. Here, Jig reveals his fear of Celestine's sexuality. 'He didn't', writes Armstrong, 'want this woman in his bedroom'.[89] However, irrespective of what Jig 'wants', his male gaze is galvanized by Celestine's 'lean [...] body' that is, rather phallically, 'hard and taut [but] would yield in the right places' (217). This said, Jig struggles 'to absent himself from his responses to her' (217). But he finds 'it [...] so damned hard to shut [his] eyes and ignore [her] compelling beauty and [...] the faint notion that he [...] could go to her now and slip the robe from her body and draw her down in bed with him' (217).

As the plot develops, Jig leaves his father's house and tracks down all the Fund-raisers except for the senator whose involvement is only revealed to Jig in the final pages. While Jig hunts for the Fund-raisers, the British counter-intelligence agent (Frank Pagan) hunts for Jig. Eventually, Jig phones home and is told by Celestine that his father has suffered a heart-attack. Circumstances triggered by McInnes and Houlihan enable Pagan and Jig to join forces, confront McInnes then track down Houlihan. Jig kills Houlihan but is, in turn, wounded. He returns to his father's house where, once again, Celestine tempts him with seduction. Now, in the closing chapters, Jig discovers that Celestine has lied about his father's illness. She informs Jig about the senator's involvement with the Fund-raisers. The senator is shocked, had no idea that she knew about his illegal activities. Her further revelations expose how she helped to steal the money from the ship. She shoots the senator, then Jig. Pagan arrives at the house, is closely followed by McInnes. The narrative ends with Pagan confronting Celestine and McInnes. Pagan learns that Celestine is McInnes's wife and has been living in a bigamous marriage with the senator for two years in order to help McInnes with his anti-Irish Republican campaign. Fatally wounded, Jig shoots both Celestine and McInnes dead. Pagan, the moral British law, is left musing over the events: 'Treachery, he thought. It bruised you, left you shaken' (579).

---

88   Zizek, *The Sublime Object of Ideology*, p.120.
89   Armstrong, *Jig*, p.216. Further consecutive references to this novel are given after quotations in the text.

Finally, a career-minded, hard-nosed FBI agent called Zuboric catches up with Pagan who then bribes Zuboric with the stolen money and the opportunity to take the credit for the killings in the house. 'You'd be a big bloody hero', says Pagan, 'you can use me to back up the authentic story of your heroic deeds' (582, 583). Here, Zuboric seems to provide a Fortinbras figure who completes the tragic Hamletian narrative through pragmatism rather than emotion.

Pagan is an interesting character, a doppelganger to Jig as well an Horatio-type ally who senses that 'all [is] out of balance' or, perhaps, 'out of joint' (439). For instance, Pagan learns that McInnes has masterminded the bombings and shootings in America. He then finds Jig and persuades him that they both have 'matching objectives' (487). Thus, Armstrong creates an Irish mirror for British identifications, an Irish Hamlet for a British Horatio. 'Pagan and Jig', thinks McInnes, 'now there was a combination that God and Scotland Yard and the FBI hadn't exactly intended' (505). McInnes has a point. But, irrespective of what 'God and Scotland Yard and the FBI [...] intended', this bizarre mirroring of British masculinity via Irish masculinity does, indeed, seem to have been intended by Armstrong.

Following the respective destinies of Hamlet and Horatio, the plot concludes with Jig's death and Pagan's survival. At the senator's house, Pagan grieves for Jig, thinks about the 'inestimable treasons' and the 'narrative of deception and violence [that] had been going on in [the] large gloomy house' which, like the castle at Elsinore, is left scattered with four dead bodies: Jig, Celestine, McInnes and the senator (the same casualty statistic presented by Shakespeare's tragic denouement) (571, 580).

As suggested, Pagan is a doppelganger as well as an Horatioian comrade to Jig. Therefore, Pagan's mirroring symbolizes both life and death. Not surprisingly, this life and death opposition implies that Armstrong's British identification with an Irish Hamlet is an ambivalent construct. Jig is heroic and moral, the ideal British Hamletian self. But he is also sexually active and violent, the Irish PIRA other. When Pagan's British identity becomes fused with Jig's Irish identity, Armstrong makes explicit (or conscious) this implicit (or unconscious) problem for British male subjectivity. Indeed, Pagan contemplates how 'whenever he plunged into the maze of Irish terrorism he had the sensation of being locked within a labyrinth of mirrors' (23). 'Frank Pagan and Jig [...] together?', thinks McInnes, 'how had this pair managed to find one another, and who was the quarry, who the hunter now?' (505). McInnes's question concerning how Pagan and Jig had managed to find one another could perhaps be answered within Armstrong's own psychological 'labyrinth of mirrors' which might reflect his own, inevitable identification with his own Irish Hamlet. This sense of the inevitable whereby Britishness fastens on to Irishness is manifested prior to Jig's first meeting with Pagan. For instance, Armstrong shows Pagan thinking about 'moments when he wondered if Jig actually existed' (29). The British agent then goes on to imagine Jig in terms of an Irish gunman who *does* 'exist'. But, it might be argued, Jig can only really 'exist' as an ideal construct or mirror image for the British self. Hence, we learn that Pagan 'actually *admired* Jig, albeit in the most grudging way [because] the man *never* did anything that would harm an innocent bystander' (29). To Pagan, Jig is 'an artist [in] a crude war, but [...] gave [this war] his own civilised flourish' (30). Furthermore, Jig is 'unlike the regular IRA rabble [...], those butchers who gave no thought to children and women and anybody else who just happened to get accidentally caught in the crossfire' (29, 30).

Reinforcing and reversing the idea of the inevitability of British identifications with Irish Hamlets, Jig experiences a kind of prescience about his involvement with Pagan. 'He wondered about this Pagan, [thought] it was interesting to know your adversary's name' (36). In fact, Jig regards Pagan as being 'the man [...] always behind him like some kind of dogged spectre' (388). Armstrong, then, appears to suggest that Jig wants to *be* Pagan, wants *to be* British. For instance, Jig considers how Pagan 'had insights [and] a deeper human understanding, an ability to cut through lies and deceptions and misleading statements' (404). Conversely, Armstrong also appears to suggest that Pagan wants to *be* Jig, wants to *be* Irish. Pagan 'has a great fondness for the Irish' (30). He wonders about 'some revelation [...] in the mystery of Jig's soul' (312). He 'want[s] an *understanding* of the assassin' (312). And, crucially, he imagines what it would be like to *be* Jig (312, 472). As observed by Zuboric, Pagan is 'consumed by Jig. Probably dreamed Jig at nights. Had Jig for breakfast' (200).

This coupling of Jig and Pagan becomes intensified when Armstrong implies that the two men share the same thoughts. Thus, a bizarre psychological paralleling occurs after the school-bus killings when Pagan 'couldn't help thinking of the dead girls' and then, a mere ten pages later, Jig is 'thinking' about 'those [...] dead girls [and] trying not to' (367, 378). Both men are loners. Both men are 'sleuth[s]' and, as observed by Jig, 'asked to *investigate* a crime' (75). Both men are 'expendable', a fact articulated by a second FBI man named Korn who says: 'Pagan's expendable, just as expendable as Jig' (449). Both men are similar personality types. Pagan has 'the kind of face that [is] difficult to read' while Jig is 'enigmatic', 'mysterious', 'a shadowy figure forever on the farthest edges of [Pagan's] vision' (245, 334, 25). Jig is 'melancholy', Pagan is 'maudlin' (58, 97). And, finally, both men have similar physical characteristics. Hence, Jig describes himself as being 'a navvy with a purpose' and Pagan describes himself as having 'inherited his father's [...] bricklayer's hands' (60, 23). Bearing these points in mind, Armstrong's creation of Pagan submits a conscious or unconscious desire for a heroic if deadly ideal ego, a British identification that, once again, seeks to Anglicize as well as Hamletize the Irish gunman.

Expanding upon these ideas, there follows a more detailed analysis of the main themes and characters. This analysis suggests how Armstrong creates a subtext for Jig's fatal destiny, a subtext that depends upon a key dilemma over Mother Ireland and Celestine's desire as well as what Lacan terms 'the hour of the Other', The Three Fathers, and *che vuoi?*.[90]

As mentioned earlier, in his essay entitled 'Desire and the Interpretation of Desire in *Hamlet*', Lacan claims that Hamlet's revenge is thwarted because of the question *che vuoi?*: what does the (m)other want from me? This said, Lacan also claims that Hamlet's revenge is thwarted by 'the hour of the Other'. 'Whatever Hamlet may do', writes Lacan, 'he will do it only at the hour of the Other'.[91] For instance, 'when [Hamlet] stays on [at Elsinore], it is the hour of his parents [and] when he [consistently] suspends his crime [thereafter] it

90   Jacques Lacan, 'Desire and the Interpretation of Desire in *Hamlet*', p.18.
91   Ibid.

134

is the hour of the others'.[92] So, 'when he leaves for England, it is the hour of his stepfather'.[93] And 'it is still at the hour of the Other', as well as 'for the sake of the Other's wager', that Hamlet 'rushes into the trap laid by the Other'.[94]

The 'trap laid by the Other' is Hamlet's duel with Laertes, an event whereby 'the Other's wager [is] Claudius's stake, [a] stake against death' which functions as *objet petit a*; 'not the object of desire but the object *in* desire', the object that 'unleash[es]' desire.[95] For Hamlet, the real object of desire is of course 'the phallus', 'the fatal signifier' which resides 'in that realm beyond [where], ultimately, the encounter with the other serves only to enable Hamlet to identify himself with the fatal signifier' which is Laertes 'poisoned' foil.[96] Although altered in significant ways, Lacan's observations about the hour of the Other are relevant to Jig, his three fathers and his deadly journey towards the phallus a propos the figure of Celestine.

For Jig, the *objet petit a*, the Other's deadly stake that unleashes desire, is the money belonging to Finn.[97] When this *object petit a* is stolen, a chain of events is prompted: the initial crime, revenge and Jig's journey towards the deadly signifier: Celestine. Indeed, this chain of events is anticipated when Finn tells Jig that the theft represents an 'awful crime' and interpellates Jig who has no *choice* but to seek revenge.[98] Irrespective of Jig's suitably Oedipal misgivings that Finn 'expected him to go into America blind', he knows that 'if Finn commanded [...] he'd obey'.[99] In this way, Jig's action is set in motion at the hour of Finn as the Other.

The next hour of the Other occurs when Jig reaches America and seeks refuge at St. Finbar's Mission where a priest, Father Tumulty, instructs Jig to 'vanish from here and come back in two days'.[100]

---

92   Ibid.
93   Ibid.
94   Ibid.
95   Ibid., pp.18, 30, 28.
96   Ibid., p.32.
97   Armstrong, *Jig*, p.69.
98   Ibid.
99   Ibid.
100 Ibid., p.134.

Therefore, it is the hour of Tumulty which causes Jig to visit his father and meet Celestine, the step m(other) who incites the *che vuoi?* dilemma and becomes the 'impossible as object of desire', the 'fatal signifier', the 'veiled phallus' as death.[101]

The unfathomable and deterministic nature of Celestine's sexual desire is made explicit. For instance, after a scene where she masturbates and feels 'as if she [is] destroyed by [an] astonishing ferocity of pleasure', she looks in 'the mirror' and sees a 'smile' that is 'enigmatic', or unfathomable, 'even to herself'.[102] Later in the narrative, while searching for the Fund-raisers, Jig phones home and speaks to Celestine. He does so against his better judgement, is compelled by the desire of the (m)other and finds himself 'going towards' the phone 'even as he resisted. Even as he thought *No, I don't need this now. I don't need this ever*'.[103] Celestine lies to Jig, tells him that his father has suffered a heart-attack. Her lie is deterministic, submits Jig, once again, to the hour of the Other, Celestine's hour, an imminent hour infused with Oedipal guilt and the question of her desire. And she knows this. 'He would come home', muses Celestine, 'because he felt guilty about what had happened, because he wanted to see her again, and because of his father. Yes he'd come back'.[104]

After the phone call, Jig lies in wait for one of the Fund-raisers and captures Pagan. Here Jig has an advantage. Yet, rather than 'shooting' Pagan, he is persuaded by the British Agent to join forces with him against McInnes. So, at Pagan's hour, Jig moves on to McInnes's hour. This happens when Pagan takes Jig to see McInnes whose information about Finn's death inflicts Jig with 'some awful' Hamletian 'inner turmoil' and the equally Hamletian awareness that 'he was ready to do violence' and 'needed to shed blood'.[105] At McInnes's hour, he learns that Houlihan murdered Finn and discovers

101 Jacques Lacan, 'Desire and the Interpretation of Desire in *Hamlet*', pp.36, 32, 38.
102 Armstrong, *Jig*, pp.260, 262.
103 Ibid., p.442.
104 Ibid., p.455.
105 Ibid., pp.513, 514, 530.

Houlihan's current whereabouts. From now on Jig's fate is sealed. Wounded in a shoot-out with Houlihan, thinking his father is dying, he returns to his father's Elsinorian mansion. This mansion is 'a monstrosity sprawling across the landscape like an immense mausoleum'.[106] Armstrong writes that if the house had been 'given a smokestack, it might have passed as a crematorium'.[107] In 'childhood', thinks Jig, 'he'd convinced himself that [the] house was haunted [with] all kinds of apparitions'.[108] Ultimately, Armstrong begins and ends his Irish Hamlet's fated journey with a suitably ominous space for the enactment of a tragic and treachery-ridden finale.

Just prior to this finale, Jig is rapt by the 'exquisite pain' of *jouissance*, a *jouissance* whereby his incestuous fantasy about Celestine becomes the unbearable real.[109] 'At her mercy', 'struggling to control the pain', 'feeling so damned feeble in front of her', he experiences both 'Desire and Pain'; 'a strange interlocking of sensations [...] as if desire and pain had fused together in one feeling'.[110] For Jig, this 'feeling [is] indescribable and fresh and beyond any emotion he'd ever registered'.[111] However, his feeling of being 'beyond any emotion' is merely a prologue to his being 'in that realm beyond' where he will experience his real 'encounter [with] the phallus' (Celestine) and death.[112]

When Celestine announces her involvement in the theft of the money, she also announces her involvement in the 'awful crime' that unleashed Jig's desire in terms of the Other's stake and *objet petit a*. Even so, Jig remains confounded by the question 'what does the (m)other want from me?' He gazes at her 'face, trying to associate what he [sees] there with the woman who'd whispered *Trust me, trust me* on the sofa downstairs'.[113] Now, Jig's confusion over Celestine's desire escalates: 'he had thought that if she was capable of sexual

106   Ibid., p.143.
107   Ibid.
108   Ibid., p.214.
109   Madan Sarup, *Jacques Lacan* (New York: Harvester Wheatsheaf, 1992), p.99.
110   Armstrong, *Jig*, p.553.
111   Ibid.
112   Lacan, 'Desire and the Interpretation of Desire in *Hamlet*', p.32.
113   Armstrong, *Jig*, p.563.

treachery, what else could she bring herself to do? There were no limits, no boundaries. Anything was possible'.[114] At this moment, Celestine becomes 'the uncanny', a Thing causing 'an imbalance that arises in the fantasy when it decomposes, crossing the limits originally assigned to it, and rejoins the image of the other subject'.[115] No longer just a sexual 'fantasy', and therefore 'crossing the limits originally assigned', Celestine 'rejoins the image of the other subject' who is, in this narrative, a traitor. And Jig is seized with this sense of the uncanny when he asks her 'who the fuck are you?'.[116] His question is answered when she shoots him. She is, of course, the phallus.

Celestine's function as the phallus relates to her symbolic function as Mother Ireland, a female em(body)ment of the nation as the north of Ireland. So, through a reworking of the *Hamlet* formula, Armstrong grapples with the real political and psychological trauma of the north of Ireland to manifest a British fantasy. This fantasy is the sublime and terrifying Irish (m)other-Thing that dominates the text and implies that the woman is always the one to blame. Linked to these ideas, I conclude this section with an analysis of Jig in terms of Finn, his biological father, and McInnes, together with their significance to the notion that Mother Ireland is the sublime body around which orbits the question: what does woman want from me?

When the narrative introduces Jig in Dublin, his sexual enjoyment of Rhiannon is interrupted by memories of an 'absentee father [...] in Washington [who] returned each summer to Roscommon to indoctrinate his son in the melancholic songs and stories that were part of the Irish tradition, tales of defeats and victories' (56). Jig's memories include his father's past and present 'memories' which are 'preserved in amber' and summon the fathers of the Republican Cause from the 1916 Easter Rising to the Long Kesh 'political prisoners' (59, 60). Indeed, King Hamlet's injunction to constantly 'remember' applies to Jig, his father, and Finn who throughout the text are haunted by an excess of memories that, ultimately, produce the obscene: death.

---

114   Ibid.
115   Lacan, 'Desire and the Interpretation of Desire in *Hamlet*', p.22.
116   Armstrong, *Jig*, p.565. Further consecutive references to this novel are given after quotations in the text.

Jig is inflicted with an archetypal, Hamletian memory through the injunction that he receives from Finn, 'a task to carry out' that returns Jig to his Elsinorian family home and his deadly step-mother (348). As suggested, Finn and the senator are also plagued by memories. These memories relate to their Irish Republican forefathers and Mother Ireland. Hence, we are told that Jig's father had 'fallen into the habit of [...] ransacking his memory [and] reminiscing [about] his favourite subject: Ireland' (137, 138, 334). For the senator, Ireland is 'a darkly brooding mistress [...], the motherland' (49). In a similar way, Finn broods upon memories of the '1920s' and a father-figure from 'the Third Tipperary Brigade of the IRA' named 'Dan Breen' (108). Finn is devoted to the Republican cause and therefore mother Ireland.

Associated with the (m)other as Other, three women fulfil three different symbolic functions for Jig. For instance, in her capacity as a nurse and a sexual partner, Rhiannon offers Jig a nurturing yet good whore-mother figure whereas his dead mother, aptly named Kathleen, summons a woman *lovely and fair*': a 'real mother' as redemptive angel (41). The third mother is Celestine, the woman his father has 'unexpectedly married', the bad whore-mother, a ferociously ethical Antigone figure symbolizing *the Old Woman of Beare*' (58, 57). This third woman is 'an abstraction called the Cause' to whom both Jig and Finn remain 'married' even though they are aware that 'freedom from the marriage lay [...] in the last divorce of death' (442).

Jig's three mothers provide a symmetrical balance to Jig's three fathers: an imaginary father (Harry Cairney); a symbolic father (Finn); and a real father of enjoyment (McInnes). These three fathers relate to Lacan's notions about crime and the law. Lacan claims that the real father is the 'primordial' father ('Father Enjoyment'), 'the obscene, castrating father of *jouissance*', 'the Great Fucker'.[117] Appearing at the moment of Jig's death, McInnes is the licentious and murderous villain whose political and sexual gratification through Celestine manifests 'a match made in hell'.[118] This suggests that McInnes is

---

117 Jacques Lacan, *The Ethics of Psychoanalysis*, 1959–1960, trans. Dennis Porter, notes Dennis Porter (London: Routledge, 1992), p.7.

118 Armstrong, *Jig*, p.575.

Jig's 'Real father', the one 'whose existence appears only retro-spectively in fantasy'.[119] Next, the imaginary father. This is the biological father who triggers 'the inevitable object of an aggressive identification from his off-spring'.[120] But the imaginary father is 'him-self castrated by the Law'.[121] So, Jig's imaginary father is the senator and 'the one that fuck[s] [Jig] up'.[122]

At both a conscious and unconscious level, Jig seems to be aware of the senator's lack. Consequently, we learn that Jig 'never wanted to be anything like [his] father [...], felt contempt for the old man and everything he represented [and] as if he were stalked by the ghost of Harry Cairney's younger self, a spectre'.[123] Yet Jig's symbolic father functions differently to his real and imaginary fathers. This is because 'the symbolic father is the dead father whose power and authority resides in the dead letter of the law incarnated in language and the Name of the Father'.[124] Therefore, the good father is necessarily the dead father.

An unconscious desire for the senator to become his symbolic dead father is inferred when Jig answers a phone call from Finn but lies to Rhiannon by saying that the phone call concerned his father who had suffered 'a mild heart attack'.[125] But the senator is not dead, is not the law. This authority resides with the martyred fathers of the Irish Republican Cause. While living, Finn is the mouth-piece of these dead fathers, a 'surrogate father [and] mentor' (234). But, in death, Finn becomes Jig's ultimate symbol of authority. 'Dear Finn,' grieves Jig, 'he had loved him more than he'd ever loved his father. More than any other human being' (578).

Unlike *Hamlet*, if Finn 'introduces the principle of the law', this law reinforces rather than forbids 'the all powerful relationship with the mother' vis-à-vis Ireland who, in turn, becomes hideously and

119 Scott Wilson, Unpublished Paper, Lancaster University, 1999.
120 Ibid.
121 Ibid.
122 Ibid.
123 Armstrong, *Jig*, pp.274, 231, 183.
124 Wilson, Unpublished Paper.
125 Armstrong, *Jig*, p.61. Further consecutive references to this novel are given after quotations in the text.

uncannily symbolized by Celestine. Jig's recollection about 'Finn's own maxim' in respect of 'the Cause' compounds this idea (234). '*The cause is a killing mistress*', insists Finn, '*It seeks your total devotion and never excuses your weaknesses. It demands your complete commitment and it rewards your infidelity not with forgiveness and understanding, but with death*' (234).

When Celestine becomes the apotheosis of the killing mistress and shoots Jig, he imagines his symbolic father's voice repeating this prophecy and saying: '*when you took the oath, you committed yourself to death*' (578). And Finn's prophesy is accurate.

'Fearfully cold, and ruthless [with] a tiny spark of amusement in her eyes [...], Celestine, the lovely, venomous Celestine', becomes the apotheosis of Finn's words in terms of the maternal superego, the punishing conscience whose desire remains unfathomable (560, 578). But at the hour of his own death, Jig is able to strike at the sublime maternal body which then becomes no longer beautiful: is finally just the real body that is 'clumsy in death' (578).

At a conscious level, the cause of Jig's fate is his political involvement in the Republican Cause. Yet, at an unconscious level, the Cause of Jig's fate is a political 'mistress', 'a whore'.[126] However, this section has shown how the real cause of Jig's fate can be explained by the Lacanian dilemma termed *che vuoi?* Here, the mother as Other, the mother as the 'killing mistress of death', the mother as the unconscious made 'real' in terms of Celestine, splits the son's will to revenge. In *Hamlet*, the woman may or may not want Claudius and 'the rank sweat of an enseamed bed' whereas Hamlet may or may not want revenge for the death of his father and sex with his mother. In *Jig*, Celestine, intensifies this dilemma. She makes Jig confront the question of her incestuous desire, she makes the unconscious conscious. Ultimately, the payoff (death) is inexorable, has '*been a close companion all along*'.[127] As I have argued, Celestine signifies the fatal Thing which cannot be escaped, 'the lost object which must be continually refound [...], the prehistoric, unforgettable

---

126 Zizek, *The Sublime Object of Ideology*, pp.118, 112.
127 Ibid., p.578.

Other [...], the forbidden object of incestuous desire, the mother'.[128] This mother is a Thing of *jouissance*, a 'Thing [...] presented to [Jig] as his Sovereign Good'.[129] But when he 'transgresses the pleasure principle and attains this Good, it is experienced as [...] evil'.[130]

The words 'death [...] sorrow and treachery' and a setting described as a 'regular funeral parlour' announce *Jig*'s finale.[131] This finale completes a replay of *Hamlet*'s 'carnal, bloody, and unnatural acts'. Through *Jig*, Armstrong submits a Lacanian Irish Hamlet. And, perhaps more importantly, he also submits a Lacanian Mother Ireland whose desire is horrifying yet irresistible. As this mother is constructed from the psyche of a British author, it might be suggested that she is the spectre who threatens and traumatizes the British, rather than the Irish, male unconscious with the question: what does the woman want from me?

2.3: 'Would you die for me?':[132] Cal's Good Gertrude

> He was in love with the one woman in the world who was forbidden him. He was suffering for something which could not exist. [...] She was an unattainable idea because he had helped kill her husband.[133]

In *Jig*, the hero is damned because the sexually desirable Celestine is, metaphorically, 'the old sow who eats her farrow'.[134] Alexander Walker notes how a film-still from Pat O'Connor's 1984 Celluloid

128 Dylan Evans, *An Introductory Dictionary of Lacanian Psychoanalysis* (London: Routledge, 1996), p.205.
129 Ibid.
130 Ibid.
131 Armstrong, *Jig*, pp.584, 579, 582.
132 Bernard MacLaverty, *Cal* (London: Penguin, 1984), p.136.
133 MacLaverty, *Cal*, p.92.
134 'Old Sow who eats her farrow': Klaus Lubbers quoting 'Stephen Dedalus's bitter quip about Ireland'. Klaus Lubbers, 'Irish Fiction: A Mirror for Specifics, *Eire-Ireland*, 20.2 (1985), 90–104 (p.92).

version of Bernard MacLaverty's 1983 novella entitled *Cal* supplies a visual image of the fated relationship between another sexually desirable Irish 'mother' and another sexually desiring Irish 'son'.[135] The mother, a character named Marcella Morton, is performed by Helen Mirren while the son, a character named Cal McCluskey, is performed by John Lynch. This section considers how and why Mac-Laverty, a writer from the north of Ireland, presents a Troubles narrative through an Hamletian theme and, more specifically, an Hamletian eponymous hero. Further, this chapter also considers how, for different yet compatible reasons to Gertrude and Celestine, Marcella represents 'the one woman in the world who [is] forbidden' to Cal.[136]

In the film-still discussed by Walker, a young and naked Cal protectively embraces an older and semi-naked Marcella. Their gazes are averted away from the camera: the other in terms of the audience as well as the other in terms of each other. Their inability to 'look one other (and the audience) in the eye' may suggest guilt. This said, while Marcella appears to be gazing at a specific object, Cal appears to be gazing at his own, internal melancholic self which, in addition to experiencing Oedipal and Hamletian guilt, might be repeating Hamlet's and Jig's male-voiced and universal Lacanian question: what does the (m)other want from me? Therefore, it is fitting that the following analysis of *Cal* should further develop important psycho-analytical issues concerning fictive Irish Hamlets and the desire of the (m)other. During this analysis, alternative critical arguments that focus upon the various political and ideological implications of Mac-Laverty's novella as well as Pat O'Connor's 1984 film version will also be considered. O'Connor's film is included because its faithful adaptation visualizes many central psychological issues found within the novella. Firstly, however, a brief synopsis of the narrative as well

135 Still photograph from the film *Cal*, Dir. Pat O'Connor, 1984. This is reproduced in a feature article by Alexander Walker, 'Peek-A-Boo, Ballyhoo & Bigotry', *Causeway*, 1.1 (September 1993), 31–5 (p.33).
136 MacLaverty, *Cal*, p.92. Further consecutive references to this novel are given after quotations in the text.

as some of its motifs, themes and general affinities with Shakespeare's *Hamlet* provides the context for a more in-depth theoretical debate.

Cal is a young, unemployed Catholic. He lives in a Protestant enclave of Derry with his widowed father (Shamie) who works at an abattoir. Their council house and their lives exist under threat from the UVF (Ulster Volunteer Force). This threat becomes evident early in the narrative when Cal finds 'a note folded and caught by the sprung metal tongue of the letterbox' (27). The note reads:

GET OUT YOU FENYAN SCUM OR WE'LL BURN YOU OUT. THIS IS YOUR 2ND WARNING. THERE WILL BE NO OTHER UVF (27).

But unemployment and sectarian victimization are not Cal's only problems. He misses his mother (Gracie) enormously and is 'constantly at war with his father' who is disappointed with Cal for not being able to sustain work at the abattoir (33). 'I moved heaven and earth to get you in there', complains Shamie, 'and you go and jack it in before the week's out' (31).

In section 1.2, I highlighted the way in which the abattoir offers an important motif for the beginning of *Cal*. For instance, Cal stands outside the abattoir listening to the sound of the 'the humane killer' (8). He then sees 'the killing pen tip over and tumble a beast on to the floor' (8). The beast is 'immediately winched up by one of the hind shanks and its throat cut' (8). But as 'Cal turn[s] away', Shamie 'appear[s], holding two halves of a hanging carcass apart like a curtain.' (8). So, like King Hamlet, Shamie is a father who inflicts horrifying images of death upon his son.

A character named the Preacher augments these opening images of death which also introduce a determinist formula. According to John Hill, the Preacher signals 'the [...] logic of fatalism'; and this 'logic', I argue, corresponds with Shakespeare's *Hamlet*.[137]

In MacLaverty's opening pages, Cal sees 'the Preacher standing waiting' outside the abattoir 'with his glass [...] to catch the spout of blood [that is] the local doctor's prescription for any anaemic with a

---

137 John Hill, 'Images of Violence', in *Cinema and Ireland*, ed. Kevin Rockett, Luke Gibbons and John Hill (London: Croom Helm, 1987), pp.147–93 (p.182).

strong stomach'.[138] Emphasizing these Gothic images, Cal regards the Preacher as being 'a vulture [who] cycle[s] the countryside on his breadcart of a bicycle [...] nailing tracts made from tin lids to trees and telegraph-poles'.[139] These tracts read: 'The Wages of Sin is Death. Romans 8.5.'[140]

Here we can recall Ronan Bennett's observations about how 'the charnel house' or 'abattoir [is a] recurrent metaphor in fiction about' the north of Ireland; a metaphor enabling 'blood [and] carcasses [to be] laid out for inspection by the horrified reader'.[141] And Mac-Laverty's choice of 'the same metaphor' in relation to 'Cal's reluctance to enter the abattoir', as well as his disgust for the Preacher's vampiric blood-lusting, offer 'a symbol for Cal's reluctance to get involved with the IRA'.[142] So, as a sensitive young man who gets involved in paramilitary activities then a sexual relationship with an older woman, Cal is a 'powerful' Oedipal Hamlet as well as a 'sweet' Goetheian Hamlet, a 'split' subject whose Olivierian carnality competes with 'the classic [...] young Hamlet [and] beautiful teenaged boy' performed by English actors such as John Gielgud.[143]

Cal's involvement with the PIRA haunts his romantic affair with an older woman called Marcella. This is because Cal was the driver during a PIRA assassination in which Marcella's husband (an RUC officer called Robert Morton) was killed. Marcella is Roman Catholic, has a young daughter, is attractive and born of Italian parents. She works in a library in Derry, lives with her Protestant in-laws at their farm. Her mother-in-law presents a tough matriarchal figure while her father-in-law, who was also shot in the same incident as her husband, survives as a semi-coherent invalid with a lung-bubbling cough. Throughout the story, Marcella is unaware of Cal's involvement in the death of her husband. Although Cal resolves to leave the PIRA, he is hounded for his inaction by an accomplice (Crilly) and a PIRA

---

138 MacLaverty, *Cal*, pp.8, 7.
139 Ibid., pp.8, 7.
140 Ibid.
141 Ronan Bennett, 'An Irish Answer', *Guardian Weekend*, 16 July 1994, p.8.
142 Ibid.
143 Rosenberg, *The Masks of Hamlet*, p.119.

commander (Finbar Skeffington). After a Protestant Loyalist mob burn Cal and his father from their council house home, Cal finds work at the Morton farm and stows away in a deserted cottage near the farmhouse. He visits his father who, because of the fire and resultant homelessness, eventually suffers a nervous break-down. When Cal is discovered in the cottage by the RUC and beaten up, Marcella persuades her mother-in-law to let Cal remain working on the farm and living in the cottage. After a brief courtship instigated then suspended then instigated again by Marcella, Cal and Marcella have sex in the cottage. Here, Cal indulges in 'country matters' with a Gertrude rather than Ophelia figure. The end of the text brings a 'sudden' dramatic 'climax'.[144] This happens when, as noted by Margaret Scanlan, 'Crilly forces Cal to accompany him to an IRA gathering, which is raided [and] Cal escapes only long enough to inform the police of' a 'bomb's location' before the RUC 'arrive to arrest him'.[145] Finally, then, Cal rather abruptly rehearses Hamlet's 'tragic inevitability'.[146]

In her capacity as a sexual yet maternal figure, Marcella could be regarded as Cal's 'Gertrude'. The complexity of her identity is intensified through her nationality because, although the widow of an Irish Protestant, she is Italian: an exotic female other. However, like Cal, she is both a powerful and sweet replay of Shakespeare's fictive character. This is because she performs a sexually active as well as a spiritually redemptive role in Cal's fate. Marcella's significance to the text will be discussed in more detail later. At this point, though, it is important to introduce her significance to MacLaverty's re-working of the *Hamlet* formula.

In Shakespeare's text, the symbolic father (King Hamlet) summons Hamlet to avenge his death, a crime in which Gertrude may or may not be implicated. Her guilt or innocence is never really made

---

144 Margaret Scanlan, 'The Unbearable Present: Northern Ireland in Four Contemporary Novels', *Etudes Irlandaises*, 10 (December 1985), 145–61 (p.150).

145 Ibid., p.150.

146 Patten, *Peripheral Visions: Images of Nationhood in Contemporary British Fiction*, p.129.

clear. Alternatively, in MacLaverty's text, it could be argued that Robert Morton is the symbolic father who summons Cal to avenge his death, a crime in which Cal is implicated. Morton, the dead father who, quite literally, symbolizes the law, is the ghostly apparition existing within Cal's memory, an obscene excess of memory processed into guilt. For Cal, sexual gratification and spiritual redemption from Marcella seem, at first, to be impossibilities. Thus, she dwells in his psyche as 'an unattainable idea because he [...] helped kill her husband'.[147] Cal is tormented by the fact that 'slaying her husband put him on the outer edge of the galaxy', that 'the ugliness of what he had done show[s] in his face' (124). We learn how Cal's 'sin clawed at him, demanding attention [when he] saw again the terrible thing that he had done' (83). Here, 'Murder most foul', a key phrase from Shakespeare's *Hamlet*, looms large. So, when Cal does eventually have sex with Marcella, shame caused by his initial impotence fuses with shame caused by the death of Robert Morton. 'He saw her husband genuflect', writes MacLaverty, 'and the sudden soiling of the wallpaper behind him' (138). And when 'Marcella touch[es] between his thighs [...], he [experiences] shame' over Morton until 'the shame of his [sexual] weakness blot[s] out the sickening visions of her genuflecting husband' (138, 139). 'You're not on trial', says Marcella, referring to Cal's sexual impotence yet unconsciously proclaiming the possibility of legal as well sexual absolution (138). Then, like a good and sympathetic mother, she tells him 'never mind'; and with a nurturing gesture 'hold[s] his ashamed head to her breasts' (139). It is Marcella who temporarily quells 'the shame of his [sexual] weakness' and the shame of his 'sickening visions' so that 'with boyish amazement and touches' he is enabled to 'take an interest in her again', to enjoy 'the fragrance of her juices on his hands', to learn from her about how 'to time his thrusts' (139).

So far, it is evident that both *Cal* and *Hamlet* show how sin and the repercussions of sin, such as guilt, conscience and shame, might affect the human psyche; a potentially universalizing, liberal humanist ethic that might serve to bypass the political. Linked to these ideas, the

147 MacLaverty, *Cal*, p.92. Further consecutive references to this novel are given after quotations in the text.

name of Cal's imaginary Lacanian father (Shamie) inflicts Cal with a linguistic echo of 'shame' and guilt. At a more explicit level, Shamie makes Cal feel shame and guilt over his resignation from the job at the abattoir. 'It sticks in my throat', grumbles Shamie, 'that [Crilly] got the job [...] because you hadn't a strong enough stomach [...]. Not to mention the embarrassment it caused me' (18). And when Cal suggests moving to England, Shamie voices Hamletian disapproval through an announcement that: 'England's rotten to the core' (32). Shamie's role as an enforcer of shame and guilt is also implied when he takes Cal on a job to chop down 'a couple of dead trees [...] and make a bit of money if Cal would sell the blocks around' (41). Here, the film version shows Cal unable to start the chain-saw and therefore anticipates his later physical impotence. Emphasizing this impotence, Shamie is depicted as being a physically powerful father: he seizes the chain-saw, immediately fires its motor and hacks huge branches off the trees. This implicit castration metaphor precedes Shamie's destitution and nervous break-down, the latter implying a psychological death. And Cal witnesses this death. 'The minute Cal saw his father', writes MacLaverty, 'he knew there had been a terrible change in him' (111). Cal observes the way in which 'the man' seemed to have 'aged twenty years': 'he sat [with] his arms lying limply. [...] The flesh of his face [...] almost disappeared and what was left [...] slipped and sagged' (111).

Lying limply, slipped and sagged; at this point Cal's perception of his father switches from identification with a paternal other as an ego ideal to identification with an Oedipal self as a despised and impotent subject. 'Like iron to Plasticine overnight', says Cal's uncle about Shamie then, moments later, adds: 'You're as like your father as two peas in a pod' (144). It therefore appears that Shamie's loss of paternal authority does not empower but, instead, further disempowers Cal.

Paternal authority and shame and guilt can of course be associated with the symbolic order and language. But the manipulation of language is something that Cal uses in two distinct ways. Firstly, as a form of self-punishment through his habit of 'cursing himself [...] in made-up French' (109). '*Cochon, merde*', says Cal with a 'mutter', 'dirty *vache*. You big *crotte de chien*' (10). And, secondly, as a form of escape through the Hamletian device of punning. 'Do you play the guitar?', enquires Marcella, noticing his 'long nails' (26). 'On the one hand they are long', quips Cal: 'Yet on the other hand they are not' (26). 'I'd like to go and live in Italy', announces Marcella (117). And Cal's reply? 'There's no place like Rome' (117).

Lacan's emphasis upon 'textuality' reinforces these ideas because 'textuality' reveals 'discourses in which unconscious processes may be concealed'.[148] Moreover, textuality as language *inscribes* the law, the 'law of the father', the 'law of the state', and the 'law governing the unconscious'.[149] Thus, while Cal's Hamletian manipulation of language is symptomatic of self-punishment, his 'miching mallecho' is also 'mischief': a device enabling an escape from the law through 'words, words, words' (to quote Shakespeare).

Guilt, shame, redemption, the paternal law and the desire of the mother. These psychoanalytical issues will be explored in more depth towards the end of this section. Firstly, because *Cal* is a text that has over the years attracted much critical commentary, I want to consider some alternative perspectives and arguments that focus upon the various political and ideological implications of MacLaverty's novella as well as O'Connor's film.

In section 2.1, Patten's observations about the ways in which Troubles' fictions have 'tended to universalize rather than particularize the [political] situation' in the north of Ireland were associated with the use of *Hamlet* as a sub-text.[150] For Patten, remember, 'a series of slim novels set against the violence of the 1970s and early 1980s established a determinist formula [whereby] a well-meaning individual [struggles] within a debilitating and ultimately damaging political context'.[151] This 'determinist formula', writes Patten, is ideologically dangerous because it manifests 'fictional essentialism'.[152] MacLaverty's novella about a young and ill-fated Hamletian hero

148   Raman Selden, *Practising Theory and Reading Literature: An Introduction* (London: Harvester Wheatsheaf, 1989), p.86.

149   Ibid.

150   Patten, *Peripheral Visions: Images of Nationhood in Contemporary British Fiction*', p.132.

151   Ibid., p.131.

152   Ibid., p.132.

seems to comply with Patten's description of a determinist formula, a formula that is, as suggested earlier, depoliticizing and universalizing. For Cal, there is no escape from his violent past, not even through sex with Marcella.

Linked to Patten's observations, Alexander Walker comments upon O'Connor's Celluloid version of MacLaverty's text.[153] According to Walker, 'while attempting authenticity', films such as *Cal* have 'generally used the Ulster situation as pretext for more conventional fiction'.[154] Walker's call for 'authenticity' is problematic because any divided community will contain different notions about authenticity.[155] This said, Walker's comment that *Cal* is 'a love-against-the-odds story which just "happens" to be set in Northern Ireland' suggests that, even though O'Connor is an Irish film-maker, he too has opted to depoliticize the Troubles.[156] '*Cal*', writes Walker, is 'about a reluctant IRA accomplice, who takes up with the victim's widow [and] turns aside from political considerations' to enact a narrative of 'Oedipal tensions [concerning] a teenage terrorist and an "older woman"'.[157] Brian McIlroy is likewise critical of O'Connor's Celluloid approach to the political situation in the north of Ireland. According to McIlroy, *Cal* is representative of 'films [that] repress history and politics for fear of distancing the non-Irish audience'.[158] From a materialist perspective, the source of this fear could be located within commercial considerations of financial profit. The film industry is, after all, a capitalist enterprise. Further, submitting an accusation that resonates with Patten's explanation of a 'determinist formula', McIlroy censures O'Connor for communicating 'the sense that the IRA leadership easily manipulates young and violent men

153 Alexander Walker, 'Peek-A-Boo, Ballyhoo & Bigotry', *Causeway*, 1.1 (September 1993), 332–5 (p.34).
154 Ibid., pp.33, 34.
155 Ibid., p.33.
156 Ibid., p.34.
157 Ibid., pp.33, 34.
158 Brian McIlroy, 'The Repression of Communities: Visual Representations of Northern Ireland during the Thatcher Years', in *British Cinema and Thatcherism*, ed. Lester Friedman (London: UCL, 1993), pp.92–108 (p.107).

who are little more than gangsters'.[159] John Hill offers more dissenting words when he writes that *Cal*'s 'adoption of the vocabulary of fatalism must work against a political explanation' and this is why 'the society which the film evokes is largely one of victims, passively enduring or futilely defying a world outside of their control'.[160] In *Cal*, 'derangement, disability or simply death are all that most of the characters can hope for'.[161] Hill also condemns how '*Cal* imposes a religious interpretation on the meaning of political violence', an interpretation that fails 'to invest its view of the "troubles" with any degree of political complexity'.[162]

Interestingly, though, Scanlan approves of the way in which *Cal* 'focuses on a single character destroyed by overwhelming political forces'.[163] She does not censure MacLaverty's Hamletian hero for being a character who 'lacks political sophistication and imagination' but, instead, applauds how 'the story of Cal and Marcella's impossible love affair is set within an almost flatly realistic social context'.[164] Barry Sloan also praises MacLaverty's novella for sustaining the 'expectation of inevitable disaster' which is prompted by 'the sitting of the initial scene in an abattoir where killing is actually in progress'.[165] For Sloan, 'the novel is perhaps above all else an impressive chronicle of the workings of a guilty conscience [whereby] Cal's sense of sin dominates his thoughts' to produce a character 'whose guilt and alienation are memorably explored' within a text of 'considerable achievement'.[166] These diverse critical engagements with *Cal* cast further doubt upon assumptions that fictions concerning the north of Ireland are able to yield some type of ultimate political 'authenticity' or transcendental truth. This said, in an essay entitled

159   Ibid., p.99.
160   Hill, *Cinema and Ireland*, p.181.
161   Ibid.
162   Ibid.
163   Scanlan, 'The Unbearable Present: Northern Ireland in Four Contemporary Novels', p.150.
164   Ibid.
165   Barry Sloan, 'The Wages of Paramilitary Sin: a comment on two recent novels by Northern Irish writers', *Honest Ulsterman*, 80 (Spring 1986), 21–31 (p.25).
166   Ibid., pp.29, 30.

'The Politics of Bernard MacLaverty's *Cal*', Stephen Watt offers a shrewd and intelligently argued account of the ideological issues embedded within MacLaverty's novella and O'Connor's film.[167] In addition, Watt's essay provides a means through which to further explore *Cal*'s re-working of the Lacanian Hamlet structure.

According to Watt: 'no politics can overlook the human subject and his or her formation within society'.[168] 'History' plays an important role here.[169] But '"history" can never again be construed as a record of objective fact' and is often 'barely distinguishable [...] [from] "Mythology"'.[170] Watt suggests how the politics of the north of Ireland which are embedded within 'the politics of [...] *Cal*' include and are shaped by history and mythology or fact and fiction.[171] Cal's recollections of his late mother's ardent Irish republicanism as well as the moral and political pontifications from 'the smug teacher and IRA leader' named Finbar Skeffington make this clear.[172] But, from a Lacanian point-of-view, history and mythology are also shaped by memory as an 'obscene excess'.[173] This excess is fortified by the dilemma regarding the desire of the (m)other: Cal's real mother and, importantly, Mother Ireland. Consequently, Cal 'remember[s]' his mother singing him 'rebel songs' such as 'The Croppy Boy or Father Murphy' whereas Skeffington remembers Padraic Pearse and 're-cite[s] [...] Pearse's poem [entitled] "Mother"', a text that portrays an Irish mother who does 'not grudge [her] two strong sons' their death for 'a glorious thing' named Mother Ireland.[174] Skeffington wants Cal to continue acting for the republican cause, to be, like Hamlet, a revenger for remembered events that merge the 'far' past, the 1916

---

167   Stephen Watt, 'The Politics of Bernard MacLaverty's *Cal*', *Eire-Ireland*, 28.3 (1993), 130–46.
168   Ibid., p.130.
169   Ibid., p.131.
170   Ibid.
171   Ibid., pp.130, 131.
172   Ibid., p.132.
173   Slavoj Zizek, *Tarrying with the Negative: Kant, Hegel, and the Critique of Ideology* (Durham, USA: Duke University Press, 1993), p.210.
174   MacLaverty, *Cal*, pp.37, 66.

Easter Rising, with the 'near' past, Bloody Sunday.[175] As Skeffington's demands for revenge also 'promote the "son's" self-sacrifice', his demands are likewise 'emblematic of a holy fidelity to Cathleen Ni Houlihan'.[176] This said, Watt also acknowledges how Skeffington displays a sophisticated perception of the far and near past.[177] Skeffington is aware that certain events and individuals are excluded from history. So, recalling the violent events of Bloody Sunday, he tells Cal that 'an old man [was] lying in the open. In the rush one of his shoes had come off [...] [to reveal] a big hole in his sock'.[178] The PIRA commander then asks: 'Will that be recorded in the history books?'.[179] At this point, 'Cal look[s] away', is resigned to the fact that any attempt to escape the past will be thwarted by the more educated man.[180] So, when Cal insists that the present 'is not like 1916' Skeffington replies: 'It wasn't like 1916 in 1916'.[181]

Although Skeffington has been dismissed by some critics as being 'a base metal stereotype', he actually supplies a more complex ideological phenomenon, denies the notion of there being a simple binary opposition between the British self and the Irish other.[182] Watt appears to acknowledge this when he suggests that, because 'Skeffington represents the bourgeoisie', MacLaverty shows how British? 'elitism and [Irish?] Nationalism are [...] inseparable'.[183] In a sense, Skeffington as well as the British signify an other for Cal and his peer: Crilly. This is because Cal and Crilly represent 'the working class' whereas Skeffington 'is a middle-class intellectual who manipulates thugs like Crilly into doing his dirty work'.[184] 'I'm a teacher, Cal, and I know that in England it's no different', says Skeffington, 'it's all the

---

175 Ibid., pp.66, 67.
176 Watt, 'The Politics of Bernard MacLaverty's *Cal*', p.132.
177 Ibid., p.102.
178 MacLaverty, *Cal*, p.67.
179 Ibid.
180 Ibid.
181 Ibid., p.66.
182 Patrick Magee, '*Gangsters or Guerrillas: Representations of Irish Republicans in 'Troubles Fiction'* (Belfast: Beyond the Pale, 2001), p.119.
183 Watt, 'The Politics of Bernard MacLaverty's *Cal*', p.143.
184 Ibid.

boys at the runt-end of the school who are going to end up in the army. The idiots, the psychopaths – the one class of people who *shouldn't* be given a gun'.[185] Here, Skeffington describes the demonic PIRA stereotypes identified in section 1.1. But, as implied by Sloan, the desire of the mother penetrates even the most lumpen of Irish gunman. Sloan observes how Crilly is 'in some sense [...] shown as a true mother's boy [who] is willing to accept orders and enjoys the sentimental thought that he is doing something for Ireland'.[186] The fact that Crilly is frequently depicted at home with just his mother reinforces this idea. So too the description of Crilly's domestic setting where hanging 'in the front room [is] a [sentimental] picture of a ragged child with one glistening teardrop [...] on his dirty cheek', an image evoking a son's traumatic desire for mothering.[187] Next to the picture is 'a plaque of wood' displaying the words: 'MADE IN LONG KESH CONCENTRATION CAMP. [...] IRELAND UNFREE SHALL NEVER BE AT PEACE' (58). This message evokes a son's traumatic patriotism towards Cathleen Ni Houlihan. However, the symbolic meanings of the sentimental picture and the political plaque are fused by a third item, that being, 'a brass picture [...] of an old woman sitting sideways wearing a bonnet and beneath her [...] a poem called "A Mother"' (58). The poem lists 'all the good things a mother ever did [then] end[s] with the line "The only bad thing she ever does is to die and leave you"' (58). This cluster of maternal icons suggests that Crilly is not only a 'true mother's boy' but also a 'true Mother Ireland's boy'.

Unlike Crilly, Skeffington's bourgeoisie status could be perceived as being the vehicle through which the PIRA leader is liberated from the desire of the punitive Irish mother. And the absence of Skeffington's real mother from the narrative gives further credence to this notion. But his reciting of Pearse's 'Mother' implies that he is not in fact liberated from a profound and matriarchal influence. And although Skeffington hero-worships his 'Daddy', this imaginary Irish republican father is nothing more than a senile old man whose long

185   MacLaverty, *Cal*, p.64.
186   Sloan, 'The Wages of Paramilitary Sin', p.23.
187   MacLaverty, *Cal*, p.58. Further consecutive references to this novel are given after quotations in the text.

since faded memories about the Cause, such as 'the story [...] of Dev in O'Connell street', have to be verbally prompted (64). Highlighting the old man's psychological lack through inversion, Cal sarcastically dubs him 'the wit' (146). All this said, though, Cal and Skeffington do have something in common: their fathers who suffer physical and psychological lack.

Cal's father has both a nervous and physical breakdown while Skeffington's senile father is 'knocked down by' a 'drunken bastard [in a] *stolen* [...] car' (47). When informing Cal about the incident, Skeffington says: 'I believe we share a problem, Cahal [...]. Our fathers being ill' (147). But Skeffington is mistaken. This is because, in spite of his hierarchical social status, Skeffington's real 'problem' is the desire of Mother Ireland, the (m)other who does not exist, the (m)other who Cal rejects. Perhaps this is why Cal thinks about the futility of 'suffering [...] for something which didn't exist [...], like Ireland' (83). Yet, later in the narrative, the 'suffering [...] for something which didn't exist' a propos Ireland is displaced by 'suffering for something which *could not* exist', that being, sex with Marcella [my italics] (92, 83). But while Cal is of course right in the first instance, he is wrong in the second instance. Sex with Marcella is the redemptive something that *can* exist, albeit only fleetingly and within a pastoral setting.

In terms of Mother Ireland being an ideological concept, the pastoral versus the urban is important. Away from the threatening and violent urban landscape where he is beaten up by Loyalist youths and hounded by the PIRA, Cal's brief residence and employment on the Morton farm lead to his redemptive relationship with Marcella and spiritual purification. 'Although he ended up each day physically filthy', writes MacLaverty, 'work had a cleansing effect on him' (57). This 'cleansing effect' opposes his former urban 'idleness [which] had allowed dirt to accumulate on his soul' and the former urban relationship with Mother Ireland which had led to the murder of Robert Morton (57). For Cal, the rural 'was Ireland – the real Ireland' (39). However, this temporary escape to the cleansing locale of the pastoral and 'country matters' does not fully liberate Cal from memories of Gracie, his aptly and religiously named dead Irish republican mother who will not permit her son freedom through amnesia.

Accordingly, when he thinks about how 'he missed [...] washing his teeth', he recalls 'a recipe of his mother's' then steals 'some cooking salt' and, like a good son, obediently cleans his teeth (93). His punitive memory also looms when he follows Marcella to Mass at her local country church. Here he prays for 'the soul of his mother' and, 'remembering her', channels 'the rest of his prayers [into] telling himself how vile he' is: another statement of guilt over Morton's death (36, 37). All this culminates in Cal's masochistic not to mention Oedipal self-torment when, punishing his own scopophiliac gaze at Marcella, 'he press[es] the knuckles of his thumbs into his eyes' and even though 'patterns merged into pain [...] continued to press' (37). Indeed, following Laura Mulvey, John Hill writes that MacLaverty's 'passive, rather than active, hero [...] finds a clear expression in masochism'.[188] But Cal's guilt-induced masochism is implied as existing prior to his involvement with the PIRA and to have actually commenced with the death of his real mother. This is evident from the fact that 'not long after Gracie's death Shamie [...] found a purple bruise mark in the crook of Cal's elbow'.[189] The bruise is the result of Cal's self-inflicted 'love-bites', his 'sucking until he tasted the coppery blood coming through the skin'.[190] Unlike King Hamlet, the ghost haunting Cal seems to be maternal. Therefore, it could be argued that, like Hamlet, the shame and guilt associated with his Oedipal desire is *reactivated* rather than *caused* by the death of his symbolic father: Robert Morton.

At an ideological level, although the pastoral setting and its association with Marcella provide a partial refuge and purification of Cal's mind and body, Watt suggests that MacLaverty avoids the creation of 'a narcoticizing dose of romantic Ireland' and the 'advancing [of] yet one more idealization of pastoral Ireland' which, as mentioned above, Cal mistakes for the real Ireland.[191] And 'O'Connor's film also registers [an] understanding of this deromanticizing

---

188   Hill, *Cinema and Ireland*, p.181.
189   MacLaverty, *Cal*, p.33.
190   Ibid.
191   Watt, 'The Politics of Bernard MacLaverty's *Cal*', p.135.

tendency.[192] For Watt the film shows that 'a modern highway system [...] can transport sectarian violence right to the cottage's front door'.[193] This is evident through the flashbacks which show Cal driving Crilly to enact the assassination at the Morton farm. So too at the end of the film when the RUC drive along the 'modern highway system' to arrest Cal who, 'stood in a dead man's Y-fronts', is masochistically 'grateful that at last someone was going to beat him to within an inch of his life'.[194] Away from the abattoir where the 'crack of the humane killer' threatens the 'queuing beasts [who] bellow in the distance as if they knew', Cal finds 'mucking out the byre [and] the nasal moan [...] of [...] the cattle [...] a comfort to him'.[195] But the countryside does not protect Cal from images of slaughtered carcasses and the prophetic, guilt-inducing words of the Preacher for long. Utopia becomes disrupted while Cal, Marcella and her daughter are blackberry picking and 'suddenly the air [is] ripped apart by an explosion'.[196] Cal goes to the fields to investigate and discovers 'half a cow – udders, hindquarters [...] muscles red-raw and still jigging'.[197] He also discovers 'the Preacher's red tin plaques which read: 'The Kingdom of God is within You'.[198] Here, the urban scene from the Derry abattoir commencing the narrative is more or less reproduced within Cal's rural refuge. If Cal thought he could escape images of death (the carcasses), and reminders of sin (the preacher), he is mistaken. Perhaps, then, Cal was right all along about the rural being the real Ireland: the real Ireland of trauma and death.

Recalling Zizek, Watt claims that ideas about 'belief [and] "forced choice of freedom"' can help to explain Cal's 'excessive feelings of guilt' and masochism.[199] According to Zizek, when subjects 'act *as if* [they] already believe [...], belief will come by itself'.[200] This means

192   Ibid., p.135.
193   Ibid.
194   MacLaverty, *Cal*, p.153.
195   Ibid., pp.7, 81.
196   Ibid., p.120.
197   Ibid., pp.120, 121.
198   Ibid., p.121.
199   Watt, 'The Politics of Bernard MacLaverty's *Cal*', pp.137, 138, 139.
200   Zizek, *The Sublime Object of Ideology*, p.39.

'the stronger [a] belief in something, the less it is the result of conscious selection or rational decision making': we believe without consciously choosing to believe.[201] In terms of the north of Ireland, 'unquestioning allegiance to the nationalist agenda is akin to religious belief'.[202] Therefore, Skeffington's allusions to Pearse fuse 'personal sacrifice for the nationalist cause [with] Christian martyrdom'.[203] Put simply, 'we find reasons attesting our belief because we already believe; we do not believe because we have found sufficient good reasons to believe'.[204] Such a belief in terms of unquestioning allegiance to the nationalist cause is likewise associated with Cal's dead mother. Paradoxically, though, Cal's *lack* of belief in the nationalist cause is a source of his guilt.

Watt expands upon this idea, claiming that although 'Cal's excessive feelings of guilt appear to be connected to his complicity in [the] attack on the Mortons [...], other explanatory models [define] his frequently severe self-castigation'.[205] Granted, some level of guilt is obviously prompted by Morton's death. This is evident when Marcella gives Cal some of her late husband's clothing ('a dead man's things') and, 'getting into' these clothes, Cal thinks about 'the monks and hermits with their hair shirts designed to cause suffering'.[206] However, Watt observes how Cal's 'wish to learn more languages so as to be able to "curse himself more thoroughly" [...] seem[s] to predate Morton's murder'.[207] So, rehearsing T.S. Eliot's notion about Hamlet and an 'emotion in excess of the facts as they appear', Morton's death 'cannot totally explain [Cal's] excess [...] of guilt'.[208]

Watt identifies the root of Cal's guilt as being the product of 'two [...] "forced choices"' which, in turn, 'challenge the entire liberal-humanist notion of a freely choosing subject'.[209] These two forced

201   Watt, 'The Politics of Bernard MacLaverty's *Cal*', p.137.
202   Ibid.
203   Ibid.
204   Zizek, *The Sublime Object of Ideology*, p.37.
205   Watt, 'The Politics of Bernard MacLaverty's *Cal*', p.140.
206   MacLaverty, *Cal*, pp.101, 102.
207   Watt, 'The Politics of Bernard MacLaverty's *Cal*', p.139.
208   Ibid.
209   Ibid., pp.140, 139.

choices are made when, firstly, 'much to his father's dismay', Cal leaves 'his job at the abattoir' and when, secondly, he 'abandon[s] the nationalist cause' which he associates with his mother and Mother Ireland.[210] As 'a political concept', Zizek's 'forced choice of freedom' insists that 'you have freedom to choose, but on condition that you choose the right thing'.[211] In effect, Cal 'must freely choose the community to which he already belongs, independent of his choice'.[212] Like Hamlet, who must freely choose the Elsinorian community to which he already belongs, Cal 'must choose what is already given to him'.[213]

Linked to these ideas, Zizek's notions about '"forced choice of freedom" [positions] guilt in the interstices between Cal and the social order that surrounds him'.[214] Reinforcing the analogy to Hamlet and the Danish Court, 'part of that social order is [...] marked by [Cal's] family – his father's valorization of the butcher's trade; his mother's of nationalism'.[215] Moreover 'another crucial part [of that social order] is situated more broadly in Northern Irish society itself, and particularly in ideology'.[216] This can all be related to Zizek's claim that 'by being a good member of my family, I thereby contribute to the proper functioning of my nation-state'.[217] Such 'proper functioning of [this] nation-state' occurs when 'primary identifications undergo a kind of transubstantiation [...] and start to function as [...] the universal secondary identification'.[218] Bearing these points in mind, Watt explains how MacLaverty shows the way in which 'desire is usually manifested in a character's opposition to one or another component of

210 Ibid., p.140.
211 Zizek, *The Sublime Object of Ideology*, p.165.
212 Ibid.
213 Ibid.
214 Watt, 'The Politics of Bernard MacLaverty's *Cal*', p.140.
215 Ibid., pp.140, 141.
216 Ibid., p.141.
217 Slavoj Zizek, *The Ticklish Subject: The Absent Centre of Political Ontology* (London: Verso, 1999), p.90.
218 Slavoj Zizek, *The Ticklish Subject*, p.90.

the dominant ideology'.[219] Following Gayatri Chakravorty Spivak, Watt describes the dominant ideology as being '"what a group takes to be natural and self-evident" and the "condition and the effect of the constitution of the subject (of ideology) as freely willing and consciously choosing in a world that is seen as background"' (141). But 'the world' in terms of the north of Ireland 'is not "mere" background' and Cal is not able to 'by an act of will simply *choose* to be free from the influences of such subjugating forces as church, schools [...] family' and, indeed, the PIRA (141). Hence, 'MacLaverty [...] attempts in his fiction to depict the ways in which these institutions exert control' (141).

Although Cal does break away from one component of the dominant ideology (his father's trade), he cannot entirely break away from the other component (his mother's nationalism). Perhaps, then, his 'desire for punishment' as expressed through guilt over Morton's murder is exacerbated by guilt over failing to comply with the desire of his mother's ideological demands (141). Murder of a father and disobedience to a mother, Cal is doubly damned. Ultimately, Watt's reading of Cal in terms of belief, guilt and forced choice implies that MacLaverty deliberately created a sophisticated and coherent political agenda. This agenda demands that Cal's '"sin" remains with him', corrupts and ameliorates 'any happiness [that] he and Marcella might enjoy' (141). Cal's 'dis-ease' is not the product of something '*specific* or *material*' but, instead, the product of 'ideology and those institutions that serve to communicate it' (141). All this said, Watt does acknowledge how MacLaverty supplies 'his reader with brief moments of emancipation and locales supportive to alternative practices' (144). These 'brief moments' occur through 'Cal's temporary escape to the Morton's cottage [and] his brief affair with Marcella' (144).

Marcella 'represents the [...] *femme de trente ans* [...] the older, exotic woman, who can inspire through her sexuality and foreignness' (145). She tells Cal about her Italian background, about her holiday in Rome, about her education within 'a great Elsinore of a place built

219   Watt, 'The Politics of Bernard MacLaverty's *Cal*', p.141. Further consecutive references to this novel are given after quotations in the text.

overlooking a cliff in the Atlantic'.[220] She is the stuff of fairy-tale, a 'Sleeping Beauty' to his 'Quasimodo'.[221] She cooks and serves him a candle-lit meal of '*spaghetti alla carbonara*' and '*costolette di vitello alla modenese*'.[222] She is 'strange [...] like a film star in an old movie'.[223] She is Cal's 'fantasy', the imaginary 'mistress' whom he wishes to 'serenade [...] beneath her window'.[224] Yet Cal's obsessional desire for Marcella is, perhaps, a *displacement* rather than a *re-placement* for his obsessional desire for his real mother: the primordial maternal figure.

Interestingly, Watt associates both Shakespeare and Stephen Dedalus with Cal and this type of displacement. At an aesthetic level, Marcella is 'the seductive and older Anne Hathaway whom Stephen Dedalus in *Ulysses* regards as so fundamental to Shakespeare's developing artistry'.[225] She is also 'Molly Bloom inspiring Stephen, the young poet, to greater heights'.[226] But, at an ideological level, Marcella is the good Gertrude, 'the matriarchal' figure who can 'oppose the violent symbolic domain [...], albeit momentarily and precariously [...], and supply Cal with an alternative space'.[227] Likewise, she is able to 'oppose the more punitive superegoic Mother Ireland'.[228] Cal's temporary liberation through Marcella struggles towards an 'expression of desire' while fighting against the 'modulation of this desire by larger cultural formations'.[229] Her sexuality and 'self-gratification [...] symbolise[s] [Cal's] liberation from an irrational, excessive guilt or psychic burden'.[230] Finally, though, Cal's Hamletian destiny inflicts him with 'an inexorable, punishing reality': a reality in which he is 'never able to overcome his deep sense of

---

220 MacLaverty, *Cal*, p.100.
221 Ibid., p.124.
222 Ibid., p.129.
223 Ibid., p.131.
224 Ibid., p.83.
225 Watt, 'The Politics of Bernard MacLaverty's *Cal*', p.145.
226 Ibid.
227 Ibid., p.146.
228 Ibid., p.145.
229 Ibid., p.146.
230 Ibid.

guilt, his self-image as irredeemable sinner'.[231] However, it seems to me that Cal is mistaken by this self-image. Cal is not irredeemable and, in fact, achieves salvation through Marcella. Importantly, though, his salvation is accomplished in tandem with the desire of the mother.

Gracie and an urban Mother Ireland. These two bad mothers seem to prompt for Cal the Lacanian dilemma of: 'what does the (m)other want from me?'. Gracie wants Cal to believe in Irish nationalism, wants him to make a 'forced choice' and support the republican cause through involvement with the PIRA. Urban Mother Ireland wants the same plus a 'forced choice' in terms of a fatal sacrifice. In rejecting these demands, Cal appears to make the 'wrong' choice which, ostensibly, incites guilt, masochism, the decision to become an 'informer' and the desire for punishment. When he decides to become an informer, he phones a 'Confidential' number and tells the security forces about a bomb that Crilly, acting under orders from Skeffington, has planted in the Library where Marcella works.[232] Cal knows his action, his choice, will culminate in his arrest. Ironically, then, by disobeying Gracie and an urban Mother Ireland, Cal seems to freely choose self-sacrifice. Yet there is, I suggest, an alternative Lacanian explanation.

Cal's decision to become an informer is mediated by his dilemma over the desire of his good, rural Mother Ireland: Marcella. This premise corresponds with Zizek's notion about 'the inherent impossibility of the sexual relationship'.[233]

According to Zizek, 'we elude the inherent impossibility of the sexual relationship by positing an external hindrance to it, thus preserving the illusion that without this hindrance, we would be able to enjoy it fully'.[234] Such a 'positing [of] an external hindrance' is of course epitomized by the narrative of 'courtly love' whereby the sonneteer invents numerous obstacles that frustrate the male subject's

231   Ibid.
232   MacLaverty, *Cal*, p.151.
233   Zizek, *For They Know Not What They Do: Enjoyment as a Political Factor* (London: Verso, 1991), p.264.
234   Ibid.

sexual relationship with the 'Lady'.[235] It is therefore appropriate that Cal perceives Marcella as being his courtly 'mistress'; a 'forbidden' and 'unattainable idea', an ideal (m)other.[236] His rejection of Gracie and an urban Mother Ireland in favour of the good, rural Mother Ireland means that he 'identifies [his] desire with the desire of [an] Other-mother'.[237] This Other-mother is Marcella. Hence, Cal replays the childhood role of 'the subject [who] depends totally on [...] the "primordial Other"'.[238] In doing so, he '[re]assum[es] a position of complete alienation [...] according to [his new] Other-Mother['s] [...] momentary whim[s]'.[239] Zizek goes on to explain how, therefore, 'the advent of the symbolic Law [...] entails a kind of "disalienation"'.[240] This is because 'the subject succeeds in establishing a kind of distance towards the Mother's desire' and renders that 'desire' as being 'no longer reduced to the demand for the Mother's love'.[241] For Cal, 'the advent of the symbolic law' is self inflicted through his phone call to the security forces. His subsequent arrest means that he no longer has to fret over unfathomable questions about the desire of Marcella and thereby enables him 'to disengage [...] from the rule of the Other's whim'.[242] Subsequently Cal is able to 'blame' the symbolic order for his psychologically damaging failure to satisfy Marcella's desire. Such a failure is evident shortly before his arrest. This happens when his first full sexual encounter with Marcella causes him to struggle against 'impotence'.[243] Feeling 'gelded [then] on a hair trigger', he ejaculates 'wetly on to her stomach almost immediately she touch[es] him' and his sense of sexual inadequacy is complete (138, 139).

---

235 Ibid.
236 MacLaverty, *Cal*, p.92.
237 Zizek, *For They Know Not What They Do: Enjoyment as a Political Factor*, p.265.
238 Ibid.
239 Ibid.
240 Ibid.
241 Ibid.
242 Ibid.
243 MacLaverty, *Cal*, p.138. Further consecutive references to this novel are given after quotations in the text.

Perhaps the real tragedy for Cal is that, even though he succeeds in becoming alienated from his two 'bad' mothers, he fails to become disalienated from Marcella: the good redemptive mother. His confusion over Marcella's desire is the problem, a confusion which is evident throughout the text. So, when Cal visits the library where Marcella is employed, he reads a book that tells him 'the heart of Ireland would be refreshed by the red wine of the battlefields, that [Mother] Ireland needed its bloody sacrifice' (73). Immediately afterwards, he thinks 'it might please [Marcella] if he were to take a novel out' (73). Here, the desire of the punitive mother is confused with and displaced onto the desire of the benevolent mother. Surely, then, it is ironic that Cal borrows *Crime and Punishment* (107). Later, he is confused by her sudden 'curtness', worries about her 'rejection' and thinks he may have 'interpreted' her desire incorrectly (105, 133, 105). Alone with her at the farm-house, he becomes 'childish' and 'dumb with disappointment' because she refuses his sexual advances and tells him: 'I'm a widow. With problems. You're a boy without' (133). 'The extra make-up', thinks Cal, 'the candle-lit dinner, her hand on his thigh. Was that just a woman or was she leading him on?' (133). Her enigmatic presence even stalks his sleep. Indeed, during a nightmare about a man being sacrificed on a railway track, 'Cal signal[s] frantically to Marcella but she [does not] seem interested in the plight of the man' (106). Elsewhere, Cal is not sure about whether or not 'she [has] come to see *him* [or] to get away from something' (107). His desire to uncover *her* desire makes him ask: 'Did you ever do anything – really bad?' (119). But then, because he is, perhaps, afraid of the answer, he says: 'Maybe I shouldn't ask a woman that question' (119). His curiosity about her appears to culminate when, alone in the farm-house, he creeps into her bed-room and, like a detective searching for clues, examines her belongings. He scrutinizes her 'dressing table with its array of make-up bottles [...], her lemon dressing-gown [...], her brassiere [and] explore[s] her wardrobe with its ranks of dresses' (125). Ashamed and frustrated, he finds 'her panties [and] burie[s] his face in them, on the verge of tears' (125). Even her diary, the one place where he might expect to learn some absolute truth about Marcella, remains stubbornly mysterious: 'he read some of it but could not make head or tail of it' (126). 'Could he ever admit that he had snooped in her bedroom?', thinks Cal (125). Perhaps not. This aside, what Cal surely needs to 'admit' is his dilemma over Marcella's desire. After all, she gives him plenty of opportunities to 'make head or tail of it'. We can recall how one such opportunity of course arises when he goes to the farm-house for the meal she has cooked. He admires how 'lovely' she 'look[s]', notices 'her hair [is] different' and that she is wearing 'more make-up' but merely *wonders* 'if she had prepared for him coming' (128, 129). As Cal is the only guest, the answer is fairly obvious. Even when she *tells* him that he is 'an attentive lover', his reply portrays doubt: 'How do you mean?' (140). Irrespective of her seemingly explicit actions and words, Marcella does 'not' seem to be able to 'mak[e] herself' or her desire 'very clear' to Cal (140).

On the other hand, Marcella's redemptive role as Cal's good mother is both explicit and implicit. As a result, her redemptive maternal qualities can be read at various levels. At a spiritual level, she is a signifier of purification, 'a priestess' who absolves his confession about 'sins of the flesh' with the words 'naughty – not bad' (83, 119). Her redemptive qualities are likewise evident when he thinks that 'although he hated his name, the way she said it was clean and beautiful' (74). Moreover, during Mass, his guilt and masochistic drive to blind himself becomes displaced into sexual desire as 'the back of his hand [rests] against her firm haunch' (38). At a spiritual and physical level, she is a good and beautiful mother. Her face 'hypnotize[s]' and, although she has 'a lovely mouth as well as eyes', she is not 'young, perhaps somewhere in her late twenties' (12, 13). She a caring mother who 'bathe[s]' Cal's 'wound' then provides him with the domestic items needed for his cottage: 'curtains, a Tilley lamp, a camping stove, a kettle, a card table [and] two chairs' (96, 99). He receives intellectual redemption from her encouragement to read books. She even brings the books to his cottage 'in a small wooden rack [symbolically] shaped like a cradle' (107). However, perhaps the most profound statement of her redemptive qualities happens during the night before Christmas Eve and his arrest. Knowing that his arrest is imminent, he returns to the farm-house and gives Marcella her Christmas present: her favourite picture of 'Grunewald's picture of Christ crucified' (153). Here, Cal 'look[s] at the flesh of Christ spotted and torn [...] then [...] at the smoothness of Marcella's body' (153). So, on the night before the anniversary of Christ's birth and Cal's arrest, Marcella's body displaces Christ's body and becomes Cal's spiritual redemption: a redemption consecrated when 'they [eat] supper and [...] make love again' (153).

This said, it could be suggested that notions about redemption and self-sacrifice contribute to Cal's dilemma over Marcella's desire. For instance, she talks to Cal about her childhood education at the convent where 'everything was so much more intense' (132). 'There were people you would die for', says Marcella, 'that was the test we used to apply to people. Would you *die* for him? Or her?' (132). Her nostalgic and romantic allusion to self-sacrifice then diverges into another narrative where, like a good Catholic mother, she tells Cal a religious legend about self-sacrifice. The legend concerns 'Saint Maria Goretti and how she died rather than lose her purity to an awful man' (132). Because Goretti 'didn't submit to rape', the man 'stabbed [her] to death' (132). After the murderer was released from prison, Goretti's mother 'received communion side by side [with] the guy who killed her' (132). 'Isn't that weird?', asks Marcella: 'that amount of goodness. [...] It was the mother who should have been made the saint' (132). Immediately after this account of romantic self-sacrifice and maternal forgiveness, Cal and Marcella kiss but then Marcella changes her mind and sends him back to his cottage. Alone, experiencing a state of sexual arousal and frustration, thinking about tales of romantic self-sacrifice and maternal forgiveness, it seems reasonable that Cal might again be plagued by the question: 'what does the (m)other want from me?'. This question is intensified just moments before Cal and Marcella do finally have sex. 'I think I love you,' says Cal (137). And her reply? 'Would you die for me?' (137).

Bearing the above points in mind, Marcella's repeated allusion to self-sacrifice might be the unintentional catalyst to the reactivation of the ghosts of Cal's two bad mothers or, perhaps, a sign that she was (or is) an incarnation of the same 'bad' mother all along: every mother requires the supreme and inescapable sacrifice. Consequently, in mis-recognizing Marcella's desire, Cal might fear that the good (m)other wants the death of her son, an inversion and reworking of Saint Maria Goretti who died rather than lose her purity. After all, 'desire in its

166

purity is of course "death-drive"'.[244] If this is the case, we can recall points raised earlier in respect of Cal's decision to become an informer and invite arrest as well as Zizek's notions about 'the inherent impossibility of the sexual relationship', 'the desire of the Other-mother' and 'alienation'.[245]

For Zizek, 'symbolic identification with the paternal metaphor' in terms of 'the agency of prohibition [...] [enables] the subject to avoid the impasse' manifested through 'desire by transforming the inherent *impossibility* of its satisfaction into *prohibition*'.[246] At an unconscious level, Cal's manufacturing of his own arrest creates an imaginary solution to the question of Marcella's desire, an impossible maternal desire which *seems* to threaten death. Hence, through his physical appropriation by the symbolic law, Cal's psychological appropriation by the Other-mother becomes an imaginary state 'as if desire would be possible to fulfil if it were not for the prohibition impending its free rein'.[247]

What does the (m)other want from me? For Cal, like all male subjects, this dilemma remains unfathomable. However, Marcella's role as the rural and redemptive Mother Ireland, the Sovereign Good, is *not* unfathomable, is *not* connected with self-sacrifice, is *not* the real source of the question: 'would you die for me?'. That source belongs to Cal's bad mothers. In conclusion, MacLaverty's tragic hero is unable to rid himself of Gracie and an urban Mother Ireland. These two mothers prevail within their Hamletian son's psyche as intractable dilemmas of desire – dilemmas circling around the desire of Mother Ireland and what does this (m)other want from me?

244   Zizek, *For They Know Not What They Do*, p.266.
245   Ibid., p.265.
246   Ibid., p.266.
247   Ibid., pp.266, 267.

Chapter 3
VAMPIRA

3.1: 'The Sexy Steps of Terror'[1]

> She heard the engine turn over, then walked down the
> street, stopped by the car, and bent over the driver's
> door.
> 'Going to give us a good time?' The soldier laughed
> and wound down his window.
> 'Perhaps'.
> She raised the Ruger and fired four times.[2]

Though fiction, this has been the sort of cautionary tale regularly told by the British Army to recruits new to the north of Ireland: beware the deadly consequences of casual fraternization; there is no rest and relaxation in Belfast. British author Gordon Stevens's novel shows how this threat sprawls to Berlin where the dangers of an imperceptible foe are also ever present. Such fatally brief encounters provide metaphors for England's bloody historical romance with Ireland and the inescapable geographical intimacy of the field of conflict. The function of this sort of anecdote in popular fiction, in this case Stevens's *Provo* (1993), is slightly different. Its purpose is not simply cautionary, it is supposed to entertain – give the reader a 'good time'. It does this by exploiting the potentially dark ambiguity surrounding 'Perhaps'. Perhaps in the world of fiction and fantasy, dying at the hands of a beautiful assassin is the very acme of a good time. Media images do of course flout this fantasy; a fantasy created for the male gaze. To cite one of many examples, appearing a few years after Stevens's fiction, photographic images appearing in the art section of *Observer Life* showed a series of semi-naked female torsos adorned

---

1   *Daily Mirror*, 23 June 1996, [n. page]. Article supplied by the Linenhall Library, Belfast, 1997.
2   Gordon Stevens, *Provo* (London: Harper Collins 1993), p.261.

with guns and bullet-packed, gun-belts.[3] The media is today still prolific in summoning such fantasies for the male spectator; effectively fusing sex with death, or Eros with Thanatos. Therefore, because the visual as well as the cognitive (or what can be imagined) is so relevant to representations of the Irish female paramilitary, this section draws upon images from the media in addition to fiction and film. Also, while I focus upon the male-authored British texts and the male British psyche, male-authored Irish texts are, where relevant included.

For as long as there has been fiction, writers have exploited the age-old metaphorical equivalence between death and orgasm. At the same time though, a necessary psychological distance from this equivalence is required. As shown in the extract from *Provo*, the suspicion that the soldier has been kerb-crawling introduces the necessary distance that protects the reader from identifying too closely with the soldier's death-driven desire, and heightens the reader's pleasure with a little morality. 'If he hadn't been looking for prostitutes [...]'. But in seeking satisfaction in morality, a reader, especially a British reader, would already be on the way to reversing the meaning of the anecdote. The female assassin becomes an avenging 'angel of death'[4]: a phantasm of liberal guilt concerning the immorality of British soldiers, male exploitation of women, the social and economic deprivation suffered by women in the north of Ireland and, by extension, British exploitation of Ireland itself.

Patrick Coogan's novel, *The General* (1994), charts PIRA activist Siobhan Maeve McCaillim's murderous and machiavellian seductions of British soldiers and Irish male republican comrades.[5] These comrades include a man named Seamus Long and a PIRA chief of staff named Gerry Madden. After McCaillim has lured a British soldier into a 'dirty entry', Long 'kneecaps' the soldier and gives 'the gun to' McCaillim whom the 'keening' soldier calls: 'Bitch. Fucking bitch' (162). The soldier then pleads with her saying: 'Sweet Jesus

---

3   *Observer Life*, 9 November 1997, pp.14, 15.
4   Stevens, *Provo*, p.8.
5   Patrick Coogan, *The General* (London: Mandarin, 1994). Further consecutive references to this novel are given after quotations in the text.

have mercy on me. Do it. Do it you fucking bitch. Get it over. [...] Oh my god I am heartily sorry for all my sins' (162). With these words, the soldier is not asking for sex but rather death from McCaillim who 'move[s] slowly, almost caressing, straddling the man on the ground, sitting on him' (162). Next, she 'slide[s] the gun barrel over the weeping man's face, forcing it between his teeth' (162). Finally, 'shuddering, she pull[s] the trigger, her whole body shaking with the lust of it' (162). As the plot develops, she performs 'her [sexual] duty' to the chief of staff (Madden) by providing him with oral sex (186). Afterwards she becomes his common-law-wife and, in order to gain PIRA leadership status, betrays him. Eventually, McCaillim is sacrificed to atone for her crimes when she is shot in the 'head [...], blood exploding from its side as the bullet rip[s] through it' (424).

With *The General*, Coogan illustrates characteristic representations of female members of the PIRA. Obviously, this is not to say that individual political attitudes fail to influence these representations. Coogan's antipathy towards the PIRA is a case in point as, although Belfast-born to a working-class family, he attended the Royal Military Academy, Sandhurst, has no truck with paramilitary violence, and now lives in Essex. Moreover, apart from individual political attitudes, representations of the Irish republican female paramilitary are certainly also influenced by the commercial requirements of genre fiction for thrills, 'glamour' and sex. However, these points aside, I am more concerned with the way a certain structure of fantasy repeatedly recurs across a variety of generic conventions including non-fiction. One look at press reporting of the activities of female members of the PIRA is enough to reveal this fantasy at work: 'The Sexy Steps of Terror' (*Daily Mirror*, 23 June 1996); 'Bomb Gang Beauty on Wanted List' (*Belfast Telegraph*, 3 October 1991); 'Pals are Shot by Love – Trap Killers' (*Sunday Mirror*, 6 September 1981); 'Love for Provo led to Murder' (*Irish Independent*, 8 October 1981); 'Terror in Blue Jeans' (*Daily Mail*, 13 November 1984); 'Blonde Bomber' (*Evening Standard*, 12 November 1984).

A curious thing about the press in the United Kingdom seems to be its expectation and demand that female terrorists be young, beautiful, sexy and preferably blonde. Clearly something quite strange, albeit very recognizable, is being suggested here about the proximity between fear and desire in which the signifying potential of women in a predominantly male media becomes an important stake in 'the propaganda war'. As Liz Curtis observes: 'Her Irish eyes may be smiling but her trade is fear and death. [...] Consider this female of the species, but keep well clear. For Margaret McKearney is certainly more deadly than the male'.[6] If female paramilitaries are claimed to be so very 'deadly', it is little wonder that the 'instruction [...] "shoot the woman first"' is alleged to have been 'given to recruits to West Germany's armed anti-terrorist squad' as well as 'other European squads'.[7]

Bearing the above points in mind, I suggest that the collective noun 'Vampira' might be used to denote the fantasmatic nature of these types of representations. Though they are shaped and characterized by a variety of popular genres of fiction, representations of female members of the PIRA share, metaphorically, the seductive and deadly qualities of Gothic vampires, draining the will and feeding off the blood of British soldiers and citizens. The term Vampira is also designed to situate these images in a familiar cinematic genre. As Deborah Jermyn writes, in an essay on female psychopaths in the cinema, 'from the vamps of early silent cinema, to the countless *femmes fatales* of *film noir*, the threatening woman, or the woman who kills, has long been an object of simultaneous horror and fascination'.[8] No wonder that, in 2006, the blonde and sexually potent actress named Sharon Stone made a comeback as a murderous nymphomaniac in *Basic Instinct 2*. But these 'threatening women' can also summon the 'simultaneous horror and fascination' of a diabolical disease or contagion. For Julia Kristeva, this idea can be linked to the 'abject [through] *jouissance* [whereby] so many victims of the abject are its fascinated victims'.[9]

6   Liz Curtis quoting from *Daily Express*, 5 September 1975. Liz Curtis, *Ireland the Propaganda War: The British Media and the Battle for Hearts and Minds* (London: Pluto, 1984), p.123.

7   Eileen MacDonald, *Shoot the Woman First* (London: Fourth Estate, 1991), p.4.

8   Deborah Jermyn, 'Rereading the Bitches from Hell: A Feminist Appropriation of the Female Psychopath', *Screen*, 37.3 (Autumn 1996), pp.251–66 (p.251).

9   Julia Kristeva, *The Powers of Horror: An Essay on Abjection*, trans. Leon S. Roudiez (New York: Columbia University Press, 1982), p.9.

Following Kristeva, John Lechte explains how the abject signals 'above all the ambiguous, the in-between, what defies boundaries [and is] resistant [to patriarchal] unity'.[10] The abject is symbolized by 'the corpse which is both human and non-human, waste and filth which are [like vampires] neither entirely inside nor outside the [male] socio-subjective order'.[11] As such, however, Vampira are often significant as phantasms of a certain deadly, or deathly, desire on the side of the British themselves. They constitute an interesting point that connects cultural anxieties about the dangers of 'unstable' women with anxieties about terrorism. Thus, proceeding with a psychoanalytical framework, I will attempt to point towards the significance of Vampira to culture through their proliferation in fiction, film and the media.

It would be easy to suggest that the often lurid representations of Vampira are designed, in the press, to deflect attention away from the political and social basis of the Republican cause. For the liberal press every bombing outrage drains sympathy, though the cases of female Republicans like Roisin McAliskey and Evelyn Glenholmes succeeded in making things appear a little more complex. In instances like these, Vampira clearly do function to occlude the real female activist. With McAliskey, the fact that she was pregnant at the time of her imprisonment certainly aroused sympathy even within the British press such as the *Guardian* where Jeremy Hardy protested that 'her [proposed] extradition' to Germany was 'certainly not in the interests of justice'.[12] As for Glenholmes, David Miller's observations about her 1980s status as 'Fleet Street's most wanted', or desired, 'terrorist' include an account of *Irish Press* columnist John McEntee's 'reported witnessing [of] the "creation of a little bit of history" in Gibraltar's Holiday Inn'.[13] This 'little bit of history [manifested] "the invention of Evelyn Glenholmes as the missing fourth IRA member in Gibral-

10   John Lechte, *Julia Kristeva* (Routledge: London, 1990), p.160.
11   Ibid.
12   Jeremy Hardy, 'On the disturbing case of Roisin McAliskey', *Guardian*, 30 September 1997, pp.6–7.
13   David Miller, 'The Media on the Rock', in *The British Media and Northern Ireland: Covering the Troubles*, ed. Bill Rolston (Basingstoke: Macmillan Academic and Professional, 1991), p.72.

tar'".[14] At the time, the 'missing fourth member' was thought to have been male. So McEntee asked 'a colourful colleague if he believed the story of the third man' and was told by a 'craggy veteran [...]: "Oh it's a woman and we are saying it's Evelyn Glenholmes"'.[15] The press insisted upon this identification because they had 'a nice picture of her and she [would not] sue'.[16] For the British press in Gibraltar, Glenholmes appears to have signified a temporary plug to a tantalizing gap created by the ever absent Irish female terrorist.

It is vital to stress that Vampira do not represent Irish women, they are figures that arise as an effect of the Troubles that function, especially in the case of British representations, to shield through fantasy the trauma of the violent conflict that unfolded for over thirty years. The lyrics from a song by the Irish performer Sinead O'Connor summon this idea rather effectively: 'I never said I was tough, that was everyone else, so you're a fool to attack me for the image that you built yourself'.[17] Given this, it is perhaps not surprising that, in films, so many actresses playing Irish female terrorists have been English. Vampira who are played by quintessentially English actresses include Miranda Richardson and Polly Walker, the latter described by the press as a 'smouldering English Rose'.[18] Walker appeared in the film version of Tom Clancy's 1987 novel, *Patriot Games*.[19] Within this film Walker, performing a 'temptress terrorist', brandishes a gun, a Lancashire accent and black lingerie. According to Partick McGee, this 'Hollywood adaptation of Clancy's best-seller [is] moronic' and Walker's Vampira is 'a role reprised [from Miranda] Richardson's "killer-bitch" in *The Crying Game*'.[20]

British, or indeed Irish, representations of Vampira do not spring fully-formed from the individual psyche of a novelist, journalist or screenwriter. Rather, they are selected and assembled from a reservoir

14   Ibid.
15   Ibid.
16   Ibid.
17   Sinead O'Connor, 'You cause me as much sorrow', in *I do not want what I haven't got*. Ensign Records, London, 1990.
18   *Daily Mail*, 18 August 1999, p.45.
19   *Patriot Games*, Dir. Philip Noyce, UIP/Paramount, 1992.
20   Patrick McGee, 'Do they mean us?', in *Guardian*, 3 September 1997, pp.12–13.

of images that already exist. That is why it is possible, through analysing the repeated use of certain images, to speak of cultural obsessions which shape, feed and articulate shared anxieties. So, for instance, British representations of Irish women also exist in relation to other representations produced by other nations. Evidence for this is apparent in the image displayed on the cover of French author Gerard De Villiers's novel entitled *Furie a Belfast*.[21] The image speaks, or rather fails to speak, for itself. No doubt created to galvanize the reader's scopophiliac drive, De Villiers's publisher supplies a picture of a cat-suited, and highly dangerous, *femme fatale* who brandishes an Armalite and wears a crucifix. Functioning 'at the symbolic level', she is a '*masquerade*' of costume and cross, an '*object a*' manifesting a strange Cat-woman-cum-Madonna hybrid.[22] The Armalite empowers this fantasy woman with an allegorical one dimensionality. And the phallic threat imposed by the weapon is perhaps too ludicrously obvious to be stated. However, historically, fantasy versus reality in terms of female Irishness is not so easily separated.

Most notably, representations of Irish women produced by Ireland itself can signify different meanings and refer to different versions of history in respect of the Troubles. British representations also exist in relation to real Irish women, of course. But, as mentioned in my Introduction to this book, the Irish Republican prisoner Patrick McGee has called recently on Irish writers, male and female, to 'square up to their task of writing their own accounts of the Troubles in fiction' as 'reality'.[23] Yet, I want to again emphasize that, generally, realist fiction does not change perceptions about reality, its dependence on recognizability tends to entrench received ideas. There is no access to the trauma of the Troubles in realist fiction, just as there is no access to real Irish women through Vampira. Nevertheless, these images have a history that can be traced. Through charting their development, it should be possible to follow the shifts in British and

21   Cover illustration. Gerard De Villiers, *Furie a Belfast* (Paris: Plon, 1974).
22   Jacques Lacan, *The Four Fundamental Concepts of Psycho-analysis*, ed. Jacques-Alain Miller, trans. Alan Sheridan (London: Vintage, 1998), pp.193, 194.
23   McGee, 'Do They Mean Us?', p.13.

Irish perceptions as the Troubles developed. Bearing in mind that the Provisional IRA did not exist until the late 1960s, it might be useful to briefly try to locate the origins of Vampira in representations that predate this period.

3.2: Demons of the Cause and Angels in the House

> He trusted her with important missions. Had she been a man, she would have been on the staff. But she was woman. He looked at her magnificent head and body, and the fact that she was a beautiful woman indicated one profound condition.
>
> She was pledged to her body: to her great beauty; to all the splendour of her hair, her exquisite countenance, her flesh in its woman's form; and the passions and impulses which that body dictated to her. And because of this condition, which he imagined was authentic, he never trusted her with the innermost secrets of the Organization, nor with missions of a particular kind. And never would.[24]

As I have suggested, British representations of the Irish female terrorist tap into misconceptions about women generally, relying on a 'patriarchal' framework that is common to most Western countries, including America. 'It still shocks me', claims a female 'IRA volunteer [...], that I have two battles to fight – one against the Brits and secondly with the men of my own organisation'.[25] Louise Ryan compounds the ambiguous age-old attitudes that such women have received from their 'own organzation' when she writes that:

---

24   F.L. Green, *Odd Man Out* (North Hollywood, California: Leisure Books, 1971 (orig. 1945)), p.31.

25   Eileen Fairweather, Roisin McDonough and Melanie McFadyean, *Only the Rivers Run Free. Northern Ireland: The Women's War* (London: Pluto, 1984), p.241.

> The active participation of women in the republican movement and the wide spread condemnation that they attracted proved a dilemma for many men. On the one hand, they needed the women's help and support, but on the other, their reliance on women could be seen as a sign of weakness.[26]

Dealing with these issues, the title of Margaret Ward's comprehensive history of women and Irish Republicanism, *Unmanageable Revolutionaries*, is taken from a conversation between W.H. Van Voris and Eamon De Valera in which the latter suggested that women are at once the boldest and most unmanageable revolutionaries.[27] A tribute that gives with one hand, only to take away with the other, female revolutionaries are credited with an excessive, undisciplined bravery: they are *unmanageable*. Relying as it does on the use of the term 'man' to denote the universal subject, 'unmanageable' manages to suggest that there is something un-man-like or inhuman about female revolutionaries. They are attributed with something extra, an added boldness or bravery that is not subject to the standard of rationality or discipline that determines men, or 'man', in general. As such, female revolutionaries are attributed with something that 'man' lacks; indeed, their 'unmanageableness' is the very signifier of that lack. The unmanageable female revolutionary functions, therefore, in a way analogous to the 'phallus' in Lacanian theory because 'the phallus is the privileged signifier of that mark in which the role of the logos is joined with the advent of desire'.[28] Through her excess, the female revolutionary determines for all men (friend and foe) the very standard of 'logos' (truth) to which 'man' is subject, and which she embodies as object of desire. The bold and unmanageable female is both the means and the goal of the revolution: the beauty of her unmanageable power is recognized as the power *to* manage (the power *of* management that cannot, of necessity, be subjected *to* management in the same way that the excessiveness of *la loi* cannot be subjected *to*

---

26   Louise Ryan, 'In the line of fire': representations of women and war (1919–1912) through the writings of republican men', in *Irish Women and Nationalism: Soldiers, New Women and Wicked Hags*, eds. Louise Ryan and Margaret Ward (Dublin: Irish Academic Press, 2004), pp.45–61 (p.48).

27   Margaret Ward, *Unmanageable Revolutionaries* (London: Pluto, 1983), p.viii.

28   Lacan, *Ecrits*, trans. Alan Sheridan (London: Routledge, 1977), p.287.

law).[29] This is the power necessary to subject the citizens of a new state, a power that finds its iconic image and meaning in the martyrdom of the bold and unmanageable female revolutionary. Since the French Revolution, at least, 'Liberty' leads the people with blouse unbuttoned and breasts exposed, the very image of bountiful social good (the mother's breast) to be had after the revolution. Unfortunately, for the women who survive, female 'unmanageabilty' justifies women's unequal status. Consequently, as Ward's book shows, when women were not unmanageable 'loose cannons', they had a secondary, auxiliary or domestic function in the Republican movement.

Ward begins her study with 'The Ladies' Land League' (1881–1882) and details its development into 'Cumann na mBan' that commenced in 1914. Cumann na mBan was formed to encourage women 'to act as auxiliaries for the old Irish volunteers, the forerunners of the current IRA'.[30] It was only with the advent of the current Troubles that women began to be recruited into the IRA itself and began to suggest images that produced a 'tantalizing gap'.

Prior to their recruitment into the PIRA, fictional representations of Republican Irish women paralleled their auxiliary status to men. These representations appealed solely to the domestic and romantic stereotypes that characterized films like British director Carol Reed's *Odd Man Out* (1947).[31] In this film adaptation of F.L. Green's novel, the iconically named Kathleen is first seen in her domestic role as a 'tea maker' for the male IRA activists before progressing to become the romantic interest of James Mason's protagonist (Johnny). This romance plays the crucial function of humanizing the IRA member for an, often British, audience. As John Hill writes in his essay on 'Images of Violence', the technique is 'quite a typical characteristic of

---

29   Jacques Derrida observes how the French term for the law (*la loi*) 'is [...] declined in the feminine [and signifies] not a woman [but] only a figure [or] silhouette [that is] sexually seductive'. For Derrida, '*la loi* is [...] the gender of this figure of the law [...], the law herself' rather than her [male] 'representatives'. Cit. Derek Attridge, *Jacques Derrida: Acts of Literature* (New York: Routledge, 1992), p.221.

30   Fairweather, McDonough and McFadyean, *Only the Rivers Run Free*, p.241.

31   *Odd Man Out*, Dir. Carol Reed, Two Cities, 1947.

the British cinema' (and, as discussed in this study's sections relating to *Hamlet*, quite typical of British novels).[32] According to Hill, 'if violence is generally seen to be negative and destructive, it is also contrasted with emotions and actions which are positive and constructive'.[33] Moreover, claims Hill, 'for the British cinema, it is typically romantic love, the home and the family which fulfil this function'.[34]

At the same time, however, romantic love can fail. This happens in *Odd Man Out* when the possibilities of romantic love apply a tragic gloss to Johnny's terrorist activities. Johnny has to pay a high price for his commitment to the Republican cause. His activities thwart his relationship with Kathleen and destroy any hope he might have for a conventional family life. Here, Kathleen functions symbolically as the supreme good that terrorist activity is willing to sacrifice to attain its goals. Irish Republicanism is therefore exposed as being totally destructive of human-value even, or especially, for the activist himself. Hence, *Odd Man Out* shows the ideological importance of Kathleen: she must resonate with Kathleen Ni Houlihan and become a metonymy for Mother Ireland, so that Johnny's actions can be seen as totally destructive and self-negating. Within *Odd Man Out*, Kathleen serves a symbolic function demanded by British perceptions of post-war Irish Republicanism. Resonating with an ideal image set in place for female identifications, this symbolic function is Kathleen Ni Houlihan, both mother Ireland and virgin daughter, an ideal (re)surrecting 'Woman-Ireland-Muse'.[35] Modern British popular culture preserves this ideal within images of Southern rather than Northern Irish women. The cult status awarded to *Riverdance* and Edna O'Brien's status as a woman who 'personifies all that is mystical and spiritual about the Celts' illustrates this tendency.[36]

---

32   John Hill, 'Images of Violence', in *Cinema and Ireland*, eds. Kevin Rockett, Luke Gibbons and John Hill (London: Croom Helm, 1987), pp.147–93 (p.155).
33   Ibid.
34   Ibid.
35   Edna Longley, *From Cathleen to Anorexia: The Breakdown of Irelands* (Dublin: Attic, 1990), p.15.
36   Terry O'Neill, *Daily Mail*, 15 January 1993, p 21.

In F.L. Green's novel, *Odd Man Out* (1945), the final page shows Kathleen and Johnny held at bay by the police. At this point, the badly injured Johnny 'hear[s] Kathleen's voice softly uttering his name and waylaying the terse shouts from the police'.[37] 'He felt her arms about him', writes Green, 'encircling him warmly supporting him'.[38] While Johnny senses 'the ecstasy of [her] possession', Kathleen shoots Johnny then herself.[39] The reader is informed that her deadly action arises from 'love' not malice.[40] Indeed, her iconic status as Mother Ireland absolves Johnny of his paramilitary 'sins'. Fittingly, the last line of the novel has 'the old priest' saying how (like Marcella in *Cal*) Kathleen 'redeemed' Johnny.[41] Later in this section, the important symbolic function of Mother Ireland will be more fully explored to show how this particular representation of the female PIRA is often more negative than the one portrayed in *Odd Man Out*. Quite often, in fact, Mother Ireland does not just 'boil down to [a] romantic "Mother Ireland" image'.[42]

This said, stereotypes such as *Odd Man Out*'s Kathleen still of course persist and augment more recent Vampira images. Perhaps because of its tendency towards romanticism and nostalgia, Hollywood has preserved the 'Kathleen Ni Houlihan' type in movies like Alan J. Pakula's *The Devil's Own* (1997) where Natascha McElhone supplies the support and romantic interest for the PIRA activist played by the all-American Brad Pitt.[43] Ironically, however, while *Odd Man Out* created no ripples of controversy, *The Devil's Own* was heavily criticized for 'glamorising IRA violence'.[44] Worse, photographs of the late Princess of Wales escorting her sons to a screening produced a general hue and cry about family values. 'She should take greater care about what her children see', proclaimed 'William Ross, the Ulster

37   Green, *Odd Man Out* , pp.250–1.
38   Ibid., p.251.
39   Ibid.
40   Ibid.
41   Ibid.
42   Fairweather, McDonough and McFadyean, *Only the Rivers Run Free*, p.237.
43   *The Devil's Own*, Dir. Alan J. Pakula, Columbia, 1997.
44   Kamal Ahmed and Dan Glaister, *Guardian*, 24 June 1997, p.2.

Unionist MP for East Derry'.[45] Adding to this hue and cry over Diana's 'incredibly ill-informed choice' over taking her sons 'to see *The Devil's Own*', Christopher Tookey asks: 'Why do film makers hate family life?'.[46] The contrast in press and public reaction to two films similar in theme and treatment testifies to the change that occurred with the advent of the Troubles. Now, movies are condemned as subversive precisely because of their romanticism. For the right-wing press, such films glamorize violence and encourage young women and men (even Prince William!) to live out romantic Hollywood fantasies about heroic Irish resistance. For the liberal press, these movies trivialize real suffering and promote American misconceptions about the 'reality' of the north of Ireland. In comparison, British, and sometimes Irish, film and fiction is commended by conservatives and liberals alike. More unglamorous representations and more serious treatments of death and suffering attract more vigorous approval. Realism is, it seems, the vehicle of political morality.

In contemporary film and fiction the domestic auxiliary complements the image of Vampira. Instead of being a romantic heroine, however, the domestic auxiliary is now the bearer of the reality of the violence of the Troubles. It is through her suffering body and cries of pain that the Troubles are 'realised' in realist fiction. This is even the case with feminist fiction that seeks to challenge 'the normalisation of terror' within the domestic sphere in the north of Ireland where, according to Michelle E. Evans, 'though it is the second largest cause of killings [...] violence against the female has largely been overshadowed by sectarian violence'.[47] This situation is not particularly new, a fact made evident by Christina Loughran whose 1985 report observed how 'in West Belfast [...] violence meted out by the security forces [could be] link[ed] to domestic violence'.[48] For female author

45   William Ross. cit. by Kamal Ahmed and Dan Glaister, *Guardian*, 24 June 1997, p.2.
46   Christopher Tookey, 'Why do film makers hate family life?', *Daily Mail*, 24 June 1997, p.4.
47   Michelle E. Evans, 'A Woman's Lot', *Fortnight*, May 1998, p.14.
48   Christina Loughran, 'The Woman's Movement in N. Ireland: Between Republicanism and Feminism', *Fortnight*, 27 May 1985, p.4.

Robin Morgan, 'everyone deplores the public violence in the history of Ireland [but] no one spends much time on the private violence'.[49] In her book *The Demon Lover*, Morgan cites, as an illustration, the case of 'the woman whose man poured a kettle of boiling water over her vagina just before she went into child-birth labour'.[50] While it is difficult to imagine anything more horrifying, or anything that could have been better chosen to shock and appal a reader, for other feminist writers the effectiveness of such examples tends to diminish with repetition. As Eve Patten writes:

> In addition to its dubious role in producing a collective identity, the effectiveness of confessional realism as part of a political lobby is debatable. The reality of (most) women's subjection is evident. Men smash bottles. Wives get hit. Relationships fail. Women get lonely and victimised and denied. Channelling this material into fiction may be considered an important aspect of a consciousness-raising incentive, but only up to a finite point at which it becomes reflexive and counter-productive.[51]

Patten suggests that the horrifying examples of male violence that repeatedly appear in feminist social realism eventually have the effect of conventionalizing the reality of the suffering they are meant to expose and document. Domestic brutality becomes yet another generic feature. Indeed, British author Chris Petit's novel *The Psalm Killer* (1997) describes the apparently common fate of the suffering Irish woman.[52] The woman is the partner of a character named 'Big John' who, Petit narrates, 'poured a kettle of boiling water over her vagina, when she was pregnant, and afterwards just laughed and told her to stop making a fuss'.[53] While such repetitions certainly seem to bear out Patten's point, they also beg another question, it seems to me. What does it mean that female characters have to bear the burden of the 'reality' of the Troubles in such a sexually agonizing way? As these anecdotes are repeated, and begin to function in a purely aesthetic manner, even social realism follows the trajectory of Gothic

49   Robin Morgan, *Demon Lover* (London: W.W. Norton, 1989), p.315.
50   Ibid.
51   Eve Patten, 'Women and Fiction', *Krino*, 9 (1990), p.7.
52   Chris Petit, *The Psalm Killer* (London: Macmillan, 1997).
53   Ibid., p.253.

fiction. What further horrors will need to be related in order to provoke the requisite 'consciousness-raising' outrage? More insidiously, perhaps, than in Morgan's anecdote, Petit's account concerning the scalding potency of 'Big John' seems to appeal to an unspoken Sadean fantasy. In the typical Sadean scenario the victim of sexual torture is never destroyed or dismembered, but retains the capacity of being what Lacan calls an 'indestructible support'.[54] Similarly, the repeated horrors of social realism sustain the suffering of women in the imagination of readers and audiences. Comparing the function of the Sadean victim to that of the alter-ego in psychoanalysis, Lacan writes that:

> Analysis shows clearly that the subject separates out a double of himself that is made inaccessible to destruction, so as to make it support what, borrowing a term from the realm of aesthetics, one cannot help calling the play of pain [...]. [This support] is in itself no more than a signifier of a limit. Suffering is conceived of as a stasis which affirms that which is cannot return to the void from which it emerged.[55]

While violence and death certainly are part of the reality of the Troubles, death only happens to 'the other'. We survivors fail to encounter it, fail to encounter it to the degree that we survive and do not return to the void from whence we came. This is not to say that everyone in the United Kingdom has not been emotionally, politically and socially affected by the Troubles to a greater or lesser extent. It is simply to suggest that Troubles fiction circulates obsessively as a trauma that is always a-proximate and that, for thirty years, was perpetually 'there' (and 'here') but never directly encountered except by 'the other', the victim. Consequently, Troubles fiction feeds a fascination for the 'stuff' and substance of this bloody trauma, and the void that it opens. As the previous excessive images of traumatic pain have shown, the 'void' (from which the suffering of existence emerged) is fairly conventionally signified in the form of female genitals: a boiling vagina about to give birth.

---

54   Jacques Lacan, *The Ethics of Psychoanalysis*, trans. Dennis Porter (London: Routledge, 1992), p.261.
55   Ibid.

That the fictional 'double', whose suffering horrifies, entertains and protects the reader or audience from the void it denotes and delimits, is always a woman says something about the 'male' imagination that informs these fictions – whether or not they are written by feminist authentic realists. Such examples imply an unquestioning acceptance of the supposed insensible plasticity that is often attributed to women's bodies (since women are designed for child birth they are supposed to bear pain better than men) and their enlarged capacity for auxiliary *jouissance* (sexual pleasure beyond the capabilities and endurance of men). Furthermore, the configuration whereby violence and sex are conjoined for the reader or audience, in the suffering of the Other, links the domestic auxiliary directly with her Vampira sisters. Such notions have crossed the Atlantic to settle in American-authored novels about the troubles. Thus, Jonathan Kebbe's *The Armalite Maiden* begins with the heroine 'tooling' herself up in preparation for terrorist activity: 'spreading her long legs again, she applied more lubricant, and clutching the plastic-covered cartridge in both hands, slowly worked it up inside herself. [...] This tampon was designed not to staunch bleeding but to induce it in British soldiers'.[56] Here, Kebbe makes the crude but irresistible link between menstrual blood and the blood of a victim of violence, this time a British soldier, thereby locating the female body as cause, vehicle and support for suffering and death. And of course, there is the non-too-subtle suggestion about and repetition of a woman's explosive sexuality. This trope is repeated in *Patriot Games* when Maureen Dwyer is arrested and the male detective looking at her naked body contemplates how 'a woman officer would perform a cavity search to ensure that she wasn't "holding" something that might be dangerous'.[57] 'Spread 'em, dearie', says the detective, 'you know the drill'.[58]

For Bill Rolston, it is this element that most characterizes representations of female terrorists in fiction concerned with the Troubles. According to Rolston, 'once women have taken the plunge into the unnatural and rejected their prime role as mother, anything is

56   Jonathan Kebbe, *The Armalite Maiden* (London: Heinemann, 1990), p.1.
57   Tom Clancy, *Patriot Games* (London: Collins, 1987), p.174.
58   Ibid.

possible'.[59] This is because fiction suggests that 'women embrace violence with a passion exceeding that of men'.[60] Such images imply that 'violent women [...] represent raw, unadulterated emotion'.[61] Hence, these women 'tremble with rage, shake with anger, get carried away in emotion'.[62] Rolston further observes how this 'metaphor' for female violence 'is undoubtedly sexual'.[63] 'Men are attracted to these violent women', writes Rolston, 'in as far as their raw emotion can be presumed to translate into sexual abandonment'.[64] On the other hand, though, men 'are simultaneously repulsed by women who show strength, fearing sexual and political emasculation'.[65]

As the, so far discussed, fictional examples show, it is not simply 'raw emotion' that characterizes the 'unmanageability' of women for their male friends and foe alike, it is just as often their cold, hyperrational calculation, their implacable refusal to 'play the game'. This characterization of women is as old as Western literature, running from the Courtly Lady of the Troubadours to the *femme fatale* of *film noir*. For Zizek, following Lacan, these literary woman are located in the place of 'the Thing', in psychoanalysis, since 'like the Lady, the *femme fatale* is an "inhuman partner", a traumatic Object with whom no relationship is possible, an apathetic void imposing senseless, arbitrary ordeals'.[66] While the Lady and the *femme fatale* determine the ordeals that maintain the amorous subject in a state of perpetual suffering, the same structure applies when the roles are reversed. The interminable suffering of Sade's Justine also marks the limit of the Thing. For Lacan, it is the privilege given to '*das ding*' or the Thing that articulates ethics, morality and desire:

59 Bill Rolston, 'Mothers, whores and villains: images of women in novels of the Northern Ireland conflict', *Race and Class*, 31.1 (1989), 41–57 (p.50).
60 Ibid.
61 Ibid.
62 Ibid.
63 Ibid.
64 Ibid.
65 Ibid.
66 Slavoj Zizek, *The Metastases of Enjoyment: Six Essays on Woman and Causality* (London: Verso, 1994), p.102.

In brief, Kant is of the same opinion as Sade. For in order to reach *das ding* absolutely, to open the floodgates of desire, what does Sade show us on the horizon? In essence, pain. The other's pain as well as the pain of the subject himself, for on occasions they are simply one and the same thing. To the degree that it involves forcing an access to the Thing, the outer extremity of pleasure is unbearable to us.[67]

The 'outer extremity of pleasure', pleasure so intense that it cannot be born by the body, an intensity that renders pleasure indistinguishable from pain, is another Lacanian definition of *jouissance*. It is imagined in forms of violent ecstasy, or in the ecstasy of violence. Once again, our *jouissance* can be conceived as that which fascinates us, but which we dare not go near. Consequently, most often *jouissance* is located in the Other and sublimated in images of violence and in fear, aggression and negativity: the 'surplus *jouissance*' that informs both the production and censorship of, for example, sexually violent images; or the violence directed towards those members of the community (black, Asian, Irish) who in their alleged work-shy idleness 'steal' the *jouissance* of the tax-paying white British subject by enjoying themselves at his expense. The Thing emerges, in the interstices of *jouissance* and counter-*jouissance*, in the shape of disturbing images that disclose the 'extimacy' or intimate exteriority of the *jouissance* of the Other in the subject. In Troubles fiction this occurs when the face of Vampira, screening the traumatic encounter with the real, takes on a grotesque familiarity: 'It was a killer. [...] It was not a human being. [...] Kill it. Kill it. Kill it'.[68] This frenzied interior dictum comes from a male character (a priest named John Tierney) in American author James Carroll's novel entitled *Madonna Red*. During the climax of Carroll's narrative, Tierney kills a female Vampira who is dressed as a nun and has a dual identity: a 'good girl' (Bridgit) and 'bad girl' (Juneau). Tierney strikes this Vampira 'so hard that her head came off [but although] it seemed like her head [...], it wasn't'.[69] Her Gothic demise shows 'her mouth [...] open, with blood spurting from the

---

67   Lacan, *The Ethics of Psychoanalysis*, p.80.
68   James Carroll, *Madonna Red* (London: Hodder and Stoughton, 1976), pp.265–6.
69   Ibid., p.266.

wreckage of her throat [yet] grotesque as it was, the twisted visage was familiar'.[70] Familiar? As uncannily familiar, perhaps, as Tierney's own head? An uncanny and familiar Thing.

The Thing is located in 'the place of the Real, which stretches from the trauma to the fantasy – in so far as the fantasy is never anything more than the screen that conceals something quite primary, something determinant in the function of repetition'.[71] Violent Vampira images circulate around a central traumatic event, the experience of terrorism, that they screen even as they denote as their origin, their 'reality'. The 'real', in this Lacanian sense, functions, in the experience of terrorism, 'in the form of that which is *unassimilable* in it – in the form of trauma, determining all that follows'.[72] For Lacan, 'the real is beyond the automaton, the return or the coming-back, the insistence of signs, by which we see ourselves governed by the pleasure principle. The real is that which lies beyond the automaton'.[73] In this instance, the 'automaton' is both Vampira as 'inhuman partner', doll, stereotype, object, but also the repetition that keeps her coming, as it were, that obsessively wills her reappearance. Ultimately, lying at the heart of sexual relationships and the representation of sexual relationships in fiction and film, the Thing is located at 'the imaginary limit of male narcissism, the obstacle to a sexual relation that sustains romantic belief in its existence, a screen for imaginary projections and fantasized union'.[74] The next section argues that the Blonde Vampira Thing is especially relevant to these issues.

70   Ibid.
71   Lacan, *The Ethics of Psychoanalysis*, p.129.
72   Lacan, *The Four Fundamental Concepts of Psycho-analysis*, p.55.
73   Ibid., pp.52–3.
74   Seminar for Hypertheory and Heterology (SHAH), Scott Wilson, 'Incorporating the Impossible', *Cultural Values*, 1.2 (October 1997), 178–204 (p.187).

3.3: The Blonde Thing

> Margaret Thatcher joined the IRA
> And the IRA joined Margaret Thatcher.
>
> Black dresses were worn by all for the occasion
> In which historical union was consummated.[75]

In his essay on 'Woman-as-Thing', Zizek discusses Irish writer-director Neil Jordan's film *The Crying Game*, and looks at the central relationship between Dil and Fergus as a metaphor for the political divisions in Ireland.[76] Quoting Jordan himself, who has suggested that he wanted the love story to provide the key to understanding the means of overcoming 'more profound separations of racial, national, sexual identity', Zizek focuses on the symbolic importance of the barrier determined by the Thing.[77] Love here does not consist in a romantic, imaginary fantasy of 'Oneness', but in a recognition of the 'impossibility' of Oneness, the impossibility of a sexual relation (Fergus is conventionally heterosexual while Dil is a transvestite homosexual).[78] For Zizek, their love retains its 'absolute, unconditional character' as an effect of the recognition and acceptance of the barrier rather than in the fantasy of abolishing it.[79] So, even though 'politically, the film remains faithful to the Irish cause, which functions as its inherent background', Jordan supplies his audience with a 'paradox' whereby 'in the very sphere of privacy where the hero hoped to find a safe haven, he is compelled to accomplish an even more vertiginous revolution in his most intimate personal attitudes'.[80]

---

75   Paul Durcan, 'Margaret Thatcher Joins the IRA', in *The Selected Paul Durcan*, ed. Edna Longley (Belfast: Blackstaff, 1982), p.97.
76   Zizek, *The Metastases of Enjoyment: Six Essays on Woman and Causality*, pp.89–111.
77   Ibid., p.105. See also *Neil Jordan A Reader* (New York: Vintage, 1993), pp.xii–xiii.
78   Ibid.
79   Ibid., p.109.
80   Ibid.

Surprisingly, in an essay on the *femme fatale*, Zizek fails to mention Jude in his reading of *The Crying Game*.[81] If an impossible romance with Dil constitutes an exotic detour for Fergus (the male PIRA), Jude (the Vampira) figures as an all-too-symptomatic blockage for any British viewer of the film. I have already suggested that, in a text like *Odd Man Out*, British identity is predicated on a fantasy of romantic/political union that is sacrificed, in Green's narrative, by Johnny in the thwarting of his relationship with Kathleen as a metonymy for Mother Ireland. Later, in the 1980s, the representation of the female member of the PIRA functioned as a different point of suture in an ambivalent image appropriated to justify violence. To see this more clearly, we have to look at the significance of the 'extimate' figure.

In *The Crying Game*, this extimate figure is the British actress who plays Jude (Miranda Richardson). The characterization of Jude is unequivocal. She is 'a fucking whore', 'a fucking bitch', and a 'crazy woman'.[82] Early in the film, where she recalls the domestic auxiliary making tea for her PIRA colleagues, Jude quickly moves into a more fully-fledged Vampira identity, carrying out her paramilitary duties in a pencil-skirt suit, packing a gun in her handbag. The choice of Richardson to play the part was no doubt influenced by her track record playing psychotic, unhinged, capricious or vengeful women: Ruth Ellis in *Dance with a Stranger*, Viv in *Tom and Viv*, Elizabeth I in *Blackadder* and the wronged politician's wife in *Damage*. Indeed, the intertextual nature of these other roles provides 'a residue of audience recall' for the audience through memory and expectation. However, the interesting thing about these characters is that they are all quintessentially or iconically English. Yet, like Helen Mirren who portrayed Marcella in *Cal*, Richardson's Englishness has not prevented her being dubbed a 'Human Chameleon'.[83] As claimed by Emma Dow, while Richardson 'is an expert at the changing game from straggly blonde to *femme fatale*, via a prim and serious brunette', Mirren is a 'a prime suspect when it comes to being guilty of reaching

81   *The Crying Game*, Dir. Neil Jordan, Palace/Channel 4, 1993.
82   Neil Jordan, *The Crying Game* (London: Vintage 1993), p.67.
83   Emma Dow, 'The Human Chameleons', *Daily Mail*, 16 May 1997, pp.40–1.

regularly for scissors and a large bottle of peroxide to alter her sultry looks'.[84] A key scene within *The Crying Game* supplies both a visual and psychological imaging of Richardson's chameleonality and her split identity in terms of Anglo-Irishness.[85] The scene occurs just after her character Jude's arrival in England to hunt down Fergus and implicate him in an assassination. Here we see Richardson gazing into a mirror that shows two identical reflections. Accordingly, Jane Giles observes how 'the casting of a British actress as an IRA member works ironically and subtextually, suggesting to us that this is not a person to be trusted'.[86] Quoting 'the critic Philip French', Giles implies how this lack of trust is intensified because Richardson's 'performance [represents] "sexuality transformed into lethal politics"'.[87]

Of the 'residue of audience recall' triggered by Richardson, the persona of Ruth Ellis from Mike Newel's *Dance With a Stranger* (1985) is in many ways the most interesting and pertinent to Vampira images. As a fatal 'blonde bombshell', in the media reports, myths and fictions that surrounded her as the last woman to be executed for murder in England, Ellis is both a representative and a victim of the *femme fatale* stereotype from *film noir*. The passing of forty-five years has not doused political comment upon, and media fascination with, Ellis. For Norman Tebbit, 'she was a murderess and paid the price'.[88] Whereas Russell Miller claims how 'she was hanged as much for her dubious morals as for murder'.[89] 'In truth', writes Miller, 'Ruth did little to help herself. With her lacquered curls of peroxide hair, her eyebrows painted in soaring arches and her vermilion lips, in court she looked [...] like a brassy tart [...] and appeared to show little remorse'.[90] Indeed, for Jacqueline Rose, it was precisely because Ruth

84 Ibid.
85 Still photograph from the film *The Crying Game* reproduced in Jane Giles, *The Crying Game* (London: British Film Institute, 1997), p.32.
86 Ibid.
87 Ibid., p.31. Cit. Giles.
88 Norman Tebbit, 'Ruth would still have been guilty of murder today', *Mail on Sunday*, 16 August 1998, p.37.
89 Russell Miller, 'Justice at last for Ruth Ellis?', *Daily Mail: Night and Day*, 4 October 1998, 10–12 (p.11).
90 Ibid.

Ellis '*failed*', in court, to perform the hystericized role of *femme fatale* that was expected of her, that she failed to get her sentence commuted to life for a *crime passionelle*.[91] Instead, as Rose writes, prior to her execution the trial called for psychiatric reports that condemned Ellis for not being 'hysterical *enough*'.[92] For the psychiatrists, and ultimately for the jury, Ellis proved to be 'too rational'; she failed to 'mobilise a stereotype in her defence'.[93] Such 'supreme rationality', mirroring the ideal rationality of the law, has the effect of hystericizing the law, resulting in a legal execution that replays, in cold blood, the very murder it would condemn.[94]

Linking the metonymic chain into a full circle, Rose's essay compares Ruth Ellis to another 'blonde bombshell' who was heavily involved in the military conflict in Northern Ireland in the 1980s. Inspiring headlines in the Irish press such as 'One-Woman Revolution' and 'Heaven Help Anyone Who Tries To Stand In Her Way', reporters described this *femme fatale* in familiar terms: 'Don't let the blue eyes dazzle you. [...] She is clever. She is charming. But it was sheer political ruthlessness – the devastating killer instinct of a determined woman – which won Margaret Hilda Thatcher the dangerous crown she grasps so tightly today'.[95] Fiction apes Thatcher's feminine yet phallic media persona. So, Chapman Pincher's 1978 novel, *The Eye of The Tornado*, shows a male character named Quinn admiring the physical attributes of a female British Prime Minister named Mrs Fletcher.[96] 'As Quinn rose from his seat on Mrs. Fletcher's left', writes Pincher, 'his trained eye observed that her dress had just ridden above her knees'.[97] Quinn is 'a connoisseur of female legs, and [observes] that for a woman of forty-five [Mrs Fletcher] had excellent

91   Jacqueline Rose, 'Margaret Thatcher and Ruth Ellis', *New Formations*, 6 (Winter 1988), 3–27 (p.8).
92   Ibid., p.10.
93   Ibid., p.8.
94   Ibid.
95   Articles from Northern Ireland Office Press Cutting File, 1.2 (31 October 1975), [n. pub], [n. page], Supplied by the Linenhall Library Belfast, 1998.
96   Chapman Pincher, *The Eye of the Tornado* (London: Sphere Books, 1978).
97   Ibid., p.44.

ones'.[98] But, like Thatcher, in addition to being an object of desire, Pincher's female Prime Minister is also 'flawless and business-like [with] the effervescent aura of a winner'.[99]

Helen Birch writes that, from Irma Grese's reputation as 'the "blonde Angel of Belson"' to Sharon Stone's role as 'an ice-pick-wielding murderess' in *Basic Instinct* (1992), the 'remorseless blonde' is historically as well as hysterically a 'popular' if inadequate 'cliché'.[100] For Birch, Myra Hindlay, 'who during her trial [...] sat impassive, in smart clothes, full make-up, and with newly paroxided hair', is of course included within the cliché of 'remorseless' and 'murderous blondes'.[101] Moreover, Birch argues, this cliché applies to Thatcher 'who, despite the best efforts of the spin-doctors, failed to match her softer, ash-blonde persona to her style of government – ruling her party [...] like her country [...] with a rod of iron and symbolically castrating her all male Cabinet'.[102]

First establishing her 'Iron Lady' credentials by coldly presiding over the death of the Maze Irish hunger strikers, Thatcher's 'devastating killer instinct' is directly, if unconsciously, associated with Vampira images in the press and in the fictions of the 1980s. Indeed, Rose's article (referred to earlier) borrows a visual image of this notion through a cartoon taken from the *Boston Globe* that depicts Thatcher's role as 'executioner' of three PIRA suspects in Gibraltar.[103] The cartoon shows a caricature of Thatcher announcing:

> In the matter of our shooting the three unarmed I.R.A. members [...] The media have been dreadfully irresponsible. They have set themselves up as judge, jury and prosecutor [...] and dared to question the executioner![104]

98   Ibid.
99   Ibid., p.205.
100   Helen Birch, 'If looks could kill: Myra Hindlay and the iconography of evil', in *Moving Targets: Women, Murder and Representation*, ed. Helen Birch (London: Virago, 1993), pp.32–61 (pp.52, 50, 52).
101   Ibid., p.51.
102   Ibid., p.52.
103   Cartoon by Wasserman, *Boston Globe*, 3 May 1988. Reproduced in Rose, 'Margaret Thatcher and Ruth Ellis', *New Formations*, p.16.
104   Ibid.

Unconsciously, and specifically in relation to Gibraltar, Thatcher takes the place of the unknown or 'missing' female member of the PIRA, later of course named as Evelyne Glenholmes. Functioning in such a way, Thatcher-as-Vampira provides a point of suture, a point of identification that, Rose notes, allowed British subjects to 'take pleasure in violence as force and legitimacy'.[105] Whether it be the conflict in the north of Ireland, race riots in Brixton or Toxteth, the Miner's strike or the Falklands war, Thatcher became the charismatic form 'of the violence which underpins power as such. Blatantly drawing on this violence, Thatcher legitimates and encodes it (the real risk of fascism) but she also lays bear the presence of violence at the heart of the socio-symbolic order'.[106]

Returning to *The Crying Game*, 'the presence of [Jude's] violence' evokes a metonymic link to 'a gun in her handbag'.[107] A similar metonymic link occurs with Thatcher, the presence of whose violence involved 'leading with a handbag'.[108] Indeed, on 5 July 2000, the *Daily Mail* emphasized the metonymic link of Thatcher-as-handbag with a report claiming that 'Baroness Thatcher's *stern black* Salvatore Ferragamo had gone up to £63,100 after just two days of bidding' at an auction [my italics].[109] In this sense, even though Jordan is Irish, his depiction and casting of Jude (as a British virago) is perfectly logical at an ideological, political, and psychological level. Fittingly, if paradoxically, during the 1980s it was Thatcher who became 'the boldest and most unmanageable revolutionary', tearing up the post-war social consensus, waging a pitiless war against every form of resistance, championing 'Victorian values' and insisting that Northern Ireland was 'as British as Finchley'.[110] Within fiction, film and the press, Vampira images flourished under the reign of Thatcher. Operating according to the Moebial structure of the law that enables it to function, ideologically, in the very image of its antithesis, Thatch-

---

105 Ibid., p.17.
106 Ibid.
107 Giles, *The Crying Game*, pp.61, 62.
108 'Handbagged', *Daily Mail*, 5 July 2000, p.22.
109 Ibid.
110 Dennis Kavanagh and Anthony Seldon, *The Thatcher Effect: A Decade of Change* (Oxford: Oxford University Press, 1989), pp.232, 239.

er's unmanageable, charismatic, transgressive 'lawlessness' paradoxically held together a highly authoritarian, right-wing regime.
Similarly, in the propaganda war between the British government and
the PIRA, Vampira can be seen to have been recruited to fuel the
abject fear and hatred of women (including Thatcher herself), that
characterized Britain under the reign of the first woman Prime
Minister, and to use that fear and hatred to galvanize Britain's
terrorized subjects to endorse and enjoy the violence deployed not just
against Irish Republicanism, but against 'the enemy within' in
whatever form it took.

3.4: The Mother of Suffering and Desire

> Lord thou art hard on mothers:
> We suffer in their coming and their going:
> And tho' I grudge them not, I weary, weary
> Of the long sorrow – And yet I have my joy:
> My sons were faithful, and they fought.[111]

Some Mother's Son is a film directed by Irish the film-makers Terry
George and Jim Sheridan. It commences with real news footage showing Thatcher delivering a speech brimming with Iron Lady rhetoric
and words borrowed from Saint Augustine.[112] The film concerns the
moral dilemma of the mothers of the 1981 hunger strikers. Their
dilemma is about whether or not to permit their hunger striking sons to
starve to death, a maternal trauma which the film's audience suffers
by proxy. Incidentally, as Saint Augustine was a famous hunger
striker, Thatcher's identification is rather ironic. This point aside, the
news footage clearly portrays Thatcher in her role as a British patriot
and a symbol of the British law. 'Crime is crime is crime', proclaims

---

111 Patrick Pearse, 'The Mother', in Ruth Dudley Edwards, *Patrick Pearse: The
     Triumph of Failure* (London: Victor Gollancz, 1977), pp.262–3.
112 *Some Mother's Son*, Dir. Terry George and Jim Sheridan, Rank, 1996.

194

Thatcher, 'the Lady is not for turning'.[113] As the courtly yet formidable Lady, Thatcher's refusal to submit to the hunger strikers' demands resulted in '*ten men dead*'. Yet, while these men sacrificed their lives, Thatcher sacrificed her own morality as a nurturing mother. Paradoxically, however, Patrick Bishop and Eamonn Mallie recall how the hunger strikers' misrecognition of Thatcher actually contributed to their deaths.[114] The hunger strikers 'persistently misjudged [Thatcher's] strength of will', write Bishop and Mallie, 'and credited her with a maternalism [...] that anyone outside the Maze prison would have found extraordinary'.[115] Rather than condemn her gender role breaking, 'the English press' hailed 'the immediate aftermath of the hunger strike [...] as a triumph for [...] Thatcher'.[116] 'The *Daily Mail*', observes Beresford, 'described' her stance as being a '"magnificent obstinacy" [whereas] the *Sunday Express* [hailed] a victory for common sense and firm moral purpose'.[117]

It might be claimed that Thatcher's sacrifice of the maternal relieves the British unconscious of the traumatic effect of the hunger strikes. This is because the law as Thatcher always functions more effectively if flawed. So, while the British press championed Thatcher's heroic intractability, 'inside' the H-Block prison she 'enjoyed pride of place [...] on a wanted poster declaring her a fugitive from justice for "murder and torture"'.[118] Yet, in spite of the prisoners' condemnation of Thatcher, blame for the hunger strikers' deaths became somewhat displaced from Thatcher on to the mothers of the starving PIRA sons. For instance, 'the *Sunday Times* published a bizarre report' asserting that the mother of Raymond McCreesh was 'egging Raymond on to his death'.[119] In both British and Irish male-authored fiction, negative representations of Irish mothers augment this blame; invert images of ideal Irish mothers or female auxiliaries to the PIRA and transform

113 Extract from Margaret Thatcher's speech in relation to the Hunger Strikers.
114 Patrick Bishop and Eamonn Mallie, *The Provisional IRA* (London: Corgi, 1988).
115 Ibid., p.375.
116 David Beresford, *Ten Men Dead* (London: Harper Collins, 1994), p.428.
117 Ibid., p.429
118 Ibid., p.239.
119 Ibid., pp.219, 220.

them into crones who are, in turn, allocated to the lumpen female faction. Contemporary to the Hunger Strike, ex-British squaddie Alan Judd's 1981 novel, *A Breed of Heroes*, portrays crones who are also domestic drudge auxiliaries.[120] Judd writes about 'dirty [...] lazy [...] harridans', Irish women who spike British soldiers' 'tea [with] urine'.[121] While for Irish, yet anti-republican, author Sean Herron, these females are 'fat women jigg[ing] around [a Belfast] lamp-post with their skirts hauled high, big putty thighs bouncing and jiggling like sows' bellies'.[122] Such images of grotesque Irish maternal obesity offer a stark contrast to images of emaciated Irish sons. And the implication of this contrast is fairly obvious. While PIRA sons starve to death, PIRA mothers revel in gluttony and metaphorically 'eat [their] own farrow'.[123]

Linked to these notions, in 1996, 'a mock documentary' entitled *1981* followed an agenda which attempts to 'domesticate [...] the enormity of historical events' presented by the hunger strike in a more pro-Irish republican and pro-maternal way.[124] Hand-in-hand with its desire to domesticate, the film 'proposes a "universal, common humanity"' but, according to Martin McCabe, 'fails because it doesn't interrogate its politics of representation' and instead relies upon 'spurious "objectivity"'.[125] Alternatively, the 1981 Irish hunger strikers, Thatcher, and the female body are analysed at a more sophisticated level within Maud Ellmann's text: *The Hunger Artists*.[126]

Following Lacan's ideas about the power of the gaze, Ellmann suggests that 'as the eye grows fat the world grows thin, starved by its insatiable stare' (104). For Ellmann, 'in the Irish Hunger Strike the prisoners were starving for the eyes of Mrs Thatcher, which she kept

---

120   Alan Judd, *A Breed of Heroes* (London: Hodder and Stoughton, 1981).
121   Ibid., pp.191, 71, 192, 194.
122   Sean Herron, *The Whore Mother* (London: Jonathan Cape, 1973), p.19.
123   Klaus Lubbers, 'Irish fiction: A Mirror for Specifics', *Eire-Ireland*, 20.2 (1996), 90–104 (p.92).
124   Martin McCabe, *Circa* (1996), [n. num.], [n. page]. Article supplied by The Linenhall Library, Belfast, 1997.
125   Ibid., p.6.
126   Maud Ellmann, *The Hunger Artists* (London: Virago, 1993). Further consecutive references to this edition are given after quotations in the text.

196

intransigently shut' (104). Ellmann discusses how both Thatcher and the hunger strikers 'were equally misled by sexual stereotypes' (104). For instance, when Thatcher asked if the prisoners were starving in order 'to prove their virility', she confused 'political impotence [with] sexual unmanliness' (104). Thus, 'by misreading the Irish [male] body she symbolically castrate[d] it' (104). As mentioned earlier, the prisoners' mistake about 'sexual stereotypes' occurred during the early stages of their protest when they credited Thatcher with a profound maternalism (104). Following John Berger, Ellmann claims that, upon realizing 'their error, [the prisoners] dubbed Thatcher "Tinknickers": an honorific that resembles the politer epithet "The Iron Lady", yet also brings [a] latent obscenity to light' (104).[127] This obscenity concerns the way in which the nickname 'is revealing [because] the atrocities of male politicians are usually imputed to their brains, whereas [...] Thatcher's were imputed to her genitals' (104). Equipped with the 'phallicism of these nicknames', Thatcher became 'defeminized by her rigidity [and a] power [indebted] to [the] outstiffening [of] her soft and unmetallic sisters' (104). Moreover, Ellmann suggests that the epithet 'Tinknickers [...] implies retentiveness as well as chastity [because] if nothing can get into her tin knickers, it is equally the case that nothing can get out' (105). For Ellmann, this idea can be linked to the 'dirty protest', an event that preceded the Hunger Strike (104).

The dirty protest involved the prisoners smearing their own excreta on their prison walls and their refusal to wash; a defiance of Thatcher's call for a return to Victorian values in which 'cleanliness is next to godliness'; the corollary of this being 'incontinence is sinful'. For Ellmann, 'Thatcher's tin knickers [...] symbolize the law of continence, which defines the boundaries of the body and initiates the infant into culture' (105). 'In fact', writes Ellmann, 'the continent body represents the prototype of prisons and of all the other limits [...] that define the social space' (105). This means that 'by refusing food and cleanliness and even clothes, the prisoners were attacking this demonic mother of confinement with the most effective and indeed the only weapons of the child' (105). So, 'knickerless themselves, [the

127   See also Beresford, *Ten Men Dead*, p.130.

PIRA] were rejecting the most primal signs of cultural inscription' (105). And this cultural inscription includes 'maternal authority'.[128]

According to Kristeva, 'maternal authority is experienced first and above all, after the first essentially oral frustrations, as sphincteral training'.[129] Bearing this point in mind, although Thatcher ensured the prisoners' oral frustrations continued on to a fatal climax, these doomed Irish men can be seen to have rebelled against their punitive British mother's 'sphincteral training'.[130] However, Ellmann forwards an argument which implies how to some extent the hunger strikers, metaphorically, 'changed sex'. For instance, Ellmann observes that 'hunger [...] de-genders the body': and her quotation from Wole Soyinka, a man who went on 'hunger strike [in a] Nigerian prison', makes this evident.[131] 'I made a strange discovery this morning', says Soyinka, 'I'm pregnant' (cit. Ellmann: 14). Ellmann describes how Soyinka experienced 'his lower body [...] swollen up as if he had "secreted a large egg just beneath the skin" to fill the corresponding chasm in his trousers' (14). This type of feminization of the male body through starvation is especially relevant to the Irish hunger strikers because 'the power of starvation depends upon its visibility' (67). The high level of media coverage prompted by the 1981 Long Kesh 'starvation' certainly guaranteed the Irish hunger strikers' 'visibility'; a public spectacle symptomatic of 'masquerade' (66). Hence, again following Berger, Ellmann claims that 'the prisoners in Northern Ireland were feminized by their starvation in that their bodies were transformed into images of meanings [or masquerade] rather than instruments of acts' (71, 72).[132]

Developing her argument, Ellmann suggests that 'in the Kesh, the male body was more prized for its interiorities than for its protuberances' (84). Like Kebbe's Vampira, whose vagina is depth-

128   Kristeva, *The Powers of Horror: An Essay on Abjection*, p.71.
129   Ibid.
130   Ibid.
131   Ellmann, *The Hunger Artists*, p.14. Further consecutive references to this edition are given after quotations in the text. See also Wole Soyinka, *The Man Died: Prison Notes* (London: Arrow, 1985), p.215.
132   See also John Berger, *Ways of Seeing* (London: British Broadcasting Corporation and Penguin, 1972), p.47.

charged with explosives, 'depth rather than length became the measure of genital superiority' (84). The importance of depth is evident at a literal level because 'the prisoners would tuck their comms (messages) behind their teeth, jam them up their nostrils, or stuff them up their rectal passages' (84). Indeed, 'one prisoner was reported to have set the record by carrying forty cigarettes in his foreskin [while] another [smuggled] a miniature radio, a wad of comms, tobacco, a camera, and [...] a Parker pen refill [...] in [...] his anus' (84). Quasi-pregnancy, masquerade, objectification in terms of the gaze, and valuation for depth rather than length; in some respects the male inmates of Long Kesh do seem to have been transformed into female and abject Vampira. 'The horrors of the mirror search' reinforce this premise (85). During the 'mirror search', a 'humiliating' ordeal, the aptly named 'screws [...] would force the prisoners to squat over a mirror [while] a metal detector was used to inspect the anus' (85).[133] As this British interrogation of the Irish body is, I argue, akin to rape, once again the male prisoners' bodies are 'feminized'.

Earlier in this section, I suggested how the blame attributed to Irish mothers for their sons' starvation is intensified by representations of obese mothers and emaciated sons. Ellmann problematizes this idea nicely through her interpretation of the paradox that obesity is another form of starvation. In her reading of American female author 'Mary Gordon's powerful first novel, *Final Payments* (1978)', Ellmann suggests the female protagonist 'experiences fat as indeterminacy rather than solidity' (49, 50).[134] 'Paradoxically', writes Ellmann, 'she experiences her enlargement as a form of self-erasure, as if she were eclipsed by her own fat, effaced by her own face' (50). Therefore, Herron's 'fat women [...] with their skirts hauled high [and] big putty thighs bouncing' are not necessarily vampirically feeding off their feminized PIRA sons' flesh. Instead, these Irish mothers' grotesque obesity could be 'symptom[atic]' of their unconscious 'desire [...] to [symbolically] incorporate' their wasting sons' bodies 'in order to deny [their] loss' (50). In a similar way to Gordon's heroine's reaction

---

133   See also Tim Pat Coogan, *On The Blanket: The H-Block Story* (Dublin: Ward River, 1980), pp.9–10.

134   See Mary Gordon, *Final Payments* (New York: Ballantine, 1979).

to the death of her father, it is possible that the hunger strikers' mothers were 'bingeing [...] in honour of [their sons'] faith' and the Catholic interpretation of the Eucharist, whereby the bread and wine are not supposed to *symbolize* the Saviour but actually to *be* his body and blood' (50). For the hunger strikers and their mothers, this 'faith' of course included political faith in the Irish Republican Cause and, importantly, Mother Ireland.

Representations of Mother Ireland summon fantasy figures like genies from a lamp, are projections akin to Edmund Burke's idea that 'Ireland is England's unconscious'.[135] These archetypal figures stalk the late twentieth century, and will, no doubt, endure throughout the twenty-first century. The following explores how and why these figures are products of the, specifically male, British and Irish cultural unconscious.

Immaculate, punitive, hideous and rapacious, Mother Ireland is ambivalent, maternal yet terrifyingly imperious, a chastising superego within the male psyche. In film and fiction, such as Sean Herron's *The Whore Mother* (1973), she is both a castrating and nurturing mother. Whereas, in Anglo-Irish author Martin Waddell's *A Little Bit British* (1970), she is a monstrous and mad Republican mother.[136] In Scottish author Eugene McCabe's *Victims* (1976), she is an authoritative, demon mother.[137] And, as mentioned earlier, in Terry George's *Some Mother's Son* (1996), she is a good-mother versus bad-mother.

Underlying more glamorous yet equally deadly imagoes, such as the 'dangerous seductress' or *'femme fatale'*, Mother Ireland has a long history which relates to the structure of myth and witchcraft whereby 'witchcraft confronts us with ideas about women, with fears about women, with the place of women in society [...], with women themselves [and] with systematic violence against women'.[138] Allegorical figures manifested by the Furies and the witch-whore named

135 Declan Kiberd, *Inventing Ireland* (London: Jonathan Cape, 1995), p.17.
136 Martin Waddell, *A Little Bit British* (London: Tom Stacey, 1970).
137 Eugene McCabe, *Victims: A Tale From Fermanagh* (London: Victor Gollancz, 1976).
138 Carol F. Karlsen, *The Devil in the Shape of a Woman* (New York: W.W. Norton, 1987), p.xii.

Acrasia, seen by recent Renaissance critics as Spenser's allegory of the seductive charms of Irish women in *The Faerie Queen*, do of course form part of this history.[139]

At an unconscious level, like the PIRA 'Mother Ireland' is both marginal yet mainstream, extimate yet intimate, good yet bad, and frequently the abject Other. Canadian author Lionel Shriver seems to acknowledge this fantasy within her novel, *Ordinary Decent Criminals*, when she portrays a west Belfast that is populated with 'the haggard pre-Jane Fonda generation of housewives'.[140] Moreover, like the male PIRA and Vampira, Mother Ireland often supplies British identity with an inverted mirror image, a mercurial image that effects specific ideological viewpoints about Ireland and Irishness, especially north of Ireland Republican Irishness. These viewpoints emerge through the imagining of a maternal other, an imagining that coincides with various failed attempts to establish an ideal, predominantly male, British identity, an imagining that coincides with various acknowledgements of responsibility for the trauma of violent conflict taking place within the United Kingdom, and an imagining of the question: what does the (m)other want from me?

John Darby observes that from the mid-nineteenth century to the early twentieth century, cartoon images of 'the female figure who came to represent' the north of Ireland shifted from 'the mute and helpless Hibernia' to a creature displaying 'a distinctly shrewish aspect'.[141] A helpless Hibernia is shown in a cartoon that appeared in an 1866 edition of *Punch* where an image of a 'helpless Hibernia' begs advice and physical protection from a phallic Britannia, an armour clad Iron Lady, a predecessor of Thatcher, perhaps.[142] 'O, My Dear Sister', says Hibernia: 'What are we to do with these troublesome people?' 'These troublesome people' are, of course, the Irish. In

139   See Scott Wilson, *Cultural Materialism: Theory and Practice* (Oxford: Blackwell, 1995), pp.67–72.
140   Lionel Shriver, *Ordinary Decent Criminals* (London: Harper Collins, 1992), p.78.
141   John Darby, *Dressed to Kill: Cartoonists and the Northern Ireland Conflict* (Belfast: Appletree, 1983), p.27.
142   'The Fenian-Pest', *Punch, or the London Charivari*, 3 March 1866. Reproduced in Darby, *Dressed to Kill*, p.23.

the cartoon, Britannia responds by dumping British responsibility for Ireland back on to the distraught Hibernia. 'Try isolation first, my dear', says Britannia: 'And then –'. The reader can only imagine the rest. Here Hibernia complements Yeats's *Cathleen ni Houlihan* (1902), 'a pleasant and a kind woman, a wise woman, too [whose] face is mild and beautiful'.[143] Alternatively, the *Punch* cartoonist Bernard Partridge depicted Hibernia redefined into something more 'shrewish'.[144] The caption to Partridge's visual depiction reads: 'I don't much mind all this briar stuff: it's the lady at the end that makes me nervous'. This implies how, during the early twentieth-century, Mother Ireland emerged as being ferociously phallic and demonic, the earlier Britannia's alter-ego. Darby attributes this redefinition to 'the emergence of Ulster as a complicating element in British politics'.[145] I argue that Ulster also emerged as a complicating element in the British psyche whereby Ulster, a castrated yet terrifyingly phallic region of extimacy, symbolized both the self (Britannia) and other (Mother Ireland); the latter being a mutant fantasy figure of insatiable desire. Darby observes how 'since 1969 [...] events in the' North of Ireland have inspired 'thousands of political cartoons'.[146] Newsworthy and female and Irish and Republican, Bernadette Devlin became a subject for these documents. According to Devlin, when the British media 'produce[d]' her as the '"baby of parliament" [...] everyone [...] invented their own little imaginary Bernadette Devlins. They called [her] St. Joan of Arc, and St. Bernadette, and the second Messiah, and God knows what other heresies'.[147] Cartoons from 1969 and 1970 suggest another Mother Ireland.

At Figure 3, David Langdon's submission to *Punch* shows Devlin appropriated by the British male gaze.[148] Young, demure, mini-

---

143 W.B. Yeats, *Cathleen ni Houlihan* (1902) quoted by Lubbers, in 'Irish Fiction: A Mirror for Specifics', *Eire-Ireland*, p.91.

144 Bernard Partridge, 'The Sleepless Beauty', *Punch*. Reproduced in Darby, *Dressed to Kill*, p.27.

145 Ibid., p.29.

146 Ibid., p.17.

147 Bernadette Devlin, *The Price of my Soul* (London: Pan, 1969), pp.171, 194.

148 David Langdon, 'It'll look a bit strange in "Hansard"', *Punch*. Reproduced from Darby, *Dressed to Kill*, p.34.

skirted, this Irish mother titillates yet disturbs the British establishment; an ambiguity announced by the caption: 'It'll look a bit strange in "Hansard" – The Hon. Member for Mid Ulster, bracket, long low wolf whistles, bracket'. Alternatively, in *Hibernia*, cartoonist J. Cogan supplies Devlin as a costumed superwoman, a modern mirroring of Britannia who announces: 'They seek me here, they seek me there, those Specials seek me everywhere'.[149] Also in *Hibernia*, Jim Fitzpatrick sketches an iconic Devlin, a beautiful Mother Ireland, a Celtic saint.[150] Heath went further than Fitzpatrick.[151] Thus, for the *price* of the *Spectator*, the reader glimpsed Devlin's sainted *soul*, an image of the actual 'apotheosis' of a celestial divinity. And, interestingly, in 1997 Ian Knox resurrected this celestial cartoon image for a depiction of Mo Mowlam – a British Mother Ireland.[152]

Shortly after 1970, the PIRA campaign together with Devlin's 'involvement in violence' demolished her positive 'stereotype'.[153] Especially for the British, the saintly Irish MP mother became the demon Irish criminal mother, a phallic female symbolizing the PIRA. Moreover, the British could not deny taking responsibility for the creation of this bad, this extimate, female threat. According to Devlin, 'to begin with [she] was the greatest publicity gimmick since Kraft cheese slices'.[154] However, Devlin notes, 'it wasn't long before people discovered the final horrors of letting an urchin into parliament'.[155] 'The British', writes Devlin, 'had shown what grand democrats they were' because 'anybody – even a Northern Ireland brat of twenty-two – was allowed to sit in their House of Commons'.[156] In a further

149 J. Cogan, *'they seek me here, they seek me there'*. Reproduced in *Hibernia*, 28 September 1969, p.24.
150 Jim Fitzpatrick, 'Bernadette Devlin', *Hibernia*. Reproduced in Darby, *Dressed to Kill*, p.35.
151 Heath, 'The apotheosis of Bernadette', *Spectator*. Reproduced in Darby, *Dressed to Kill*, p.35.
152 Ian Knox, 'War is Over (if you want it)'. Reproduced in *Fortnight*, December/January 1997/1998, front cover.
153 Darby, *Dressed to Kill*, p.36.
154 Devlin, *The Price of my Soul*, p.199.
155 Ibid.
156 Ibid.

parodying of British attitudes, Devlin adds: 'And what did these Irish peasants do, when you made them Members of Parliament and gave them £3,250 a year? They simply went off home and threw stones at you'.[157] Not surprisingly, then, Devlin was recreated.

In *Fortnight*, Dobson's caricature at Figure 4 shows her as a 'split personality', an image that is worthy of inclusion within *A Beginner's Guide to Lacanian Psychoanalysis*.[158] Ideal English rose, abject Irish thorn, the caption makes this clear: 'When she was good she was very, very good, But when she was bad she was horrid'. And finally, in *Riotous* Living, Rowel Friers's Devlin shows her as being a multiple personality through a triptych series of cartoon images: Devlin as Joan of Arc then Devlin as an Archetypal witch-bitch then Devlin as a Femme-fatale-cum-IRA-guerrilla.[159]

A similar transformation happened for the British MP Mo Mowlam whose demotion from saint to sinner is proclaimed by the headline: 'Outrage as Mowlam gives the IRA "a licence to murder"'.[160] So too with the headline: 'Blair's "revenge" on Mo deepens Ulster crisis'.[161] When the British accused Mowlam of being 'too close to the Republicans', she became the epitome of extimacy, a *British* Mother Ireland.[162] 'Too close to' the Irish enemy within and a potential threat to her British sons, Mowlam allowed British responsibility for the north of Ireland to be acknowledged then displaced onto a bad mother.

---

157   Ibid.
158   Dobson, 'A child's guide to Ulster politicians', *Fortnight*. Reproduced from Darby, *Dressed to Kill*, p.36.
159   Rowel Friers, *Riotous Living.* Reproduced in Darby, *Dressed to Kill*, p.37.
160   *Daily Mirror*, 27 August 1999, p.4
161   Simon Walters and Vincent Moss, 'Blair's revenge on Mo deepens Ulster crisis', *Daily Mirror*, 29 August 1999, pp.8, 9.
162   Ibid.

"It'll look a bit strange in 'Hansard'—'The Hon. Member for Mid Ulster, bracket, long low wolf whistles, bracket.'"

Fig 3: 'It'll look a bit strange in Hansard …' in *Punch*

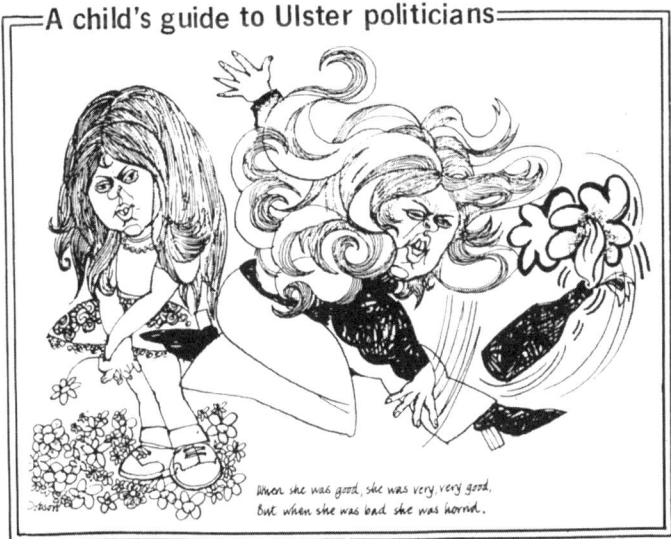

Fig 4: 'A Child's Guide to Ulster Politics' in *Fortnight*

The myth of Mother Ireland and the dilemma of her desire sustains dizzying metonymic repetitions and, ultimately, self conscious fictions. Satirizing this idea, and therefore subverting it, Irish novelist Robert McLiam Wilson portrays a fictive and eponymous tramp named Ripley Bogle who claims that 'all [...] Irish women [are] particularly hideous and [...] my mother was no exception'.[163] 'She's probably dead now,' ponders Bogle, 'I like to think [so] I don't quite know why I bother with all this [...] semi-satire [and] demi-truth [which is] the hard half of nothing'.[164]

Semi-satire. Demi-truth. The hard-half of nothing. These terms describe Bogle's image of a bad Irish mother, a hysterical harridan repeated in British documentary programmes such as *The Troubles* which shows 1970s news footage of abject Irish mothers who yell 'you bastards, you cunts' at the British Army.[165] Legally prevented from filming the PIRA, bad Mother Ireland seems to have offered a substitute. Consequently, these same images of Belfast housewives have been hysterically repeated in subsequent television documents.

Another 'demi-truth', the impossibly good Irish mother, is supplied through an interview conducted by Elizabeth Shannon.[166] During this interview, the mother of a 'Provo' is described by another woman who says: 'the mother thinks he is wonderful, only a wee bit misguided. If he just wouldn't kill people, he'd be a fine lad altogether'.[167] This woman goes on to say: 'Oh, he's his mother's darling, alright [...], an Irish mother has to be subservient to a man. [...] He could rape, plunder, steal, and murder, and at the end of the day he is still her darling son and therefore she will stand by him'.[168]

The diversity of the above examples suggests how and why not only British but also Irish readers and audiences might regard Irish women as being either good sufferers or bad sacrificers. Therefore, it is not particularly astonishing that, eventually, Thatcher functioned

---

163   Robert McLiam Wilson, *Ripley Bogle* (London: Picador, 1989), pp.7, 8.
164   Ibid.
165   *The Troubles*, Thames, Channel 4, 1981 (repeated 1989).
166   Elizabeth Shannon, *I Am of Ireland* (Boston: Little, Brown, 1989), p.108.
167   Ibid.
168   Ibid.

within this economy of motherhood. But, as mentioned earlier, her words condemning the hunger strikers ('crime is crime is crime') summon an inexorable and punitive British maternal figure. So too, a 1988 cartoon from the *Guardian* which portrays a trench-coated gun-toting Thatcher shooting a reporter for daring to question the legal status of the SAS assassinations of three PIRA activists in Gibraltar.[169] Stood beside the dead reporter, her captioned words, 'Now you can see why Our Boys might not bother to challenge!', actually equate her with the PIRA as well as a fatal phallic mother. However, a documentary film featuring Mairead Farrell, entitled *Mother Ireland*, evokes the punitive 'maternal metaphor' as a symbol for Irish Nationalism and 'makes the [British] law "regress" towards a ferocious maternal superego'.[170] Ironically, though, during *Mother Ireland*, Mairead Farrell's overtly feminist discourse criticizes such stereotyping of Irish women (Farrell was in fact one of the victims of the Gibraltar shootings by the SAS).[171] Speaking on the film, the Irish female director, Anne Crilly, claims that: '*Mother Ireland* explores the development and use of images and music which personify Ireland as a woman in Irish culture and nationalism'. These images occur in fiction where an extreme variability is manifested by the annexing of the Irish mother who is scape-goated on every side because the M(other) as Other is, ultimately, always 'the one to blame'. Accordingly, the remainder of this chapter shows how Mother Ireland informs British and Irish Troubles novels; reinforcing how gender issues can merge with political issues to conjure phallocentric narratives seeped in male paranoia about women.

Mary Beckett's *Give Them Stones* declares Ireland's 'wicked stepmother' to be 'England'.[172] But in many Troubles novels this 'wicked' female presence is often the desiring and hideously revenging spectre lurking behind and determining male paramilitary

169   *Guardian*, 1 April 1983, [n. page]. Cartoon held within the Linenhall Library, Belfast.
170   Slavoj Zizek, *Looking Awry: An Introduction to Jacques Lacan through Popular Culture* (Cambridge, MA: MIT, 1992), pp.97, 99.
171   *Mother Ireland*, Dir. Anne Crilly, Derry Film & Video, 1988.
172   Mary Beckett, *Give Them Stones* (London: Bloomsbury, 1987), p.121.

action. For instance, she is a castrating and malevolent species of Kathleen Ni Houlihan depicted in James Carrick's novel, *With O'Leary in the Grave*.[173] So too in James Barlow's novel entitled *Both Your Houses*.[174] 'This bloody country reaches out and drags you into itself,' writes Carrick, 'Like an old whore she is hungry for men'.[175] There is little doubt about the voracious desire of Carrick's 'old whore [because] when she gets [her men] she drains them of their manhood'.[176] So, according to Carrick's narrative, 'the Irish are a race of eunuchs and that's what it's all about'.[177] Barlow invents an Irish son named Tumulty whose Irish mother instils him with 'a romantic prejudiced view of his father's activities in the Border skirmishes of the late 1950s as well as a reminder of 'his death, at which she had been present'.[178] 'She could talk as powerfully as Tumulty', writes Barlow, 'and had rooted deep in her son's mind an impression of lorry loads of heroic patriots'.[179] Tumulty's Irish mother's 'nerves never broke. On the contrary, she'd grown heavy and bitter'.[180] Alternatively, Irish author Sean Herron's *Through the Dark and Hairy Wood* portrays an Irish gunman ('Dew-Boys') assailing Ulster's history as 'the comedy of Ulster's tragedy' and then enacting revenge upon his mother.[181] Herron's antipathy towards the PIRA has been commented upon previously. But it is interesting that his fictive gunman's revenge is a symbolic gelding of the maternal phallus which he performs because his mother 'was a flax-spinner's genteel wife [and] thought the only way to live was to lick the arses of your betters'.[182] In both life and death she is guilty of a failure to epitomize Dew-Boys' desires: a saintly and sacrificing Kathleen Ni Houlihan for

173 James Carrick, *With O'Leary in the Grave* (London: Heinemann, 1971).
174 James Barlow, *Both Your Houses* (London: Hamish Hamilton, 1971).
175 Carrick, *Both Your Houses*, pp.76, 77.
176 Ibid.
177 Ibid.
178 Barlow, *Both Your Houses*, pp.179, 181.
179 Ibid.
180 Ibid.
181 Sean Herron, *Through the Dark and Hairy Wood* (London: Jonathan Cape, 1972), pp.166, 197.
182 Ibid.

her son. Hence, when Dew-Boys is asked, 'why do you grow those Biblical plants?', he says, 'my mother. She used to grow them. [...] I hated the bitch. [...] Every time I cut one I [...] cut the bitch's throat'.[183]

When British Tory MP Douglas Hurd penned a novel about the Troubles, he created a sinister, treacherous, and bizarrely English, Kathleen Ni Houlihan named Clarissa Strong – she is the daughter of a Brigadier and works 'in the Parliament office, specializ[ing] in Parliamentary questions about Northern Ireland'.[184] Her involvement in a plot to assassinate the Prime Minister (an act she attempts to perpetrate herself with a cross-bow) is fuelled by her desire for an IRA activist and her brainwashing by 'an Irish grandmother [...] on the mother's side of course'.[185] According to Clarissa's father:

> Grandmothers were the root of the troubles in Ireland. [...] They keep them at home, the Catholics I mean. [...] So there they sit by the fire, night after night, telling all the old stories, spreading all the old lies. That's why the different kinds of Irish go on hating each other [...] because it's granny they take it as gospel. It's the same in Sicily, virgins and vendettas and the Mafia [...].[186]

As a British and, importantly, female traitor who is spurred on by sexual desire and a vindictive Mother Ireland, Clarissa's fate is sealed within this type of narrative. Consequently, she fails in her mission to kill the Prime Minister and dies a gruesome death 'in silence, half-way up Headington Hill'.[187] For Hurd, 'it is the novel rather than the academic work that is [...] the best medium for a political portrait with a political message'.[188] Arguably, though, such political portraits and messages about the conflict within the north of Ireland only serve to demonize the fantasy female Other.

This female imago is encoded rather more terrifyingly within Herron's novel, *The Whore Mother*, where, rather than being the hamletian 'whored mother', Mother Ireland is the 'whore mother'

---

183   Ibid.
184   Douglas Hurd, *Vote to Kill* (London: William Collins, 1975), p.14.
185   Ibid., p.109.
186   Ibid.
187   Ibid., p 213.
188   Ibid., vii.

revenger, a primordial and perpetual force.[189] For instance, early in Herron's narrative, 'the Springfield Women's Revenge Committee' are a female species described as being 'the terrible warlike women of Ulster [who] conceived hatred and vengefulness as they conceived children, and passed the venom in their blood' (23, 213). The novel's hero, Johnny McManus, falls foul of the PIRA. He is suspected of treachery and, together with a young boy, accused of informing then submitted to an interrogation. During the interrogation, a woman, whose 'bulky breasts [are] tied down against her rib-cage as if they [are] testimonies to crushed lust', threatens to geld the boy when 'she open[s] the boy's trousers and fumble[s] for his penis' (47, 48). Confronted with his 'shame and terror mingled', she takes out his penis and says: 'I could cut it off ye [...], Gimmie a knife' (48). Her depiction provides a castrating Mother Ireland and a desire that, in turn, summons a callously judicial manifestation of 'crushed lust'. She is a punitive and phallic superego, a terrifying revenger, an 'unnatural' beast-mother whose image becomes intensified through inversion when the boy announces his pitiful desire for his real mother: 'Ma [...] Ma [...] Mammy' (49).

McManus escapes across the Irish border to the countryside where he encounters a sexual nightmare. This happens after he becomes dangerously sick, plunges into unconsciousness, then is rescued by an older woman called Kate Burke. At first, he mistakes Kate for his real mother. This is made clear when he regains consciousness and discovers himself alone in a strange bed from where he 'hear[s] kitchen sounds' and imagines that he is 'a child in his own bed, curled securely in a safe and familiar place, enclosed in safe and familiar sounds' (150). He finds 'the bedclothes [...] deep and warm and reassuring', regresses to a state of infantile desire for the maternal other: '"Mammy", he said [...]. That was comforting too. His mother was close. He would call. He could hear. She would hear. She always heard' (150).

For McManus, the desire of the maternal other is grotesquely played-out when he becomes a helpless 'invalid [...] Child' to a

---

189   Sean Herron, *The Whore Mother*. Further consecutive references to this novel are given after quotations in the text.

210

maternal archetype who rehearses Carrick's 'old whore' vis-à-vis Mother Ireland (160, 167, 162). Eventually, his real mother's voice is displaced by 'her voice [and] her words' as well as her unfathomable physicality (167). 'How old was she?', thinks McManus, 'Forty? Forty-five? Fifty? It varied by the day' (162). Yet, at an unconscious level, Kate *is* his real mother in terms of a figure of impossible desire. This is evident when McManus regresses into being 'a mother's boy' whose new 'mother cradle[s] his head and put[s] her bra-less nipple to his hungry mouth. Child, she called him' (162). At first, Kate seems to gainsay Carrick's imago of a horrifying Irish, female incubus who 'drains' men of their 'manhood'. For example, we read that Kate 'gently [...] drew him and lay on her back, guiding his hand to her breasts [while] his senses birled in his head' (165). 'I'm a country,' she tells him, 'feel my hills' (165). And McManus obeys, 'grasp[s] her breasts frantically, [feels] the hard nipples in his palm, [takes] them in his fingertips [...], pull[s] his mouth from hers and suckle[s] the nipples like a feeding infant' (165). But her position as a good mother is false. Therefore, while declaring her status as Mother Ireland, she echoes Hamlet's bawdy pun to Ophelia about 'country matters'. And the 'country' is precisely the location where McManus encounters the ravenous maternal 'cunt' then becomes a Lacanian subject of this cunt's desire (166). McManus is an 'insatiabl[e] [...], resentful son and jealous lover' to the woman who is a 'Mother in the day, mistress at night' (166, 207, 204). 'The name they call me,' she tells him, 'is Cathleen the Whore-Mother' (222).

With Kate, Herron supplies an allegorical figure, a phallic Mother Ireland whose desire at both a literal and metaphorical level is rapacious, deadly and determines the fate of the male subject. This happens when McManus leaves Kate for 'Mother England' and a young woman called Brendine who is a 'happy little mother' (260, 265). Having once again alluded the PIRA, he imagines freedom whereby he can 'leap from past to future, from land to land, from skull of bard and thigh of chief to daughter company to mother company, leap from foot to foot, from old woman to young woman' (271). But he cannot escape the desire of Kate who, deserted by her 'child', resides alone where she psychologically inhabits 'some distant place [that is] created by a poet and storyteller' (222). 'We were born to self-destruction, child', says Kate (251). Her words are an omen, a hint of her status as McManus's hamletian 'strumpet fortune', the apotheosis of his desire. Now, her former sustenance mutates into a tormenting memory of 'consuming lust' which McManus tries to 'exorcise' through sex with Brendine (271). 'She was not Kate', thinks McManus, 'these were not Kate's strong cunning thighs, Kate's hips not these little hips were for lustful, luxurious wallowing, this little belly was not Kate' (271). But, in spite of his injunction to 'get out of my head, Kate. Let me go Kate', he cannot escape the desire of the Irish mother (271).

Interestingly, recalling *Jig* and *Cal*, *The Whore Mother* also supplies a protagonist who is a son to three very different but psychologically determining mothers: McManus's real mother as nurturer, Brendine as redemptive angel, and Kate as deadly whore-Mother Ireland. And all these texts show Mother Ireland as being the final and fatal determining matriarchal figure. For McManus, this happens at the end of the novel. At the same moment that he is shot dead by a PIRA assassin (Powers), he acknowledges Kate's absence as the presence of her inevitable vengeance: '*Piteous Jesus Kate no no no not you Kate*' (274).

Powers mocks his victim by calling him 'fuckin' Shakespeare' (279). Yet in Power's crazed psyche, McManus is 'resurrected' and reunited with Kate. This happens when an image of 'McManus' invades Powers 'head' and shows him 'standin' there w'his soft cock hangin' and his face twisted, lookin' like an eejit' (279, 280). But Powers is horrified when the image includes 'the widow-woman [Kate] with' McManus who is 'shoutin' [...] "Piteous *Jesus Kate no no not you Kate*"' (279, 280). Here, bizarrely, McManus's entreaty to the whore-mother is 'remembered' by Powers who, in turn, 'scream[s] [...] "*Get out of my head McManus!*"' (280).

McManus is punished for his treachery against Mother Ireland in terms of the PIRA, yes, but more so in terms of Kate. He suffers retribution through her determining desire. This desire is transferred to Powers whose hallucinations ensure that although McManus has been sacrificed for the cause, the desire of Mother Ireland remains alive and unabated. What does the [m]other want from me? Powers's reciting of

212

a prayer to the 'Motherland' implies that she wants further male sacrifice:

> O, Sacred Heart of Jasus!
> We pray to Thee today,
> To aid our sufferin' Motherland upon her bloodstained way.
> For loyalty to serve her,
> For strength to set her free,
> O, Sacred Heart of Jasus!
> We send our prayer to Thee! (280).

During his stay with Kate, McManus imagines her words sitting 'on his mind like a crow' (160). This nightmarish trope seems to have originated in Celtic mythology. For instance, Morrigan, the 'major [Celtic] goddess of war, of death and slaughter', symbolizes a revenging female whose 'favourite shape was that of a crow or raven'.[190] Morrigan 'embodied all that was perverse and horrible among the supernatural powers'.[191] Furthermore, her desire determined the fate of the mythic Irish hero named Cuchulainn because, after failing 'to incite Cuchulainn to make love to her [...], his fate was sealed'.[192] Indeed, 'when he was eventually killed, she settled on his shoulder in triumph in the form of a crow and watched while a beaver drank his blood'.[193] For McManus, it would seem, Kate is Morrigan, an Irish mother of horrifying desire made real.

In conclusion, Mother Ireland is the terrifying maternal metaphor of 'the old sow who eats her farrow'.[194] The texts discussed in this section suggest that the unfathomable desire of the Lacanian mother is perpetually manifested through narratives concerning the Troubles and Irish motherhood. Hence, manifested and repeated by various British and Irish male authors, these fantasy mothers ensure the

---

190 Peter Beresford Ellis, *A Dictionary of Irish Mythology* (Oxford: Oxford University Press, 1991), p.173.
191 Ibid.
192 Ibid.
193 Ibid.
194 'Old Sow who eats her farrow': Klaus Lubbers quoting 'Stephen Dedalus's bitter quip about Ireland'. Cit. by Klaus Lubbers, in 'Irish Fiction: A Mirror for Specifics, *Eire-Ireland*, p.92.

perpetuation of the question: what does the (m)other want from me? This again suggests that the dilemma concerning the desire of the (m)other is a crucial element of the, essentially male, human psyche, is some appalling Thing through which, paradoxically, the unfathomability of desire ensures desire will not become fulfilled in terms of death. At a political level, she preserves the north of Ireland 'as a hermetically sealed place [whereby] discrete cultural units [become] more Irish than the Irish, more British than the British'.[195] But at a psychological level, both Mother Ireland and her Vampira 'daughters' are the unattainable phallus. These female imagoes are scape-goats, not only for the British, but for the citizens of every 'Ireland' be they Nationalist or Loyalist. Thus, Mother Ireland and Vampira supply us with eternal repetitions of imaginary women who signal the Thing which is to blame, fear and desire.

195   Medb Ruane, Tribes and Prejudice, *The Sunday Times*, 27 July 1997, p.8.

Chapter 4
'It's the Valium talking'?: Fempira and Women Writing Back[1]

4.1: Politicizing the Private

> It's got a lot to do with the Troubles – a woman with 13 kids, the bother with sons at an age to join the IRA, the police and the army patrolling and searching […] it's no wonder the women are living on their nerves […] the doctors I worked for were well worried, but what could they do? Women really need the tablets.[2]

This last chapter of this study concerns 'women writing the Troubles' and compares female-authored fiction to male-authored thriller narratives about the conflict in the north of Ireland. As Christine St. Peter notes:

> What we discover in the North is how difficult it has been for Northern women to insert their 'voices' into the extravagantly militarized 'masculine' discourses that still predominate.[3]

Bearing St. Peter's comments in mind, I debate whether or not it is possible for female authors to avoid repeating fictions and stereotypes that privilege male national identity: an identity that encodes the male public and political sphere of the Troubles and subordinates gender issues. I ask the reader to consider whether or not such female authors can successfully appropriate the thriller and literary *realism* from the public domain of men, war and nation to then 'rewrite' the IRA and

1   Mary Costello, *Titanic Town* (London: Methuen, 1992), p.1.
2   Eileen Fairweather, Roisin McDonough, Melanie McFadyean, *Only The Rivers Run Free – Northern Ireland: The Women's War* (London: Pluto, 1984), p.36.
3   Christine St. Peter, *Changing Ireland: Strategies in Contemporary Women's Fiction* (London: Macmillan, 2000), p.2.

the Troubles from the perspective of the private domain of women, family and home. Crucial to this debate, and linked to previous observations about the dubious ideology of realism, is whether or not the repetition and foregrounding of negative aspects of the lives of working class women from the north of Ireland are politically enlightening, and therefore empowering, or merely a reinforcement of the patriarchal status quo.

For example, the opening title to this section contains a quote from novelist Mary Costello's *Titanic Town* – 'It's the Valium talking'. Whereas the quotation below the title is taken from a social historian study by Eileen Fairweather, Roisin McDonough, Melanie McFadyean: *Only The Rivers Run Free – Northern Ireland: The Women's War*. Before commenting upon *Only the Rivers Run Free*, there follows some observations about Costello's novel.

At various points in *Titanic Town*, Costello's female, first person narrator, Annie, refers to her mother's often hysterical, Valium-induced 'voice' that is a direct result of living in Belfast during the Troubles. This image of an emotionally fragile housewife appears to repeat a stereotype from male-authored texts. But, as observed by St. Peter, *Titanic Town* is 'a comic novel [...], a black humour mix of hilarious anecdote, caricatured characterization, and fictionalized history'.[4] Alternatively, then, it might be claimed that Costello attempts to 'address the absence of the female in the Irish comic tradition'.[5] This absence is highlighted by Theresa O'Connor who demands that we recoup the comic tradition in Irish women writers and thereby enable 'the occulted comic voices of women [...] to disturb and interrupt the writing of the [predominately male] Irish canon'.[6] Moreover, as *Titanic Town*'s subjects and objects of laughter are often female, Costello seems to complement a strategy that Hélèn Cixous advocates for women writers:

> Culturally speaking, women have wept a great deal, but once the tears are shed, there will be endless laughter instead. Laughter that breaks out, overflows, a

4   Ibid., pp.105–6.
5   Theresa O'Connor, *The Comic Tradition in Irish Women Writers* (Gainesville, FL: Florida University Press, 1996), p.2.
6   Ibid.

216

humour no one would expect to find in women – which is nonetheless surely their greatest strength because it's a humour that sees man much further away than he has ever been seen. […] And her first laugh is at herself.[7]

And her first laugh is at herself? These words hint at the prospect of there being a more positive interpretation of Annie's mother's 'Valium smile'.[8]

Throughout Costello's text, we can certainly detect Annie's narrative voice as being able to not only 'laugh at herself' but also laugh at the violence-ridden city of Belfast: a violence-ridden city that threatens the female domestic space of the home. Word-play contributes to this humour. For instance, in a chapter displaying the ironic title 'The Glamour of Violence', a young Annie sneaks off to watch 'the Orangemen marching' (13). Here, her companion, a boy named Terry, attempts to educate Annie about King William of Orange and The Battle of the Boyne:

> 'You see that banner? You know who that is?'
> […] The man had magnificent, long, curly hair and above his head waved a great hat with a long feather.
> 'Jesus?' I ventured. I knew Jesus had long hair.
> Terry roared with laughter. 'Jesus! Christ that's a good one. No, dopey! It's oul' King Billy. King William the Third. Their hero.'
> I remembered something about him. The bottle of the boing (13–14).

The pun concerning 'the bottle' is repeated when, during the march, Terry is hit on the head by a flying object which Annie thinks 'must have been the bottle of the boing' (15).

Wordplay is, of course, a key (not to mention hamletian) device for the disruption of the male symbolic order – in this case the, highly testosteroneized, male discourse of the Orangemen. Complementing this potential for disruption, although addicted to Valium Annie's mother is portrayed as being a feisty female who, against the wishes of her husband, tries to organize a peace movement, is *not* prepared to

---

7   Hélèn Cixous, 'Castration or Decapitation', in *Psychoanalysis and Woman: A Reader*, ed. Shelley Saguaro (London: Macmillan, 2000), 231–44 (p.243).

8   Costello, *Titanic Town*, p.240. Further consecutive references to this novel are given after quotations in the text.

sacrifice her sons to the Irish Republican Cause, and stands up to the PIRA when they threaten her domestic domain; this latter incident supplying another comic moment. So, when an inept PIRA sniper stations himself outside her home to shoot at a British Army helicopter, Costello provides a comic yet potent image of Annie's mother 'charg[ing] up the path, her dressing gown flapping candle-wick, the pink knickers bobbing on her head' (5). She even manages to chase the sniper away with the words: 'You get off this bloody path now or I'll shove that fucking gun up your arse' (5). There are several other moments in the novel where the private, domestic and female present an active foil to the public, political and male. Thus, Annie's Aunt Kathleen is jokingly described as 'a one-woman guerrilla campaign' (24) and 'a group of local women' join forces 'to improve living conditions' by keeping the Troubles (male violence) away from their homes:

> It seemed a harmless enough initiative – a group of local women getting together to improve living conditions. It would be like bingo, or the Con-fraternity of the Blessed Virgin, or like doing the nine Fridays. A little deft negotiation would do it nicely. The adjustment of a few timetables and every-body would be happy. The IRA could keep shooting and the women could keep shopping [...] (162).

On the one hand, it could be argued that the flippancy of this female point-of-view, a flippancy that equates 'shooting' with 'shop-ping', ingeniously undermines the phallocentric mind-set of the male dominated aggression that is prepared to sacrifice the domestic in favour of politics and national male identity. Yet, on the other hand, this female point-of-view could be regarded as being hopelessly naïve. After all, Costello's heroine does eventually concede that in spite of attempts to subvert patriarchy, it is still, ultimately, 'always the women who [stereotypically] suffer' (339). Further, Costello does tend to repeat other negative female stereotypes such as Mrs French, a 'dirty, throughother [and violent] sloven', who, in turn, repeats the Mother Ireland harridans identified in the previous chapter concerning *Vampira* (54). All this said, Annie's feisty mother and her companions do supply the reader with images of women who are forceful, defiant and spirited. And these more positive images of mothers are in contrast to those evoked within *Only the Rivers Run Free*. Totally dependent upon Valium, 'mother's little helpers', the women described in *Only the Rivers Run Free* are passive victims of the Troubles, confronted with a social, economic and political impasse they cannot breach.[9] Paradoxically, then, Costello's 'fiction' provides a more ambiguous portrayal of how women cope with male aggression than Fairweather and others' 'fact'. Indeed, Stephen Howe has criticized the authors of *Only the Rivers Run Free* for being 'cheerleaders for armed Republicanism, bizarrely identifying its cause with that of women's liberation'.[10]

Women writing the Troubles versus men writing the Troubles. As previously discussed in this study, when women do make an appearance in male-authored texts, they tend to conform to a series of stereotypes. These, we can recall, include the long-suffering domestic drudge, or, as Catherine Shannon notes, the repetition of clichéd figures churned out by 'the British tabloid press to portray northern women as passive victims of para-military mobsters or bomb-throwing viragoes and godmothers of hate'.[11] Then there is the *femme fatal*, or *'vampira'*, the fantasy female who splices Eros with Thanatos to 'give the male reader a good time' by proxy.[12] The work from women writers I discuss below submit attempts to challenge the stereotypical ways in which the north of Ireland has been written as a male text. Some of these attempts are successful, some less so. For instance, several of the female-authored novels considered in the following pages do (like Costello) partly reject patriarchal notions about a national identity which subordinates gender issues. Such novels also often attempt to *politicize the private* (the home, the body, the self) to thus create a more vigorous feminist agenda. However, in other

9   McFadyean, *Only The Rivers Run Free – Northern Ireland: The Women's War*, p.36.

10   Stephen Howe, Ireland and Empire: Colonial Legacies in Irish History and Culture (Oxford: Oxford University Press, 2002), p.188.

11   Catherine Shannon, 'The Woman Writer as Historical Witness', in *Women and Irish History*, eds. Mary-Ann Giclanella Valinis and Mary O'Dowd (Belfast: Wolfhound Press, 1997), 239–335, (241).

12   Jayne Steel, *'Vampira:* Representations of the Irish Female Terrorist', *Irish Studies Review*, 6.3 (1998), 273–83.

respects the narratives sometimes 'fail' at a number of levels. As with *Titanic Town*'s Mrs French, women writers from the north of Ireland are quite capable of reproducing the metonymic stereotypes so far identified within British and Irish male-authored thriller novels. Here, we might look to female and British author Doris Lessing's 1985 novel entitled *The Good Terrorist*.[13]

Lessing's novel is set in London during the 1980s and rampant right-wing Thatcherism. The narrative centres upon a commune of young, disaffected British men and women who are prepared to attach themselves to any political cause so long as it is anti-Tory and far left. Lessing's main protagonist is called Alice. From the beginning of the novel, it is clear that Alice's subjectivity and sense of identity is imposed by her parents and fellow commune dwellers so that she sees herself as the 'good woman', 'good girl', 'good daughter', and 'good terrorist': a female 'carer' who diligently cooks, cleans and 'mothers' the commune's shifting population.[14] Constructed by others, Alice's impossibly multifarious, ideal identity is of course a fantasy that she acts out in her imaginary 'Wonderland'; a highly domestic communal space where political stances are 'ready-to-wear' but have little bearing on reality.

The other characters in Lessing's narrative include upper middle-class, intellectuals, quasi-revolutionaries and feckless working-class would-be-anarchists. And various objects displayed in their slum house dwelling makes the ridiculously hybrid nature of their politics evident. For example:

> A picture of Lenin was on the wall opposite the flag. Next to Lenin, and several times the size, was a poster of a Whale: 'Save the Whales!' On other walls posters said: 'Save our Countryside!', 'Remember the women of Greenham Common!' and an IRA poster with a picture of a British soldier hitting a young boy whose arms were tied. On a table in the hall were pamphlets: 'The case for the IRA', all the Greenpeace pamphlets, several books about Lenin, a long poem in free verse about Greenham Common, a large variety of pamphlets from the Women's movement, and on vivisection, vegetarianism, the use of chemicals in foodstuffs, Cruise, Trident, the dumping of radio-active waste in

13   Doris Lessing, *The Good Terrorist* (London: Jonathan Cape, 1985).
14   Ibid., pp.22, 36, 46.

the sea, the ill-treatment of calves and chickens, and the conditions inside Britain's prisons.[15]

Notice how the 'picture of Lenin' is dominated by a 'Save the Whales!' poster, suggesting that the commune's affiliation with communism is merely paying lip-service to the actual political manifesto therein. Even more importantly, 'the case for the IRA' is counterbalanced with a sense of preserving Britishness: 'Save our Countryside!' – not to mention 'a long poem' about 'Greenham Common'.

Added to this, Lessing's characters and their, almost comical, political 'flirting' with various causes rehearse important stereotypes identified in *Dempira*. These, we can recall, include attempts to splice what are perceived as negative aspects of male Britishness (communism and homosexuality) with the IRA and Irishness. In *The Good Terrorist*, however, these attempts also fail. This is made apparent at various points in the narrative. For example, separated from the commune, it is the occupants of an adjoining slum who are the shadowy group of 'real' communists and 'real' Irish republican activists. And when Alice's erstwhile boyfriend (a scrawny and homosexual layabout) travels to Ireland to offer support to the PIRA, this support (and his Britishness) is promptly rejected by the movement. Ultimately, in *The Good Terrorist*, although British far left militancy and homosexuality is *associated* with communism and Irish Republicanism, this association is deconstructed to show that the British self cannot achieve a fully authentic identity from the fully elusive Irish other. As for Alice, psychologically submerged in an amalgam of political causes imposed on her *by* others, physically submerged in cooking and cleaning *for* others, she has little opportunity to fashion her own autonomous self.

Five years after publication of *The Good Terrorist* Britain was still in the grips of Tory rule and, consequently, another important stereotype that we can recall from *Dempira* emerged: the PIRA entrepreneur. This stereotype, as with Lessing's commune dwellers, signalled a displacement of rampant Thatcherism and therefore Britishness. Coincidently, first published in 1990, female author Lionel

15   Ibid., p.218.

Shriver's novel titled *Ordinary Decent Criminals* demonstrates how this stereotype is not just the preserve of the male imagination. Thus, Shiver shows how a character named Farrell O'Phelan appropriates the PIRA by 'sometimes' imagining the Army Council 'mapping out the year's campaign much like any advertising firm with a job to do'.[16] O'Phelan's Irish gunmen are not in fact 'ordinary decent criminals'. Instead, they are keen professionals who study 'foolscap black with crossed-out ideas [and], drumming their fingers, [seek] a new angle [while] racking their brains for a catchy gimmick to sell the Struggle like any other product whose billboards had gone stale'.[17] Here, O'Phelan constructs a PIRA work-party through images akin to a 1980s Saatchi-and-Saatchi-campaign. Written in the wake of the 1980s, Shriver's novel attributes the PIRA with the type of consumer conscious ruthlessness adopted by British Tory capitalist ideals that were contemporary to this former decade. Shriver presents the PIRA as 'an advertising firm with a job to do', a firm who needs 'a catchy gimmick to sell the Struggle' which is apoliticized into being a 'product'.[18] This 1990 PIRA is 'as hard to get into as the Malone Golf Club' and suffers 'paramilitary redundancies' inflicted by 'Big Daddy Provo'.[19]

Bearing the above examples in mind, can we locate writing by women that does not appropriate to just repeat stereotypes, especially the female stereotypes charted in *Vampira* and which Shannon identifies as being the 'sacrificial Mother Ireland'.[20] We have seen how Costello and Lessing appear to respectively supply an Irish and British sample of the 'sacrificial Mother'. But Shannon examines how women writers such as Anne Devlin offer alternative sites for female identification. Shannon discusses Devlin's 1986 play, *Ourselves Alone*, and explores how Devlin 'refuses to consider the hunger-strikers unblemished heroes' while, at the same time, portraying a

---

16   Lionel Shriver, *Ordinary Decent Criminals* (London: Harper Collins, 1992), p.128.
17   Ibid.
18   Ibid.
19   Ibid., p.189.
20   Shannon, 'The Woman Writer as Historical Witness', in *Women and Irish History*, p.251.

female character who 'rejects the whole republican enterprise by declaring her total indifference to the goal of Irish unity, and insists that British withdrawal will do nothing to liberate [women] from a life of service and sacrifice for their men'.[21] Historically, this life of service and sacrifice repeated in fiction is often linked to the private in terms of the home where women *service* men and *sacrifice* female autonomy at both a sexual and domestic level, where 'personal sacrifice' becomes 'a metaphor for general sacrifice'.[22]

When it comes to Irish women and history, Margaret Ward notes how 'men have written women out of history'.[23] 'Women are not', says Ward, 'seen as part of Irish history, and neither are the causes they fought for'.[24] Significantly, here, Liam Harte and Michael Parker observe how some novels:

> engage deeply with private and public histories in Northern Ireland, whose principle characters struggle for release from the disabling legacies of the past and challenge the legitimacy of received discourses of identity that have sustained the sectarian divide in the region.[25]

History and gender identity – these important social, political and cultural issues are, as we shall see, addressed by female novelists. Indeed, in the 'Author's Note' to *Titanic Town*, Costello writes:

> I don't pretend that *Titanic Town* contains all the facts of my life and times, but Annie McPhelimy is certainly part of me. [...] The story imposed its own form on character, events and circumstances, and shaped out the truth and untruths, misunderstandings, myths and rumours which, in Belfast, ferment into history.

This said, while some might champion the emergence of a 'female' discourse about history and gender identity, French Feminist theorists

---

21   Ibid.
22   Colm Tóibín, 'Martyrs and Metaphors', ed. Dermot Bolger, *Letters from the New Island* (Dublin: Raven, 1987), pp.44–55 (p.46).
23   Margaret Ward, *The Missing Sex* (Dublin: Attic, 1991), p.4.
24   Ibid., p.7.
25   Liam Harte and Michael Parker, 'Reconfiguring Identities: Recent Northern Irish Fiction', eds. Liam Harte and Michael Parker, *Contemporary Irish Fiction: Themes, Tropes, Theories* (London: Macmillan, 2000), pp.232–54 (p.233).

such as Julia Kristeva have 'deep suspicions of identity' as a fixed or singular concept and 'reject any idea of an *écriture féminine* that would be inherently feminine or female'.[26] For Kristeva, as a form of writing available to male *and* female authors *écriture féminine* can 'develop a notion of signifying practice [...] that covers both the [phallocentric] symbolic order of rational language [the domain of realism] and the marginal, repressed feminine discourses of poetry, irrationality, art and so on'.[27] Writing that draws upon fairy-tale, myth, the surreal, stream of consciousness, 'madness, the body, the uncanny, and female sexuality' can all be included here.[28] In terms of poetry, writing that utilizes devices such as rhythm and tone can unleash the repressed 'semiotic *chora*' which, in turn, can disrupt the symbolic order of language.[29] This theoretical approach also favours the dismantling of binary hierarchies which tend to privilege one concept over another: 'male over female', 'voice over silence', 'presence over absence', 'logos over pathos', 'head over emotion', 'reality over fantasy'.[30] So, while not totally abandoning literary realism or the material, these ideas from French Feminism might usefully support a methodological strategy that offers an alternative, less patriarchal, form of discourse. Moreover, this discourse could have the potential to breach repetitions of male-authored history and the social which become so normalized that other views are neglected.

This chapter has so far explored various methodological strategies in which novels concerning the Troubles and written by women may, or may not, offer alternative discourses to those written by men. Beginning with Jennifer Johnston's 1977 novel, *Shadows on our Skin*, the following sections develop these strategies.[31]

26   Madan Sarup, *Jacques Lacan* (New York: Harvester Wheatsheaf, 1992), p.142.
27   Ibid., p.141.
28   Ibid., p.143.
29   Ibid., p.141.
30   Ibid., pp.141, 133.
31   Jennifer Johnston, *Shadows on our Skin* (London: Headline, 2002).

4.2: How *not* to Appropriate Social Realism: Jennifer Johnston's *Shadows on our Skin*

> 'I know well,' said his mother. 'Nothing ever changes.
> It only gets worse'.[32]

Jennifer Johnston's novel, *Shadows on our Skin*, is set in a conflict-besieged 1970s Derry. Johnston's themes focus upon childhood, the Troubles, memory, the past (or history) and the domestic (the home). Published during the peak of the Troubles in 1977, *Shadows* is a product of its turbulent time. The narrative concerns a young Catholic boy, Joe Logan, who is growing up in a war-weary city where Provo snipers and army raids are everyday events. Joe's Dad is a bed-ridden, whining invalid who exists on cigarettes, beer and rose-tinted memories of his 'heroic' Republican past whereas Joe's Mum is a long suffering domestic drudge who works long hours both inside and outside the home. This ontological dichotomy between husband and wife is emphasized throughout during scenes in which Joe's Dad is shown reminiscing about the past while Joe's Mum cooks and cleans for the family. Lonely, unhappy, Joe befriends a young woman named Kathleen, a schoolteacher engaged to a British soldier. Not surprisingly, she asks Joe to keep her engagement a secret. Meanwhile, Joe's older brother, Brendan, returns from London and becomes involved with the PIRA. He also becomes romantically involved with Kathleen. Joe is jealous of his brother's relationship with his special friend and, in a fit of temper, informs Brendon about her fiancé. This results in Kathleen receiving a punishment beating from the PIRA – a result of Brendan's jealousy not, as he claims, his nationalistic loyalties to Irish republicanism. The novel ends with Kathleen leaving Derry and, of course, Joe.

The dubious plot aside, (Kathleen has moved from the South to Derry knowing that, because of her engagement to a British soldier, her life will almost certainly be in danger), does *Shadows* supply a gender politics that challenges more patriarchal representations of the

---

32   Ibid., p.43.

Troubles? Well, Johnston's Kathleen is no iconic ní Houlihan – the latter would never be engaged to a British squaddie. And her tongue-in-cheek version of a poem that mockingly links her name to 'Ireland' suggests she has no truck with notions about 'woman' being a symbol for 'nation':

> 'Kathleen Doherty is my name,
> Ireland is my nation
> Derry, referred to by some as Londonderry, is my dwelling place,
> And heaven, my destination'.[33]

All in all, then, it seems that Kathleen might supply the reader with a female image that is more subversive than male representations of mother Ireland figures. After all, she is a free spirit: Joe calls her 'mad', she admits to having 'no damn self-control', and, as noted by Ann Owens Weekes, thinks marriage is a 'mindless ritual'.[34] Weekes also highlights the fact that Kathleen is an orphan and, therefore, free from familial ties.[35] Further, although Kathleen is an English teacher, she rejects the rules of language and favours the semiotic *chora*, the pulses found in poetry and song:

> 'What do you teach?' [asks Joe]
> 'English ... at least that's what I'm supposed to teach. In fact I find myself spouting out whatever happens to be in my mind that day. Do you know what is a past participle?'
> 'No.'
> 'Or a semi-colon?'
> 'No.'
> 'Or why you mustn't split an infinitive?'
> 'No. No. No.'
> 'Neither do I. Nor do I think it matters much.'[36]

---

33   Ibid., p.28.
34   Ann Owens Weekes, *Irish Women Writers: An Uncharted Tradition* (Lexington, Kentucky: The University of Kentucky, 1990), p.60. Cit. Weekes, pp.31, 30, 198.
35   Ibid.
36   Johnston, *Shadows on our Skin*. Further consecutive references to this novel are given after quotations in the text.

Adding to her subversive mindset, Kathleen rejects religion and instructs Joe that he 'mustn't be too rigid about things. Look at every object with an open mind' (52).

Joe likewise struggles with the symbolic order. He finds Gaelic, a signifier of national identity, unfathomable and gets in trouble at school for writing poetry, a signifier of the imagination, instead of concentrating on 'equilateral triangle[s]' (29). In fact, the idea that language is unable to reliably construct the past or present is an important philosophical premise throughout the novel. As one of Joe's poems informs us:

> Words run
> In and out of your mind
> Like children playing.
> And then
> When you really need them,
> Like children,
> They disappear (200).

And, characteristically, Kathleen echoes Joe's viewpoint about language when she announces that 'words are aggravating, the way they hide on you when you need them most' (57).

As mentioned earlier, another important theme in Johnston's narrative is that of 'memory'. However, the memories in *Shadows* are male, not female, and these memories belong to Joe's Dad who tearfully languishes in a romanticized past colonized by republican heroes. According to Joe's Dad, this is a past where he 'was […] whole', suggesting that he is now symbolically castrated (39). This feminization, or infantilization, of Joe's Dad is emphasized when he weeps for lost youth and reminisces about a past that is a 'fairy tale' (39). The phoney nature of his memories (which are shared by Joe's elder brother Brendan) are fiercely denounced by his wife who recognizes that material inequalities are often ignored by male discourses:

> It's old buggers like you should be shot, with your talk and your singing of glory and heroes […] women [are] scrubbing floors to keep home together because stupid, useless old men are sitting round gassing about freedom? Singing songs about heroes? Take your bloody fairy tales out of this house (171).

It could be argued that such a rejection of patriarchal discourses (nationalism, religion, language and history) by Kathleen and Joe's Mum, together with the focus upon home and domestic, infuses *Shadows* with a potent feminist viewpoint. Indeed, according to Mark Mortimer, the narrative contains 'a powerful story' that is 'vivid compassionate and beautifully written'.[37] This may be so. Yet Weekes observes how Johnston rejects feminism on the basis that, like 'the Provisional Irish Republican Army', feminists 'alienate rather than gain […] support'.[38] Additionally, even though the novel was short-listed for the Booker Prize, in an interview with Richard York Johnston claims that *Shadows* is a 'wasted book'.[39] So, irrespective of Kathleen's and Joe's Mum's anti-patriarchal stances, might *Shadows* ultimately fail in terms of being a radical challenge to male-authored narratives?

Addressing this question, it could be suggested that the text's realism slams the door on female agency. For example, even though Joe's Mum despises her husband's romanticized Irish Republicanism, she still performs her relentless ritual of domestic duties and cannot escape the economic and working class shackles that bind her to her role as a domestic drudge performing 'menial tasks'.[40] What is more, although she attempts to prevent male-dominated and public violence from entering her female-dominated and private domestic space, this space eventually succumbs to such violence. This is apparent when the British Army raid the house and force her and Joe to leave their home while they search inside. Ironically, Joe's Dad is spared from being ejected from the domestic space because of his illness. As for Kathleen, although she and Joe are able to escape to the countryside, where Joe feels like 'God', this escape is short-lived. Thus, as mentioned earlier, when Brendan learns that she is engaged to a British soldier, he arranges for her to receive a punishment beating

---

37   Mark Mortimer, 'The World of Jennifer Johnston', *The Crane Bag*, 4.1 (1980), 88–94 (p.88).

38   Owens Weekes, *Irish Women Writers: An Uncharted Tradition*, p.30.

39   Richard York, '"A Daft Way to Earn a Living": Jennifer Johnston and the Writer's Art', ed. Bill Lazenblatt, *Writing Ulster: Northern Narratives*, no.6 (1999), (29–47), p.37.

40   Johnston, *Shadows on our Skin*, p.54.

after which she is forced to leave her home and Derry.[41] Here, rehearsing stereotypes of a demonic PIRA, Johnston supplies her reader with Irish republican racketeers and bullies who extort money from small businesses and beat-up women.

Disappointingly, then, it seems that Kathleen and Joe's Mum are unable to destabilize or escape the male-dominated, violent and public space of the social, political, national and the historical. Instead of offering an empowering alternative to female and working class oppression, Johnston merely repeats a role-call of stereotypes including the long-suffering domestic drudge, the female victim, the demonic PIRA, as well as the bitter and decrepit republican veteran (who is not unlike Eugene McCabe's hideous and invalid Irish republican mother in *Victims*). In *Shadows*, Irish women endure poverty, service men, forfeit material equality and suffer domestic as well as paramilitary violence for the 'good of the nation'.

According to Katie Donovan, however, *Shadows* succeeds as a text because it shows the realities about how 'children and women […] are […] innocent and passive victims of public machinations which are out of their control […]'.[42] Donovan goes on to claim that Johnston exposes the ways in which these children and women are 'caught up in their inner modes of escape [and] suffer more when these private worlds are intruded upon'.[43] For Donovan, Johnston targets 'the personal lives of [her] characters, so that the social is sacrificed for the sake of psychological realism'.[44] Yet, surely, and as I have argued throughout this study, when they are depicted as being inexorable such repetitions of the realities of a patriarchal stranglehold, be they social or psychological, only function to preserve the status quo. So, while I am not saying that these realities should be ignored, I am saying that they need to be challenged through the imagining of alternative outcomes, or choices, for women.

41   Ibid., p.104.
42   Katie Donovan, *Irish Women Writers: Marginalized by Whom?* (Dublin: Raven Arts, 1988), p.30.
43   Ibid.
44   Ibid., p.31.

For Joe's Mum: 'Nothing ever changes. It only gets worse'.[45] And if women who write the Troubles insist upon repeating the literary realism inherited from male authors, she might well have a point.

The next section looks at four novels from four women writers who all, in one way or another, also utilize 'realism'. However, unlike Johnston's *Shadows*, these novels summon more radical, more empowering, feminist narratives. The novels are: *One By One in the Darkness* by Deirdre Madden;[46] *No Bones* by Anna Burns;[47] *To Stay Alive* by Linda Anderson;[48] and *Give Them Stones* by Mary Beckett. [49]

4.3: More Subversive Tales To Tell …?

> 'Are you a Republican?' he asked and I shrugged. I was going to be a heroine but instead I said, 'I am a home baker.'[50]

Shifting from Johnston's city landscape, *One by One in the Darkness* concerns three sisters (Cate, Helen and Sally). As with Johnston's text, memory plays an important role. But the memories in *One by One* are not from the male and public realm of national identity or history. They are instead the childhood memories of the three sisters; memories steeped in the rural idyll of the domestic and home. And the importance of 'home' to the sisters is presented with the first word of the novel when Cate returns from London for a visit.

Home was a huge sky; it was flat fields of poor land fringed with hawthorn:

---

45   Johnston, *Shadows on our Skin*, p.43.
46   Deirdre Madden, *One by One in the Darkness* (London: Faber and Faber, 1997).
47   Anna Burns, *No Bones* (London: Flamingo, 2002).
48   Linda Anderson, *To Stay Alive* (London: The Bodley Head, 1984).
49   Mary Beckett, *Give Them Stones* (London: Bloomsbury, 1988).
50   Beckett, *Give Them Stones*, p.123.

And alder. It was birds in flight; it was columns of midges like smoke in a summer dusk. It was grey water; it was a mad wind; it was a solid stone house where the silence was uncanny.[51]

A close reading of this extract shows how Madden's writing of the private and domestic resonates with *écriture feminine* and the idea that less phallocentric discourses could emerge from a reconciliation between the symbolic and the semiotic. As the extract suggests, home is not just a phallic bastion, 'a solid stone house', not just, like the male symbolic order, an arbitrary structure. For Cate, home is also a natural space ('hawthorn and elder'), a free and fluid space ('huge sky, grey water'), an irrational space ('mad wind'), an anti-empirical space ('uncanny'); and a space that is not subordinate because it contains absence ('silence'). The prose style is also poetic – anaphoric repetitions of 'it was' supply the opening paragraph with a pulse, a rhythm, a semiotic *chora*.[52] And this recourse to the semiotic occurs at various points throughout the novel.

As mentioned, the narrative focuses upon three sisters: Cate is pregnant and works in London, Helen is a Belfast lawyer, and Sally is a schoolteacher who still lives at home with the sisters' widowed mother. All three are, therefore, women who have carved a certain financial independence, an independence that does not exclude the home, an independence that can still accommodate the domestic and private. Missing from this domestic space is Charlie, their father, whom is dead, having been murdered in error by Loyalist paramilitaries: a detail from the sisters' childhood not revealed until much later in the novel.

The structure of Madden's novel contains many flashbacks and, in consequence, disrupts the despotic linearity adopted by historical meta-narratives (an obstinate and historical linearity espoused by Johnston's depiction of Joe's Dad). With Madden, the use of flashbacks helps to create a more contingent past, a past that is constructed

51   Madden, *One by One in the Darkness*, p.1.
52   Interestingly, this feminist discourse of memories, sisters, plus a whimsical, quasi-magical, rural past recalls Brian Friel's play *Dancing at Lughnasa*. This observation suggests that Kristeva has a point about male authors being able to write the feminine.

and deconstructed through the female memory. Unlike the, ostensibly, objective histories served up by the media (which, in fact, 'tell only part of the story'), subjective memory is shown to come closer to 'the essence of things' such as 'time', 'society' and the 'self'.[53]

In terms of the self, Madden's text also challenges ideas about the nation being the main signifier of identity, a signifier that, as previously suggested in terms of the politics of the north of Ireland, is male. So, unlike the schoolteacher named Kathleen from Johnston's narrative, Cate rejects the iconic spelling of her name, changing the 'K' to a 'C' because the former is 'too Irish'.[54] And Cate's struggle towards a more autonomous identity has been commented upon by Michael Parker, who notes how 'we discover Cate […] examining in a mirror "the tiny invisible scar at her hairline", the result of an accident when she was six'.[55] For Parker, 'the scar figures as an originary emblem, lending the character "a sense of who she was, in a way that her reflection could not"'.[56] What Parker means here is that Cate's scar symbolizes a '[self-]defined' identity based on [female] agency, whereas the mirror returns just 'an image which "other people see"'.[57]

Although, initially, the sisters appear to be very different in terms of occupation and personality, they also have much in common. All are 'single' and devoted to their dead father, a gentle, non-violent man who, in contrast to Johnston's father figure, does not haunt their present through self-promoting and specious bygone heroism but, instead, through their own memories and dreams. The sisters also share a tendency to veer from the male symbolic (language) to the female imaginary (colour, art, and chaos), a tendency that deconstructs the public and private. For example, Sally's work-space, her school-room, is both public (in term time when populated with students) and private (in vacation time when she is the sole occupant). Moreover, her school-room is a delightfully chaotic space that is cluttered with a

53   Madden, *One by One in the Darkness*, p.60.
54   Ibid., p.4.
55   Michael Parker, 'Shadows on Glass: Self-Reflexivity in the Fiction of Deirdre Madden', *Irish University Review*, 30.1 (2002), 82–61 (95). Cit. Parker, p.2.
56   Ibid. Cit. Parker, p.2.
57   Ibid. Cit. Parker, p.2.

liberating childhood imagination. This childhood imagination portrays the domestic as a magical zone, displaying 'paintings of skewered mothers and fathers lolling outside vivid, pointed houses with trees like lollipops; [and a] list of words in colours written up in the colours themselves'.[58] As for Cate, she deconstructs the opposition between public and private to deal with the trauma of the past (her father's death) and the trauma of the present (the on-going political conflict). This happens when she imagines the building of a (public) monument to the dead that is akin to her memory of the (private) family home:

> She imagined a room, a perfectly square room. Three of its walls, unbroken by windows, would be covered by neat rows of names [...], and the fourth wall would be nothing but a window. The whole structure would be built where the horizon was low, and the sky huge. It would be a place which afforded dignity to memory, where you could bring your anger as well as your grief.[59]

Geraldine Higgins has also highlighted this image, claiming that the 'imagined memorial [...] suggests containment and interiority, [...] a window to the past [...] and an opening out, gesturing towards the future'.[60] Thus, Cate's feminine imagination succeeds in the unravelling of a number of hierarchal oppositions: public and private, past and future, past and present, inside and outside, confinement and freedom, culture and nature.

Even Helen, whose job as a solicitor conforms to the symbolic rule of law, has another, less regimented, side to her persona: in spite of her flat's 'clinical neatness', her bedroom is a wild zone of non-conformist chaos that displays 'a floor littered with unwashed coffee cups, compact discs, books and stray shoes'.[61] And, ironically, of all the sisters it is Helen, the pragmatist, who can 'slip into a fold in her mind somewhere between her dreams and her imagination' (178): 'By the force of her imagination she could lift herself out of her bed, and pass through the roof of the house like a beam of light passing through

58   Madden, *One by One in the Darkness*, p.137.
59   Ibid., p.149.
60   Geraldine Higgins, 'A Place to Bring Anger and Grief', *Northern Narratives: Writing Ulster*, 6 (1999), 143–59 (p.158).
61   Madden, *One by One in the Darkness*, p.45. Further consecutive references to this novel are given after quotations in the text.

water' (179). Rationality (the law) and the imaginary (dreams) are, for Helen, not polar opposites, are not diametrically opposed zones dividing the psyche into male and female. In some ways, then, Helen's psyche is probably the most compatible with ideas concerning *écriture feminine*. Helen straddles what are, culturally, politically and socially, often deemed to be distinct male and female realms and, to some extent, rejects taken for granted notions about the specificities of gender. Fittingly, then, the novel ends with Helen and her imagining of a past she did not witness, a past for which she has no 'evidence' – her father's murder:

> She saw her father sitting at Lucy's kitchen table, drinking tea out of a blue mug. She could smell the smoke of his cigarette, even smell the familiar tweed of his jacket [...]. And then they shot him at point-blank range, blowing half his head away (180, 181).

Here she creates a more detailed, more poignant and, arguably, more 'real' narrative of the murder than the so-called facts reported in the male-dominated media. Further, her narrative also defies historical linearity by bringing the novel, full circle, back to 'the solid house [where] the silence was uncanny [and] one by one in the darkness, the sisters slept' (181).

Madden's novel is, of course, a material product of a specific historical moment. First published in Britain during 1996, the story was composed at the same time as the declaration of the first IRA ceasefire in August 1994. But the *One by One* narrative unfolds just prior to the ceasefire and the Good Friday Peace Agreement. Arguably, though, the reader at the time of the publication might have brought a certain optimism to the novel that was based on a type of 'reality': the less volatile situation in the north of Ireland. But this is not the case for Madden's fictive sisters. Their present day reality within the novel contains no ceasefire. Rather, their reality remains haunted by the conflict of the 1960s and 1970s, their father's death and the recorded history of the Troubles: the transcendental, symbolic, and masculine narratives of the historian and the media. Thus, Madden inserts real events such as Bloody Friday and real political figures such Bernadette Devlin (129, 94).Yet, as with male-authored novels, no matter how graphic, the inclusion of these real events and real political figures cannot replicate the actual trauma experienced by those who suffered death or bereavement during the Troubles. As usual, language is not sufficient to the job. And Madden seems to be aware of this failure of language when she implies how the real trauma of the 1960s, 1970s and early 1980s (being shot, blown up, or beaten by paramilitaries) resists authentic repetition through the symbolic order, through media-speak, or through the language of fiction. Indeed, the bogus nature of the so-called facts, histories, or historiographies, articulated by the media are summed up by Helen when she recalls the press reports about her father's murder:

> Taking things and making stories about them [...], that's all it amounts to: making up stories out of a few facts and presenting them as though that interpretation was the absolute truth (50).

Ultimately, *One by One* contests ideas about absolute truth. Pertinently, then, the novel ends with silence, with absence, with the notion that contingent versions of the past and constructed or imagined memories are just as valid, perhaps more valid, than ostensible facts. And this silence, absence, contingent past, these imagined memories are, in *One by One*, perhaps somewhere that female voices might assert a certain autonomy and 'truth'.

Returning to a more urban setting, Belfast, we can now examine Anna Burns's 2002 novel: *No Bones*. Although Burns's actual storyline is very different to Madden's, *No Bones* is, like *One by One*, analogous to *écriture féminine*. For example, I will show how Burns destabilizes binary oppositions such as reality versus fantasy and madness versus sanity. She also focuses upon the female body and, like *Shadows*, childhood.

Short-listed for the 2002 Orange Prize, *No Bones* is a disturbing black comedy that splices grim literary realism to bleak surrealism so that the reader is never really sure whether or not the events being described are 'actually happening' or a product of the imagination (or madness) of the characters. These characters include the main protagonist named Amelia Lovett. However, unlike many of the thriller texts discussed throughout this study, the narrative does not conform to one monolithic point-of-view. Alternatively, different narrative voices (in terms of characters) and different points-of-view (in terms of first-person and third-person) are permitted to articulate their different versions of reality, including fantasy as reality. One such narrative voice belongs to a boy called Vincent who is undergoing psychiatric care for 'schizophrenia', a condition that is, in itself many-voiced and thereby challenges notions about the individual subject having one fixed identity.[62] So, when a psychiatrist attempts to impose the discourse of psychotherapy (and the real world) onto Vincent's sense of self, the boy's fantasy world takes over. This happens by virtue of Mr Hunch, a product of Vincent's fantasy world, who 'blocks' the psychiatrist's words:

> As far as Vincent was concerned, although the doctor started off audibly, even if bizarre and outlandish and off-the-rails wrong, everything he said after this sounded as it usually did, indistinct, blursome and 'bla' bla' 'bla'. The reason the young man could no longer follow what the older one was saying, was because Mr Hunch had come between them and was himself now starting to speak. Mr Hunch always came between at the least sign of anyone else usurping and although Vincent could never see him, there was never any mistaking when Mr Hunch was in the room (135).

Vincent is so suspicious about language and its ability to 'betray' that he does not even 'trust' his own discourse; a fact made evident during another session with the doctor:

> Vincent still said nothing although his tongue was definitely twitching. He realised it was trying to betray him and give him away. This was a mortifying problem and his mind wondered what would be the best thing to do in the circumstances. After all, if you can't trust your own tongue, whose tongue can you trust? He took a bite out of it and it bled (145).

And Vincent is not the only young character in the novel that rejects language. His friend, a child called Mary, is not 'good at words' (139). Although she does speak, her 'words' do not conform to the rules of articulacy and are more akin to an irrational babble. Further, she, like

---

62   Burns, *No Bones*, p.144. Further consecutive references to this novel are given after quotations in the text.

Vincent, is able to retreat into an inner fantasy world which blocks out reality. Consequently, with the exception of Vincent, most of the people she encounters think she is mad. Her state of mind is due to the fact that she is a victim of incest inflicted by her father, the product of which is a stillborn baby – a psychological as well as physical trauma. Therefore, Mary's disruption of the symbolic order of language (the law of the father) and retreat from reality into fantasy is, paradoxically, entirely logical. There is further evidence for this idea within the narrative. For example, we learn how Mary pushes the dead baby (which she has put in a plastic bag) around the streets of Belfast in a pram. When Amelia discovers this and challenges Mary, the latter is adamant that it was not her but 'God' who placed the baby in the bag (70). For Mary, this grotesque fantasy is less psychologically painful than the reality of being raped by her father. However, in placing the blame upon God (the 'father' and the 'Word'), her fantasy speaks a certain 'truth'.

In terms of the media and paramilitary rhetoric, language is obviously a powerful ideological weapon and therefore an important catalyst to the violence that was so endemic to the north of Ireland; a violence that, some might say, was madness. This, I argue, ratifies the idea that Vincent's and Mary's rejection of language and their retreat into their own kind of madness is a rational act. Further, in considering the madness of the violence that was normality in the north of Ireland, it is surely ironic when Vincent's psychiatrist informs him that:

> 'Psychosis is one of the worst experiences there is,' the doctor went on. 'It is isolation deadland, it is a world of absolute horror, but worse than that, it is a place full of hate. I think it's time we talked' (134).

Surely there could be no 'worst experiences', 'world of absolute horror', and 'place full of hate' than a city where bombs and bullets are a routine part of childhood.

Although Vincent and Mary are key figures in the novel, as mentioned above Amelia is the main protagonist. Her story spans the twenty-five-year period from 1969 (when she is nine years old) to 1994 (when she is thirty-four). During this period the reader follows her bizarre and shocking public and private world that, like Mary's world, includes child abuse and extreme violence both inside and outside the home. However, rather than separating public (para-military) and private (domestic) violence (with the former being privileged), Burns reverses this binary opposition and shows how the domestic (female violence) can explode onto the public (male violence) and disrupt it. This occurs when Amelia's mother has an argument with her sister and rips off her 'scalp' (53). When the sister complains to the IRA and asks them to intervene, the IRA agree because:

> although it was trivial, domestic and risible and not as real or as grown-up as killing soldiers, this here long-running notorious feud had to be put a stop to, for it was getting on their nerves, causing mounting disturbance and attracting the wrong sort of attention just when they, the IRA, did not want any sort of attention attracted at all. The British Army [...] had taken it into their heads to pop round in their Saracens in the hope of catching gunmen every time this here family started up. The drop of a pin, never mind the crunch of a sibling's bone or familial crack of a head, was enough to saturate the area with troops and cause the budding Irish organization great, but great, inconvenience (54).

Here, and in common with Robert McLiam Wilson's *Ripley Bogle*, Burns's liberal use of black comedy subverts the bleak realism being depicted. Burns makes explicit the outrageousness and sheer lunacy of both domestic and paramilitary violence; and this tactic undermines more conventional literary realism and its tendency to reinforce violence as a taken-for-granted norm. Burns uses this tactic at various other moments in the narrative. For example, the following extract shows the reaction of a group of adolescents who have just been informed by a member of the PIRA that they must report for punishment kneecappings:

> The boys watched him go and they were upset and some said 'I'm not going!' and others said fuck, fuck and fuck, but this was all just swashbuckle for they knew what would happen if it turned seven o'clock and they didn't do as they were told and show up. That meant they had no time to lose. They had to get drunk immediately. [...] They had fifty-three minutes to get blocked. Doctors on TV warned about getting blocked. 'If you're going to get kneecapped,' they complained, 'please please please – don't get drunk! It's hard to deal with the injuries when you're drunk, it makes our job that much more difficult.'
> 'Tough!' said the boys with complete total selfishness (95).

The excruciating yet hilarious adolescent naivety portrayed here (the boys might just as easily be preparing for a scolding from their headmaster), together with the doctor's matter-of-fact kneecapping advice, has the effect of defamilarizing the boys' plight so that, paradoxically, the reader is more appalled than might be case in a more 'realistic' narrative. We are uneasy as we laugh and wince at one and the same time. And this impact upon the reader is reinforced when, on the same page, we follow another group of young boys who are just as naively enjoying a fatal game of Russian Roulette.

As mentioned at the beginning of this section, a major theme in *No Bones* is that of childhood and the impact upon childhood that is made by living in the north of Ireland during the 1970s and 1980s. But, compared to Johnston's literary realism that describes Joe's experiences, Burns's admixture of black comedy, literary realism and surrealism that describes Amelia's experiences summon a narrative that is far more disturbing.

In a similar way to Mary, Amelia suffers a psychological and physical decline that is attributable to the private (her dysfunctional family) as much as the public (the Troubles). For instance, the following scene portrays a 'typical' night at her home. The scene commences with Mick and Mena, Amelia's deranged brother and equally deranged wife, returning home 'early from the Star (pub)':

> Giggling, they squeezed into the old, fake-leather, L-shaped settee between Mick's ma, Mick's da, one sibling, four cousins, five friends, three neighbours, their own four-year-old daughter and began to slabber and paw each other as usual. Pretty soon they were having sex. Everyone kept their eyes on *Starsky and Hutch*. After a while, Mena whispered loudly that she'd soon be needing a toilet roll, a remark so witty that both she and Mick giggled all over again. At this, Mick's ma spat up a huge lump of catarrh, Mick's da twisted the poker in the fire and a neighbour turned up the TV. [...] There, something bloody and gruesome was just about to happen so everyone tried to settle to that. Except for the lovers. Nobody, it goes without saying, noticed them.
> Eventually, Mick's ma remembered she had to go upstairs and scream her head off [...], Mick's da [...] thrust his daughter-in-law's shuddering leg off his lap [...], ten year old Josie said she was going to get drunk [and] when little Orla went off to tie up her dollies and give them damn good hammerings [Mick and Mena] tore off their clothes [...] and had big, spread-out sex everywhere (119).

Shortly after this macabre sketch of the Lovett family, Burns plunges us into a more disturbing scenario. This happens when Mick and Mena try to rape Amelia. Here, because the reader is obliged to make such a swift psychological transition (from laughter to shock) the impact is all the more powerful. Moreover, the attempted rape has a surreal, insane and nightmarish tone – as Mike and Mena approach Amelia, Burns tells us that their young daughter is amusing herself by 'hitting [her] tied-up naked dolls' (126). Adding to this surreal not to mention black comic tone, the rape is prevented by Amelia's sister, Lizzie, and her 'pathological' girl-friends who are all named 'Mary' (127). Violence and the domestic looms large here when Mike suffers a *grand guignol* death:

> Lizzie drew out the poker, the long, hot poker, that trusty old treasure from so long ago, and whacked it with a 'Take that ye whore!' a whole lot of times off her older brother's head. She burnt his hair, burnt his head, burnt her hands, burnt everybody else and burnt giant holes all over the carpet. Eventually, Mick fell over and she and the Marys flung themselves on top. They ripped him apart, tore his flesh from his body and left him to die in the hallway (127, 129).

As a result of the Troubles, domestic abuse and a dysfunctional upbringing, Amelia becomes anorectic and then, later in life, drifts into madness. But, as with Vincent and Mary, this madness perhaps signals a 'logical' attempt to enter a fantasy world and thereby escape the reality of a traumatic childhood past.

Interestingly, Amelia's anorexia can be 'diagnosed' in a similar way as, according to Maud Ellmann, 'to starve is to renounce the past […], it is to rid the body of its larded history'.[63] Fittingly, then, after Mick's death Amelia goes into denial:

> As far as Amelia was concerned, it was absolutely about rape. […] But there was no way she was ever going to admit this. And how could she? She was counting calories, swallowing laxatives, shoving up suppositories, […] not being friends with food […].[64]

---

63   Maud Ellmann, *The Hunger Artists: Starving, Writing and Imprisonment* (Cambridge, MA: Harvard University Press, 1993), p.88.
64   Burns, *No Bones*, p.128.

The above extract recalls French Feminist thought about the political empowerment that might be gained when women write about the female body. So, irrespective of the physical abuse inflicted by her family, it could be argued that, finally, Amelia has sovereignty of her own body as well as (through madness) her own mind.

Linked to these ideas, for Ellmann, fasting is analogous to a terrorist act because:

> anorexia, like terrorism, attacks the social fabric indiscriminately [and] like terrorism, too, anorexia depends upon the gap between the reasons and the deed: starve now, explain later, is the terroristic temporality of this compulsion.[65]

Ellmann also notes that:

> What is tragic is that anorectics rarely explain themselves at all, and the explanations that they offer are designed to disavow their illness rather than to master its destructive logic.[66]

Perhaps, then, Amelia's anorexia could be analysed at a metaphorical level in the sense that the illness signals a failure to 'master' a 'destructive logic'; a destructive logic that can be associated with both the public violence of the Troubles and the private violence of the Lovett household. Therefore, although *No Bones* might not supply the reader with an optimistic alternative to more conventional thriller novels, through surrealism and black comedy Burns does encourage the reader to unravel ideological assumptions which tend to privilege reality over fantasy, speech over silence, sanity over madness, the public over the private, and adulthood over childhood.

In comparison to *No Bones*, Linda Anderson's novel, *To Stay Alive*, is a text that, arguably, shuns surrealism in favour of a relentless and gritty literary realism: poverty, bombs, bullets, sex and death. This Belfast narrative concerns three young working class people: a married couple (Dan and Rosaleen) and a British soldier (Gerry) who hates army life. Dan is a medical student. He and Rosaleen have a baby and are dogged with financial problems that are the catalyst for

65   Ellmann, *The Hunger Artists: Starving, Writing and Imprisonment*, p.21.
66   Ibid.

Dan's reluctant involvement with the IRA. In this sense, the public space of male national identity once again impacts, negatively, upon the private space of the female and the home. The narrative also involves a doomed affair between Rosaleen and Gerry; a scenario that in both British and Irish male-authored texts would usually lead to a tragic finale where the woman would be 'punished' for her sexual 'crime'.

However, it seems to me that Anderson offers a more feminist text through a focus upon the body and the breaking down of binary oppositions. Indeed, in terms of historical context, and like *No Bones*, the body features profoundly in Anderson's writing. The narrative is set during 1979, a period when IRA prisoners were engaged in the 'dirty protest' prior to the hunger strikes. For Ellmann, the 'dirty protest' signified an assertion of the self because:

> Although [the prisoners'] world had been reduced to four cramped walls, within that tiny compass self was everywhere. Through the dirty protest, they were striving to reclaim their cells, just as they reclaimed their bodies through the hunger strike, for they cocooned themselves into their excremental signatures.[67]

Paradoxically, through their own agency (the abjection of their own bodies) the prisoners reclaimed and, in turn, experienced greater psychological freedom than the working class Catholics in Belfast. This is because, as Anderson shows, to be working class and Catholic meant both physical and psychological imprisonment by poverty, a loss of agency, and a struggle to, quite literally, 'stay alive' within a city where *both* male and female bodies were constantly threatened.

Accordingly, St. Peter notes that 'when Dan is lifted for inter-rogation and torture, his very body [is] the signifier of helplessness'.[68] While I am not suggesting that representations of the exploitation of male bodies are necessarily politically liberating, Anderson does, unlike the majority of male-authored texts, imply how, irrespective of gender, the north of Ireland inflicted constraints upon 'every-body' – passivity and vulnerability is not just suffered by women. And

67   Ibid., pp.99–100.
68   St. Peter, *Changing Ireland: Strategies in Contemporary Women's Fiction*, p.113.

Rosaleen shows she is aware of this when she observes how: 'Dan's body was bent forward, rump jutting out like a female baboon inviting sexual entry'.[69] St. Peter comments upon how Dan's abjection, or objectification, results in the 'grotesque male version of gendered humiliation', a feminization of the male body.[70] And, as implied, this binary opposition between male and female is subverted, or deconstructed, throughout Anderson's text in which men weep, tremble, and are shown as being passive sexual objects, whereas women, particularly Rosaleen, are capable of having profound sexual appetites and are intolerant of their roles as wives and mothers.

The novel also deconstructs more abstract binary oppositions, thus challenging the often simplistic ideological constructs supplied by reactionary discourses. So, when Rosaleen copulates with Gerry in a graveyard, there is a blurring of sex (Eros) and death (Thanatos). Moreover, there is no easy distinction between good and bad, friend and foe: both the IRA and the British Army attract violent bigots as well as more compassionate figures which, in turn, refuse the taken-for-granted simplicity of stereotyping.

Congruous with the above, when it comes to the female body and identity Rosaleen provides the most interesting character upon whom to concentrate. For instance, her female body is subjected to the threat of rape by the British Army and, if her affair is discovered, a punishment beating by the IRA. And Rosaleen is shown to be aware of this when she speaks about a punishment beating which left the female victim with a 'wet slick of blood curling from the punctured womb' – a reprisal specific to the female anatomy a propos the maternal.[71] Although afraid about the possible consequences of her illicit sexual relationship, Rosaleen's defiance suggests that she is not passive but active; a woman who 'disobeys' the imposed rules of paramilitary patriarchy. Later on in the narrative, and ironically in terms of her fears about punishment for sex, Rosaleen worries that she might be pregnant again:

69   Anderson, *To Stay Alive*, p.162.
70   St. Peter, *Changing Ireland: Strategies in Contemporary Women's Fiction*, p.113.
71   Anderson, *To Stay Alive*, p.47.

> The period was so late. She hesitated, praying, willing the menstrual flow, then pressed her hand between her legs, withdrawing it smeared with blood.
> It was a reprieve. A sign. She could have a new life, scoured clean of everything that had happened.[72]

Here, the onset of Rosaleen's period signifies the opposite of the misogynistic notion that associates menstrual blood with the Kristevian abject. Rosaleen's blood is, instead, liberating and cleansing. It is a 'sign' that signifies female agency rather than male agency.

All this said, through issues explored alongside the Troubles (motherhood, money and marriage), *To Stay Alive* implies that the Irish female body is subjected at various levels. For example, although Rosaleen is sexually voracious, her body is appropriated by marriage, a fact made evident when, looking at Dan and utilizing word-play, she decides 'This is your country. And I'm your cunt' (44). She also argues against her friend's idea that Ireland, unlike China, is a 'free country':

> Free! Don't you realize it's the same here? The pressure is opposite, that's all. Priests and neighbours meddling into your sex lives, turning you into biddable little breeders.[73]

'Biddable little breeders'? For working class Catholic women like Rosaleen, the female body is not just subjected to threats of rape and punishment but also appropriated by patriarchy in respect of marriage and religion.

Critics such as Padraig O'Malley claim that, in terms of Rosaleen, Anderson's novel 'conveys an over-riding sense that there is no way out, no future, and no hope'.[74] However, I am more convinced by St. Peter's observation that Anderson 'refuses her readers any kind of closure'.[75] This is because, although Anderson's female protagonist remains within Belfast and her unhappy marriage, 'Rosaleen's fierce

---

72   Ibid., p.94.
73   Ibid., p.45.
74   Padraig O'Malley, *The Uncivil Wars: Ireland Today* (London: Blackstaff, 1983), p.7.
75   St. Peter, *Changing Ireland: Strategies in Contemporary Women's Fiction*, p.114.

desire to stay alive in the face of so much death [...] marks a heroic struggle against the false forms of [male] heroism current in Belfast society'.[76] *To Stay Alive* leaves the reader with a certain pessimism, granted, but, unlike Johnston's *Shadows*, it also leaves the reader with a sense that Irish women will never wholly capitulate to patriarchy either.

The last novel I want to consider is also one that draws upon literary realism: Mary Beckett's *Give Them Stones* (1987). Briefly, the narrative's protagonist is called Martha (a biblical name that resonates with domestic duty and the opposite in terms of desire and female sexuality – that being Mary (Magdelene)). Martha is from a poor, Catholic, working class, Belfast family. Her story begins in the 1980s then shifts back to the 1940s and a childhood when, because of the Blitz, she is sent into the countryside; a rural retreat often depicted as an alternative to the threat of the urban space. And, of course, this type of rural retreat is often associated with the feminine: a trope appropriated for hackneyed images of Mother Ireland. But in the following analysis of *Give Them Stones* I suggest how, through her portrayal of Martha, Beckett rewrites this trope.

For a number of years Martha lives with two her elderly female relatives, Bessie and Maggie, who teach her how to bake bread – a commercial as well as domestic skill that will, later on, grant her a certain amount of economic independence. Eventually, Martha inherits Bessie's and Maggie's small property, sells it, secretly places the money with a solicitor and returns to Belfast. Here she marries Dermot because he owns a 'gas cooker' and she will be able to 'bake'.[77] At this point, Martha claims her inheritance from the solicitor and uses the money to open a bakery within her marital home. Throughout the text, Martha's first person narrative voice supplies a haunting, lyrical tone, a feminine discourse similar to the one created by Madden, especially as the 1940s back-story is set in rural Ireland.

Although, again like Madden, Beckett draws upon real historical events such as the General Strike, the Falls Road Curfew and Bloody Sunday, she rewrites these events from a female perspective that

76   Ibid.
77   Beckett, *Give Them Stones*, p.76.

avoids a monolithic, phallocentric discourse and firmly places working class, Catholic women from the north of Ireland and *their stories* back into the Troubles. As noted by Megan Sullivan, the novel charts the main protagonist, Martha, and her psychological journey from 'a national identity to a gender-based class politics'.[78] This gender-based, class politics revolves around the material, especially employment and wages. For instance, although Martha and Dermot have young children, Dermot keeps most of his wages. Yet, through her bakery, Martha is able to prevent this material reality from inflicting deprivation upon herself and her children. Her self-sufficiency is a female legacy from Bessie and Maggie who have taught Martha to be 'in charge of [her] own life', and supplied her with the skills (bread-baking) as well as the financial means (the sale of the property) to act independently.[79] Materially empowered by her late female relatives, Martha has enough money to launch her own bakery from home and thus create an autonomous, not to mention profitable, source of income. Her female domain breaks down the binary opposition of public equals male and private equals female: Martha's home is both a public, commercial space (the shop) and a private, domestic space (the home) (98).

This said, Martha's shift away from a national, male-dominated identity is not recognized by either the British Army or the IRA. So, when Martha refuses to serve British squaddies, the army assumes she is an IRA sympathizer, raid her bakery and ruin her precious 'bins of flour' (127). Thus, a patriarchal imposition of national identity deprives Martha of her livelihood and the local working class women of her cut-price bread. For, as Martha tells us, she 'never made much more than [she] needed for housekeeping' (148).

The incident with the British Army is later echoed by The Falls Road Curfew of 1970 and Martha's sense of 'pride' when 'a whole army of women with bread and milk came marching down [the] streets [...] and pushed the soldiers away, shouting at them to go

---

78   Megan Sullivan, *Women in Northern Ireland* (Gainesville: Florida University Press, 1999), p.42.

79   Beckett, *Give Them Stones* p.54. Further consecutive references to this novel are given after quotations in the text.

home to England and learn manners' (121). Both Martha and the female army are providers of bread not bullets; they are an active collective that, once mobilized, sustains rather than maims the working class Catholic body. As suggested above, though, resistance to patriarchy gets punished. Hence, Martha is victimized by the British Army twice.

The second incident happens after she has been given a record player by her sister and then acquires a taste for classical music. This music 'lift[s] her spirits', 'calms' her, provides her shop and her 'body' with a semiotic *chora* (134, 133). Thus, Martha collapses the economic and material with the spiritual; the latter signified by her ceremonial baking of, as opposed to breaking of, bread. But her flights into the semiotic are soon thwarted when 'a crowd of [...] soldiers [...] open the door in the middle of the "1812" Overture and sho[o]t a rubber bullet at [her] record player, knocking it off its shelf, breaking it in smithereens and fusing the electricity' (134). Note the Costelloian humour at this point though? In spite of her loss, and like Anderson's Rosaleen, Martha remains defiant and recounts the incident with subversive female laughter.

However, it is not just the British army who inflicts male animosity on to Irish female autonomy. So, when the IRA knee-cap a youth outside her shop, Martha protests by refusing to donate protection money. This defiance results in the IRA burning down her business and home, which leaves her feeling 'worthless [because] if [she is] not baking bread [she is] nobody and nothing' (147). Once again, then, the bread that she baked and supplied to the women in her community appears to merge the economic and the material with the spiritual. This is because if 'not baking' leaves her as 'nobody and nothing', the bread must surely symbolize the female body and sense of identity; a quasi-transubstantiated body that gives the working class bread (not 'stones'). Indeed, Sullivan touches upon these ideas concerning Martha and the female body when she writes:

> The [kneecapped] boy's body *stands in for* Martha's bakery, and Martha the worker and business owner is aligned with 'transgressive' youth. [...] When the IRA threatens Martha's shop/body, it acknowledges that it knows the way in

which a woman's body can be used by and for her; the IRA want to use Martha's body for its own purposes.[80]

The novel ends, paradoxically, with Martha and Declan receiving compensation from Sinn Fein and hoping to start over again. Whether or not Beckett's domestic heroine will be able to open a new business is left for the reader to decide. Finally, though, *Give Them Stones* suggests that national identity is patriarchal and that, like the Cuchulain myth which Martha criticizes because she does not 'believe all this "honour" stuff', national identity reinforces a male-dominated history that takes no account of gender and class.[81]

The women writers that I have discussed in this final chapter of this study have all, to a greater or lesser extent, attempted to challenge the ways in which the north of Ireland has been written as a male text. Such modern female voices enable both men and women from the north of Ireland to consider how politicising the private (the home, the body, the self) together with the deconstructing of binary oppositions can provide a politically empowering feminist agenda and, even through devices borrowed from literary realism, dispute the notion that 'nothing ever changes'.

80   Sullivan, *Women in Northern Ireland*, p.50.
81   Beckett, *Give Them Stones*, p.73.

Conclusion

> The unconscious [...] is a site of ambivalence: if Ireland is raw, turbulent, destructive, it is also the locus of play, pleasure, fantasy, a blessed release from the tyranny of the English reality principle. Ireland is the biological time-bomb which can be heard ticking softly away beneath the civilized superstructures of Pall Mall clubs.[1]

Terry Eagleton's suggestion that, at an unconscious level, Ireland supplies ambivalence in terms of 'fantasy' and 'reality' is entirely pertinent to the metonymic representations of the PIRA and the Troubles created by British and Irish, male and female writers. Granted, and as I have acknowledged throughout, these represent-ations are summoned in different ways and for different reasons depending upon the gender and national identity of the writer. Nevertheless, the high frequency of recurring themes and images identified in fiction, film and the media does supply strong evidence for the argument that the 'traumatic' Troubles had a profound and reciprocal impact upon the British and Irish, male and female psyche.

An important feature of this book has been the revealing of how representations of the PIRA and the Troubles bear the traces of, to quote Eagleton, an Irish 'time-bomb' of fear and fantasy that is always threatening to explode in the face of British pragmatism, human subjectivity and common sense. Repeating 'the later sixteenth century, when Edmund Spenser walked the plantations of Munster', images of the PIRA often provide 'the perfect foil to set off [...] virtues [such as] controlled, refined and rooted [against] hot-headed, rude and no-madic'.[2] Ironically, though, perhaps the 'hot-headed', 'rude' and

---

1   Terry Eagleton, *Heathcliff and the Great Hunger: Studies in Irish Culture* (London: Verso, 1996), p.9.
2   Declan Kiberd, *Inventing Ireland: The Literature of the Modern Nation* (London: Vintage, 1996), p.9.

'nomadic' are traits that can also be associated with an ideal image of macho masculinity.

Alternatively, though, images which Hamletize and sentiment-alize the extimate 'enemy within' reveal more complex figures so that what seem to be binary notions of 'good British self' versus 'bad Irish other' are deconstructed by both nations. Importantly, the same crit-ical methodology that I have used (to explore the ways in which binary notions of the British self versus the Irish other as well as the male self and female other are unravelled by Troubles narratives) can be applied to a whole series of divergent ideological constructs in order to disclose how commonplace oppositions, such as crime versus deviance, madness versus sanity, and black versus white are, quite often, products of reciprocal identities.

In terms of fantasy and reality, Eagleton's allusion to 'the tyranny of the English reality principle' is both highly relevant yet ironic. This is because, when appropriating the PIRA and the Troubles, literary realism itself *becomes* the 'blessed release' whereby 'pleasure' and 'fantasy' are played out through figures which have been shown to be a product of Ireland as well as Britain – the Irish female paramilitary as a vampire being an obvious example. More-over, as mentioned in my Introduction, the 'pleasure' produced by 'literary realism' is often the 'fantasy' of the stereotype, the fantasy which psychologizes, apoliticizes, demonizes, sentimentalizes and eroticizes Ireland and the Irish.

For those who still insist that readers can recognize and dismiss stereotypes, I want to again recall Zizek's ideas concerning 'cynicism as a form of ideology'.[3] Hence, of course, we all 'know that' believing in metonymic constructs of the PIRA is the same as 'following an illusion, but still [we] are doing it'.[4] A key reason why 'we are still doing it' results from our continuing fascination with the Troubles which, in turn, produces more and more stereotypes that all function through the reality principle but, inevitably, are fantasies that fail in various ways. This said, the 'light on the horizon' could, potentially, be located through women writing the political conflict within the

3   Slavoj Zizek, *The Sublime Object of Ideology* (London: Verso, 1989), p.28.
4   Ibid., p.33.

north of Ireland. I await more evidence of this – particularly in terms of 'polictizing the private'.

In recent years the fragmentation of the PIRA into groups such as the Real IRA and the Continuity IRA has made the Irish 'enemy' within even more elusive. Frustrating British and Irish, male and female, appropriations of the PIRA, this fragmentation has served to exacerbate desire through lack (where have they gone?) and, in turn, produce a 'surplus' of metonymic representations which act as sub-stitutes in the search for the real Irish Thing. Bewilderingly mercurial, the PIRA refuses homogeneity, is now, in some respects, a post-modern concept whereby a series of 'little narratives' refuse to be contained within one 'big narrative'.[5] More than ever before, it is impossible to circumscribe the PIRA with a transcendental signifier. They have vanished, ghost-like, into the liminal cease-fire zone via amnesty, disarmament, peace – but they will always be 'there' in the cultural unconscious.

On the other hand, Ireland *itself* is no longer amenable to hack-neyed images of, for example, an urban Gothic (Belfast) or a romantic and fey (Dublin). Both Belfast and Dublin are modern cosmopolitan cities, and, in the case of Dublin, utterly European: unlike Britain which seems to be entrenched within a constant backward glancing to a sense of quintessential Britishness.

If an enduring fascination with the Troubles endures, so too will the creation of diverse stereotypes for diverse reasons which fail in diverse ways yet share common denominators or preoccupations: national identity (particularly male national identity), self and other, and gender politics. Such stereotypes are consistent with Zizek's notions about the 'phallic [...] detail that "does not fit", that "sticks out" from the idyllic surface scene and denatures it, renders it un-canny'.[6] Zizek describes this type of phallic detail as being 'the point of *anamorphosis* in a picture: the element that, when viewed straight-forwardly, remains a meaningless stain, but which, as soon as we look

5   *Modern Literary Theory: A Reader*, eds. Philip Rice and Patricia Waugh, 3rd edn. (London: Arnold, 1996), p.289.

6   Slavoj Zizek, *Looking Awry: An Introduction to Jacques Lacan through Popular Culture* (Cambridge, MA: MIT, 1992), p.90.

at the picture from a precisely determined lateral perspective, all of a sudden acquires well-known contours'.[7] In Troubles narratives, these well-known contours are often the British and, maybe surprisingly, Irish male self (such as demons, Mafiosi, communist traitors, homosexuals, the SAS and Hamlets) or objects of desire and fear (such as the deadly *femme fatale* and monstrous maternal figures).

For Zizek, 'Lacan's constant point of reference for *anamorphosis* is Holbein's *Ambassadors*'[8] which shows 'at the bottom of the picture, under the figures of two ambassadors [...], an amorphous, extended, "erected" spot'.[9] However, 'a [...] lateral glance at [the] spot' shows it to be 'a skull, disclosing thus the true meaning of the picture – the nullity of all terrestrial goods'.[10] 'This', writes Zizek, 'is the way Lacan defines the phallic signifier, as a "signifier without signified" [...] and thus opens up the abyss of the search for a meaning [because] nothing is what it seems to be'.[11] Here we find 'a realm of total ambiguity [whereby] lack propels us to produce ever new "hidden meanings" [and] is a driving force of compulsion'.[12] Like metonymic representations of the PIRA and the Troubles, this compulsion causes an 'oscillation between lack and surplus meaning [which] constitutes the proper dimension of subjectivity'.[13] So, when 'the "phallic" spot' (the PIRA) enables 'the observed picture' within film, fiction and media to become 'subjectivized: this paradoxical point undermines our position as "neutral", "objective" observer, pinning us to the observed object itself'.[14] Ultimately, then, 'this is the point at which the observer [reader or audience] is already included, inscribed in the observed scene – in a way, it is the point from which the picture itself looks back at us'.[15] Like the 'phallic spot' in the *Ambassadors*,

---

7   Ibid.
8   See Jacques Lacan, *The Four fundamental Concepts of Psychoanalysis* (London: Hogarth, 1977), p.92.
9   Zizek, *Looking Awry*, p.90.
10   Ibid., pp.90–1.
11   Ibid., p.91.
12   Ibid.
13   Ibid.
14   Ibid.
15   Ibid.

metonymic repetitions of the PIRA also 'look back at us', the British and Irish, male and female, subject who is 'inscribed in the observed [Troubles] scene'.

The skull in the *Ambassadors* is the hidden trauma of death in terms of desire, a desire that is often analogous to unconscious identifications with the PIRA which attempt to 'block-out' the trauma of the Troubles with fantasies that are inadequate yet repeated in a fluctuating process of surplus and lack. Throughout, I have argued that the stereotypes and fantasy images discussed do not represent the real, 'phallic' PIRA but, instead, an *'object a'* triggering desire and supplying merely lack because the real PIRA thing can only be accessed through pain and what is beyond consciousness – often sex and death. Thus, when the trauma of the events that took place in the north of Ireland is displaced onto the PIRA (who are, in turn, de-monized, glamorized, fetishized and sometimes sentimentalized), the Troubles become pleasurable and *jouissance* replaces death: the real, unconscious fantasy.

The ways in which human subjectivity is constructed through repetitions of an imagined other offers an intriguing focus for literary criticism. However, this book has also identified the recurrence of alternative points of focus. These include the residue of audience recall stimulated by the intertextuality of various actors (such as Miranda Richardson) as well as the motif of the three 'mother' figures and three 'father' figures whose triadic structure demands further research to see if it occurs within alternative narratives. Such research might offer some interesting additional points of reference to my conviction that, through surplus and lack, representations of the PIRA and the Troubles within film, fiction and the media preserves the gap in the real trauma inflicted by the violent conflict within the north of Ireland. Part of this process, as shown, involves the desire for an ideal British or Irish self who, in turn, cannot escape the mirrored gaze of the imaginary PIRA other. In conclusion, then, like the young British soldier in *Harry's Game*, Troubles texts have 'never seen an IRA man, or anything like one' except for the traumatic Anglo-Irish variety.[16]

16   Gerald Seymour, *Harry's Game* (London: Harper Collins, 1975), p.340.

List of Illustrations

Bibliography

Fiction

Anderson, Linda, *Cuckoo* (London: Bodley Head, 1986)

——, *To Stay Alive* (London: Bodley Head, 1984)

Armstrong, Campbell, *Jig* (London: Hodder and Stoughton, 1987)

Barlow, James, *Both Your Houses* (London: Hamilton, 1971)

Beckett, Mary, *Give Them Stones* (London: Bloomsbury, 1987)

Braddon, Russell, *The Progress of Private Lilyworth* (London: Joseph, 1971)

Brenton, Howard, *The Romans in Britain* (London: Methuen, 1982)

Broderick, John, *The Fugitives* (London: Pan, 1976)

Broxon, Mildred, Downey, *Too Long a Sacrifice* (London: Futura, 1981)

Burns, Anna, *No Bones* (London: Flamingo, 1997)

Burns, Richard, *Why Diamond Had to Die* (London: Bloomsbury, 1989)

Carrick, James, *With O'Leary in the Grave* (London: Heinemann, 1971)

Carroll, James, *Madonna Red* (London: Hodder and Stoughton, 1976)

Charles, Robert, *The Hour of the Wolf* (London: Hale, 1974)

Cheever, Susan, *A Handsome Man* (London: Weidenfeld and Nicolson, 1981)

Clancy, Ambrose, *Blind Pilot* (London: Macmillan, 1981)

Clancy, Tom, *Patriot Games* (London: Collins, 1987)

Cleary, Jon, *Peter's Pence* (London: Collins, 1974)

Coogan, Patrick, *The General* (London: Mandarin, 1994)

Costello, Mary, *Titanic Town* (London: Methuen, 1992)

Daniel, James, *They Told Me You Were Dead* (London: Pan, 1996)

De Mille, Nelson, *Cathedral* (London: Granada, 1981)

De Jorre, John, and Brian Shakespeare, *The Patriot Game* (London: Hodder and Stoughton, 1973)

De Villiers, Gerard, *Furie a Belfast* (Paris: Plon, 1974)

Dowling, Kevin, *Interface Ireland* (London: Barrie and Jenkins, 1979)

Driscoll, Peter, *In Connection With Kilshaw* (London: Macdonald, 1974)

Egleton, Clive, *The Mills Bomb* (London: Hodder and Stoughton, 1978)

Edgar, David, *Destiny* (London: Methuen, 1976)

Esler, Gavin, *Loyalties* (London: Headline, 1990)

Forsyth, Frederick, *The Deceiver* (London: Transworld, 1991)

Friel, Brian, *Dancing at Lughnasa* (London: Faber and Faber, 1990)

Gadney, Reg, *Just When We Are Safest* (London: Faber and Faber, 1996)

Gibson, Tom, *A Wild Hope* (London: Hale, 1983)

Gordon, Mary, *Final Payments* (New York: Ballantine, 1979)

Green, F.L., *Odd Man Out* (North Hollywood, CA: Leisure Books, 1971 (orig. 1945))

Hanley, Clifford, *Prissy* (London: Collins, 1978)

Harriott, Ted, *No Sanctuary* (London: Secker and Warburg, 1983)

Herron, Shaun, *Through the Dark and Hairy Wood* (London: Cape, 1972)

—— *The Whore Mother* (London: Cape, 1973)

Higgins, George, V., *The Patriot Game* (London: Secker and Warberg, 1982)

Higgins, Jack, *The Violent Enemy* (London: Hodder and Stoughton, 1969)

—— *The Savage Day* (London: Collins, 1972)

—— *A Prayer for the Dying* (London: Pan, 1981)

—— *Angel of Death* (London: Penguin, 1995)

Holland, Jack, *The Prisoner's Wife* (Dublin: Poolbeg, 1995)

Holloway, Rupert, *The Terrorist Conspiracy* (Lewis, Sussex: The Book Guild, 1982)

Honeywood, John, *The Terrorist's Woman* (London: Hale, 1981)

Hurd, Douglas, *Vote To Kill* (London: Collins, 1975)

Hutchinson, Ron, *Rat in the Skull* (London: Methuen, 1984)

Johnston, Jennifer, *Shadows on our Skin* (London: Headline, 2002)

Jordan, Neil, *The Crying Game* (London: Vintage, 1993)

Judd, Alan, *A Breed of Heroes* (London: Hodder and Stoughton, 1981)

Kebbe, Jonathan, *The Armalite Maiden* (London: Heinemann, 1990)

Keeffe, Barrie. *The Long Good Friday* (London: Handmade, 1984)

Kiely, Benedict, *Proxopera* (London: Poolbeg, 1977)

Lane, Andrew, *The Ulsterman* (London: New English Library, 1979)

Lessing, Doris, *The Good Terrorist* (London: Cape, 1985)

Lund, James, *The Ultimate* (London: Calder, 1976)

Madden, Deirdre, *One by One in the Darkness* (London: Faber and Faber, 1997)

McCabe, Eugene, *Victims: A Tale from Fermanagh* (London: Gollancz, 1976)

McNabb, Andy, *Immediate Action* (London: Bantam, 1995)

MacLaverty, Bernard, *Cal* (London: Penguin, 1984)

Martin, David, *The Task* (London: Secker and Warburg, 1975)

May, Naomi, *Troubles* (London: Calder, 1976)

Melville-Ross, Antony, *Shaw's War* (London: Michael Joseph, 1988)

Moore, Brian, *Lies of Silence* (London: Arrow, 1991)

Mullin, Chris, *A Very British Coup* (London: Hodder and Stoughton, 1982)

Oulds, Chris, *A Kind of Sleep* ((London: Deutsch, 1986)

Perry, Ritchie, *Dead End* (London: Collins, 1977)

Petit, Chris, *The Psalm Killer* (London: Macmillan, 1997)

Pincher, Chapman, *The Eye of the Tornado* (London: Sphere: 1978)

Power, M.S., *The Killing of Yesterday's Children* (London: Chatto and Windus, 1985)

Ransley, Peter, *The Price* (London: Corgi, 1984)

Rennie, James, *The Operators: Inside 14 Intelligence Company – The Army's Top Secret Elite* (London: Century, 1996)

Renwick, Aly, *...Last Night Another Soldier* (London: Barbed Wire, 1989)

Romanes, Julian, *The Cell* (London: Star, 1987)

Ryan, Chris, *Standby, Standby* (London: Century, 1996)
Scott, Hardiman, *Operation 10* (London: Bodley Head, 1982)
Seaman, Donald, *The Bomb that Could Lip-Read* (London: Hamilton, 1974)
Seymour, Gerald, *Field of Blood* (London: Fontana, 1986)
—— *Harry's Game* (London: Collins, 1975)
—— *The Journeyman Tailor* (London: Collins, 1995)
Shakespeare, William, *Hamlet* (London: Penguin, 1980)
Shriver, Lionel, *Ordinary Decent Criminals* (London: Collins, 1992)
Stevens, Gordon, *Provo* (London: Hammersmith, 1993)
Strong, Terence, *Whisper Who Dares* (Bath: Chivers, 1983)
Symons, Julian, *The Detling Murders* (New York: Viking, 1983)
Theroux, Paul, *The Family Arsenal* (London: Penguin, 1976)
Waddell, Martin, *A Little Bit British* (London: Stacey, 1970)
Wilson, Robert, McLiam, *Ripley Bogle* (London: Pan, 1990)

Film and Television

A Prayer for the Dying, Dir. Mike Hodges, Samuel Goldwyn, 1987
Auntie: The Inside Story of the BBC, 'When Auntie Met the Iron Lady', Prod. Jeremy Bennett, BBC1, 1987
Blown Away, Dir. Stephen Hopkins, MGM, 1992
Cal, Dir. Pat O'Connor, Paramount, 1984.
Harry's Game, Dir. Lawrence Gordon Clark, Yorkshire Television, 1982
In the Name of The Father, Dir. Jim Sheridan, Universal, 1994
Michael Collins, Dir. Neil Jordan, Warner Brothers, 1996
Mother Ireland, Dir. Anne Crilly, Derry Film & Video, 1988
Odd Man Out, Dir. Carol Reed, Two Cities, 1947
Patriot Games, Dir. Philip Noyce, UIP/Paramount, 1992
Some Mother's Son, Dirs. Terry George and Jim Sheridan, Rank, 1996
The Crying Game, Dir. Neil Jordan, Palace/Channel 4 Films, 1993
The Devil's Own, Dir. Alan J. Pakula, Columbia, 1997
The Godfather, Dir. Francis Ford Coppola, Paramount, 1972
The Jackal, Dir. Michael Caton-Jones, Universal, 1997
The Long Good Friday, Dir. John Mackenzie, Handmade Films, 1979
The Troubles, Thames, Channel 4, 1981 (repeated 1989)

Non-Fiction Books

Adams, Gerry, *Cage Eleven* (Kerry: Brandon, 1990)

—— *Before The Dawn: An Autobiography* (London: Heinemann, 1996)

Adams, James, Robin Morgan and Anthony Bambridge, *Ambush – The War between the SAS and the IRA* (London: Pan, 1988)

Attridge, Derek (ed.), *Jacques Derrida: Acts of Literature* (London: Routledge, 1992)

Baudrillard, Jean, *The Transparency of Evil* (London: Verso, 1993)

Bell, Ian, A. (ed.), *Peripheral Visions: Images of Nationhood in Contemporary British Fiction* (Cardiff: University of Wales Press, 1995)

Beresford, David, *Ten Men Dead* (London: Harper Collins, 1994)

Berger, John, *Ways of Seeing* (London: British Broadcasting Corporation and Penguin, 1972)

Birch, Helen, *Moving Targets: Women, Murder and Representation* (London: Virago, 1993)

Bishop, Patrick and Eamonn Mallie, *The Provisional IRA* (London: Corgi, 1988)

Bolger, Dermot, *Letters from the New Island* (Dublin: Raven, 1987)

Boswell, David and Jessica Evans (eds), *Representing the Nation: A Reader* (London: Routledge, 1999)

Cliff, Brian and Èibhear Walshe (eds), *Representing the Troubles: Texts and Images* (Dublin: Four Courts, 2004)

Coogan, Tim, Pat, *On The Blanket: The H-Block Story* (Dublin: Ward River, 1980)

—— *Michael Collins: A Biography* (London: Arrow, 1991)

—— *The IRA* (London: Harper Collins, 1995)

—— *The Troubles: Ireland's Ordeal (1966 –1995) and the Search for Peace* (London: Random House, 1995)

Crowley, Helen and Susan Himmelwelt (eds), *Knowing Women: Feminism And Knowledge* (Cambridge: Polity, 1992)

Curtis, Liz, *Ireland the Propaganda War: The British Media and the Battle for Hearts and Minds* (London: Pluto, 1984)

Darby, John, *Dressed to Kill: Cartoonists and the Northern Ireland Conflict* (Belfast: Appletree, 1983)

Devlin, Bernadette, *The Price of my Soul* (London: Pan, 1969)

Doane, Mary, Ann, *Femmes Fatales: Feminism, Film Theory, Psychoanalysis* (London: Routledge, 1991)

Dollimore, Jonathan and Alan Sinfield, *Political Shakespeare: New Essays in Cultural Materialism* (Manchester: Manchester University Press, 1985)

Donovan, Kate, *Irish Women Writers: Marginalized by Whom?* (Dublin: Raven Arts, 1988)

Dowling, Taylor and others, *The Troubles: The Background to the Question of Northern Ireland* (London: Thames Macdonald Futura, 1980)

Eagleton, Terry, *Heathcliff and the Great hunger*: Studies in Irish Culture (London: Verso, 1996)

Easthope, Anthony, *Englishness and National Culture* (London: Routledge, 1999)

Edwards, Ruth, Dudley, *Patrick Pearse: The Triumph of Failure* (London: Victor Gollancz: 1977)

Ellmann, Maud, *The Hunger Artists* (London: Virago, 1993)

Ellis, Peter, Beresford (ed.), *A Dictionary of Irish Mythology* (Oxford: Oxford University Press, 1991)

Evans, Dylan, *An Introductory Dictionary of Lacanian Psychoanalysis* (New York: Routledge, 1996)

Everson, William, K., *The Bad Guys: A Pictorial History of the Movie Villain* (New York: Cadillac, 1964)

Fairweather, Eileen, Roisin McDonough and Melanie McFadyean, *Only the Rivers Run Free: Northern Ireland, the Women's War* (London: Pluto, 1984)

Felman, Shoshana, *What Does a Woman Want?: Reading And Sexual Difference* (London: Hopkins, 1993)

Foucault, Michel, *Madness and Civilisation: A History of Insanity in the Age of Reason*, trans. by Richard Howard (London: Tavistock, 1971)

Friedman, Lester, *British Cinema and Thatcherism* (London: UCL, 1993)

Gantz, Jeffrey, trans. by, *Tales of Cu Chulaind: Irish Heroic Myths* (London: Penguin, 1981)

Giclanella, Valinis and Mary O'Dowd, *Women and Irish History* (Belfast: Wolfhound Press, 1997)

Giles, Jane, *The Crying Game* (London: British Film Institute, 1997)

Harte, Liam and Michael Parker (eds), *Contemporary Irish Fiction: Themes, Tropes, Theories* (London: Macmillan, 2000)

Hawkes, Terence, *That Shakespeherian Rag: Essays on a Critical Process* (London: Methuen, 1986)

Howe, Stephen, *Ireland and Empire: Colonial Legacies in Irish History and Culture* (Oxford: Oxford University Press, 2002)

Jones, Ernest, *Hamlet and Oedipus* (London: W.W. Norton, 1976)

Jordan, Neil, *Neil Jordan: A Reader* (New York: Vintage, 1993)

Kaplan, Ann, E. (ed.), *Psychoanalysis and Cinema* (New York: Routledge, 1990)

Karlson, Carol, *The Devil in the Shape of a Woman* (New York: W.W. Norton, 1987)

Kavanagh, Dennis and Anthony Seldon, *The Thatcher Effect: A Decade of Change* (Oxford: Oxford University Press, 1989)

Kennedy Andrews, Elmer, *(De)constructing the North: Fiction and the Northern Ireland Troubles* (Dublin: Four Courts, 2003)

Kiberd, Declan, *Inventing Ireland: The Literature of the Modern Nation* (London: Jonathan Cape, 1995)

Kirkland, Richard, *Identity Parades: Northern Irish Culture and Dissident Subjects* (Liverpool: Liverpool University Press, 2002)

Kristeva, Julia, *Powers of Horror: An Essay on Abjection*, trans. by Leon S. Roudiez (New York: Columbia University Press, 1982)

Lacan, Jacques, *Ecrits*, trans. by Alan Sheridan (London: Routledge, 1977)

—— *The Ethics of Psychoanalysis*, 1959–1960, trans. by Dennis Porter (London: Routledge, 1992)

—— *The Four Fundamental Concepts of Psycho-analysis*, ed. by Jacques-Alain Miller, trans. by Alan Sheridan (London: Vintage, 1998)

Lechte, John, *Julia Kristeva* (London: Routledge, 1990)

Lee, Alfred, McClung, *Terrorism in Northern Ireland* (New York: General Hall, 1983)

Longley, Edna (ed.), *The Selected Paul Durcan* (Belfast: Blackstaff, 1982)

—— *From Cathleen to Anorexia* (Dublin: Attic, 1990)

—— *The Living Stream: Literature and Revisionism in Ireland* (Newcastle-upon-Tyne: Bloodaxe, 1994)

MacDonald, Eileen, *Shoot the Women First* (London: Fourth Estate, 1991)

Magee, Patrick, *Gangsters or Guerrillas?: Representations of Irish Republicans in 'Troubles Fiction'* (Belfast: Beyond the Pale, 2001)

McRobbie, Angela, *Postmodernism and Popular Culture* (London: Routledge, 1994)

Miller, David, *Don't Mention the War: Northern Ireland, Propaganda and the Media* (London: Pluto, 1994)

Morgan, Robin, *Demon Lover* (New York: W.W. Norton, 1989)

Mumford, Lewis, *The City in History: Its Origins, Its Transformations and Its Prospects* (London: Secker and Warberg, 1961)

Newsinger, John, *Dangerous Men: The SAS and Popular Culture* (London: Pluto, 1997)

O'Connor, Theresa, *The Comic Tradition in Irish Women Writers* (Gainesville, FL: Florida University Press, 1996)

O'Malley, Padraig, *The Uncivil Wars: Ireland Today* (London: Blackstaff, 1983)

Paget, Derek, *True Stories?: Documentary Drama on Radio, Screen and Stage* (Manchester: Manchester University Press, 1990)

Palmer, Gerry, *Thrillers: Genesis and Structure of a Popular Genre* (London: Edward Arnold, 1978)

Parekh, Bhikhu, *The Parekh Report* (London: Profile Books, 2000)

Paulin, Tom, *Ireland and the English Crisis* (Newcastle-upon-Tyne: Bloodaxe, 1984)

Pincher, Chapman, *Their Trade is Treachery* (London: Sidgewick and Jackson, 1981)

—— *The Secret Offensive* (London: Sidgewick and Jackson, 1985)

Poster, Mark (ed.), *Jean Baudrillard: Selected Writings* (Oxford: Polity, 1988)

Purdie, Bob, *Politics in the Streets* (Belfast: Blackstaff, 1990)

Rabinow, Paul (ed.), *The Foucault Reader: An Introduction to Foucault's Thought* (London: Penguin, 1984)

Rice, Philip and Patricia Waugh, *Modern Literary Theory: A Reader*, 2nd edn (London: Edward Arnold, 1989)

—— *Modern Literary Theory: A Reader*, 3rd edn (London: Arnold, 1996)

Rivkin, Julie and Michael Ryan (eds.), *Literary Theory: An Anthology* (Malden: MA: Blackwell, 1998)

Rockett, Kevin, Luke Gibbons and John Hill (eds), *Cinema and Ireland* (London: Croom Helm, 1987)

Rolston, Bill (ed.), *The British Media and Northern Ireland: Covering the Troubles* (London: Macmillan, 1991)

—— *Drawing Support: Political Murals in Northern Ireland* (Belfast: Beyond the Pale, 1992)

Rolston, Bill and David Miller (eds), *War and Words: The Northern Ireland Media Reader* (Belfast: Beyond the Pale, 1996)

Rosenberg, Marvin, *The Masks of Hamlet* (Cranbury, NJ: Associated University Press, 1992)

Ryan, Louise and Margaret Ward (eds), *Irish Women and Nationalism: Soldiers, New Women and Wicked Hags* (Dublin: Irish Academic Press, 2004)

Shelley, Saguaro (ed.), *Psychoanalysis and Women: A Reader* (London: Macmillan, 2000)

Sarup, Madan, *Jacques Lacan* (London: Harvester Wheatsheaf, 1992)

Schlesinger, Philip, Graham Murdoch and Philip Elliott, *Televising Terrorism: Political Violence in Popular Culture* (London: Comedia, 1983)

Selden, Raman, *Practising Theory and Reading Literature: An Introduction* (London: Harvester Wheatsheaf, 1989)

Selzer, Michael, *Terrorist Chic: An Exploration of Violence in the Seventies* (New York: Hawthorn, 1979)

Shannon, Elizabeth, *I am of Ireland: Woman of the North Speak Out* (Boston: Little, Brown, 1989)

Smythe, Gerry, *Decolonization and Criticism: The Construction of Irish Literature* (London: Pluto, 1998)

Soyinka, Wole, *The Man Died: Prison Notes* (London: Arrow, 1985)

Spivak, Charlotte, *The Comedy of Evil on Shakespeare's Stage* (London: Associated University Press, 1978)

St. Peter, Christine, *Changing Ireland: Strategies in Contemporary Women's Fiction* (Basingstoke: Macmillan, 2000)

Sullivan, Megan, *Women in Northern Ireland* (Gainesville, FL: Florida University Press, 1999)

Taylor, Gary, *Reinventing Shakespeare* (London: Vintage, 1991)

Theroux, Paul, *The Kingdom by the Sea* (London: Hamish Hamilton, 1983)

Ward, Margaret, *Unmanageable Revolutionaries* (London: Pluto, 1983)

—— *The Missing Sex* (Dublin: Attic, 1991)

Waugh, Patricia, *Harvest of the Sixties: English Literature and its Background (1960–1990)* (Oxford: Oxford University Press, 1995)

Weekes, Ann, Owens, *Irish Women Writers: An Uncharted Territory* (Lexington, Kentucky: The University of Kentucky, 1990)

Wilson, Scott, *Cultural Materialism: Theory and Practice* (Oxford: Blackwell, 1995)

Wright, Elizabeth, *Psychoanalytic Criticism: Theory in Practice* (London and New York: Routledge, 1989)

Zizek, Slavoj, *The Sublime Object of Ideology* (London: Verso, 1989)

—— *For They Know Not What They Do: Enjoyment as a Political Factor* (London: Verso, 1991)

—— *Everything You Always Wanted to Know About Lacan... But Were Afraid to Ask Hitchcock* (London: Verso, 1992)

—— *Looking Awry: An Introduction to Jacques Lacan Through Popular Culture* (Cambridge, MA: MIT, 1992)

—— *Tarrying with the Negative: Kant, Hegel and the Critique of Ideology* (Durham, USA: Duke University Press, 1993)

—— *The Metastases of Enjoyment: Six Essays on Woman and Causality* (London: Verso, 1994)

—— *The Plague of Fantasies* (London: Verso, 1997)

—— *The Ticklish Subject: The Absent Centre of Political Ontology* (London: Verso, 1999)

Bibliographies, Reports and Journals

Bell, Robert and Bill Rolston, 'Literature of the Troubles: Bibliography', *University of Ulster: Northern Ireland Collection* (November 1996)

Fitzgerald, Jennifer, 'The Arts and Ideology', *Crane Bag of Irish Studies*, 9.2 (1985), 60–9

Higgins, Geraldine, 'A Place to Bring Anger and Grief', *Northern Narratives: Writing Ulster*, 6 (1999), 143–59.

Hughes, Eamonn, '"Town of Shadows": Representations of Belfast in Recent Fiction', *Religion & Literature*, 28.2–3 (Summer–Autumn 1996), 141–61

Jermyn, Deborah, 'Re-reading the Bitches from Hell: A Feminist Appropriation of the Female Psychopath', *Screen*, 37.3 (Autumn 1996), 251–66

Lacan, Jacques, 'Desire and Interpretation of Desire in *Hamlet*', *Yale French Studies: 'Literature and Psychoanalysis, the Question of Reading'*, 55–6 (1977), 11–52

Lubbers, Klaus, 'Irish Fiction: A Mirror for Specifics', *Eire-Ireland*, 20.2 (1985), 90–104

McCabe, Martin, *Circa*, [n. num.] (1996), [n. page]

McMinn, Joseph, 'Contemporary Novels on The Troubles', *Etudes Irlandaises*, 5 (1980), 113–21

Mortimer, Mark, 'The World of Jennifer Johnston', *The Crane Bag*, 4.1 (1980), 88–94

Newsinger, John, 'Our Boys in the North', *Irish Studies Review*, 16 (1996) 34–7

264

—— 'Heartland: A Few Troubles More', *Irish Studies Review*, 19 (Summer 1997), 53–6

Parker, Michael, 'Shadows on Glass: Self-Reflexivity in the Fiction of Deirdre Madden', *Irish University Review*, 30.1 (2002)

Patten, Eve, 'Woman and Fiction', *Krino*, 9 (1990), 7

Roberts, John, 'Sinn Fein and Video: Notes on a Political Pedagogy', *Screen*, 29.2 (Spring 1988), 94–7

Rolston, Bill, 'Mothers, Whores and Villains: Images of Women in Novels of the Northern Ireland Conflict', *Race & Class*, 31.1 (1989), 41–57

Rose, Jacqueline, 'Margaret Thatcher and Ruth Ellis', *New Formations*, 6 (Winter 1988), 3–27

Scanlan, Margaret, 'The Unbearable Present: Northern Ireland in Four Contemporary Novels', *Etudes Irlandaise*s, 10 (December 1985), 145–61

Sloan, Barry, 'The Wages of Paramilitary Sin', *Honest Ulsterman*, 80 (Spring 1986), 21–31

Steel, Jayne, '*Vampira:* Representations of the Irish Female Terrorist', *Irish Studies Review*, 6.3 (1998), 273–83

Thatcher, Margaret, 'In Memory of Airey Neave: Ireland and the Problems Facing Our Society', *Etudes Irlandaises*, 5 (December 1980), 145–52

Titley, Alan, '"Rough, Rug-Headed Kerns": The Irish Gunman in the Popular Novel', *Eire-Ireland*, 15.4 (1980), 15–38

Walker, Alexander, 'Peek-A-Boo, Ballyhoo & Bigotry', *Causeway*, 1.1 (September 1993), 31–5

Watt, Stephen, 'The Politics of Bernard MacLaverty's *Cal*', *Eire-Ireland*, 28.3 (1993), 130–46

Wilson, Scott, 'Incorporating the Impossible': Seminar for Hypertheory and Heterology (SHAH), *Cultural Values*, 1.2 (October 1997), 178–204

York, Richard, '"A Daft Way to Earn a Living": Jennifer Johnston and the Writer's Art', ed. Bill Lazenblatt, *Writing Ulster: Northern Narratives*, no.6 (1999) (29–47)

Newspaper and Magazine Articles

Ahmed, Kamal and Dan Glaister, *Guardian*, 24 June 1997, 2

Bell, J., Bowyer, 'The Troubles as Trash: Shadows of the Irish Gunman on an American Curtain', *Hibernia*, 20 January 1978, 26

Bennett, Ronan, 'An Irish Answer', *Guardian Weekend*, 16 July 1994, 6–8

Cogan, J., 'they seek me here, they seek me there', *Hibernia*, 28 September 1969, 24

Dow, Emma, 'The Human Chameleons', *Daily Mail*, 16 May 1997, 40–1

Editorial, *Sunday Times*, 12 September 1999, 5

Evans, Michelle, E., 'A Woman's Lot', *Fortnight*, May 1998, 14

Hardy, Jeremy, 'On the Disturbing Case of Roisin McAliskey', *Guardian*, 30 September 1997, 6–7

Hughes, David and James Clarke, 'Traitor Granny may Still be Sent for Trial', *Daily Mail*, 13 September 1999, 1

Knox, Ian, 'War is Over (if you want it)', *Fortnight*, December–January 1997–1998, front cover

Lopez-Barillas, Carlos, R., *Guardian*, 2 January 1998, 1

Loughran, Christina, 'The Women's Movement in Northern Ireland: Between Republicanism and Feminism', *Fortnight*, 27 May 1985, 4

Lowther, William, 'IRA to Share in £3m US Art Theft Reward', *Mail on Sunday*, 21 September 1997, 1

McGee, Patrick, 'Do they Mean Us?', *Guardian*, 3 September 1997, 12–13

Macnab, Geoffrey, *Sight and Sound*, July 1992, 56

Macnee, Calvin, 'Terrorism: Telling It How It Is', *Fortnight*, 7 May 1976, [n. page]

Miller, Russell, 'Justice at Last for Ruth Ellis', *Daily Mail: Night and Day*, 4 October 1998, 11

Mullin, John, 'A Shattered Peace', *Guardian*, 2 January 1998, 4

O'Neill, Terry, *Daily Mail*, 15 January 1993, 21

Pincher, Chapman, 'Sex, Lies and Secrets – Why we Love the Spying Game', *Daily Mail*, 13 September 1999, 10

Quinn, Frankie, *Fortnight*, April 1998, 18

Redmond, John, 'Ordinary Madness', *Guardian*, 25 September 1997, 8–9

Ruane, Medb, 'Tribes and Prejudice', *Sunday Times*, 27 July 1997, 8

Sears, John, *Daily Mail*, 13 September 1999, 6

Sparrow, Andrew, 'Faces that Damn Mr Adams (And Shame Labour MPs)', *Daily Mail*, 26 September 1996, 6–7

Stern Chester, 'Traitor in jail plot to betray MI5 men to IRA', *Daily Mail*, 14 June 1998, 13

Tebbit, Norman, 'Ruth would Still have been Guilty of Murder Today', *Mail on Sunday*, 16 August 1998, 37

Tookey, Christopher, 'Why Do Film Makers Hate Family Life?', *Daily Mail*, 24 June 1997, 4

Toolis, Kevin, 'The Troubles with Harry', *Observer Review*, 17 March 1996, 6

Trianor, Liz, *The Irish Times*, 28 March 1998, 8

Tse, David, *Sight and Sound*, February 1998, 47

Walters, Simon and Vincent Moss, 'Blair's revenge on Mo Deepens Ulster Crisis', *Daily Mirror*, 29 August 1999, 8–9

Electronic Information, Music and Interviews

Clarke, Jeremy (1999), *The Long Good Friday*, Available: http://festive.demon.co.uk/reviews/lastminute.com

Long Good Friday (1999), Available: http://shef.ac.uk/city/showroom.html

O'Brion, Owen, *Republican News*, Belfast, July 1997 (Interview)

O'Connor, Sinead. *I do not want what I haven't got*, Ensign Records, London, 1990

Rolston, Bill, Department of Sociology, University of Ulster, July 1997 (Interview)

Index